Entanglement

This book is a message of hope and a call to action in building flourishing human–machine systems in the age of artificial intelligence (AI). It looks beyond the AI hype and advocates for humanity in an industry infatuated by machine superiority. Its focus is on empowering leaders and citizens by raising awareness and encouraging active participation in building responsible technology and resilient organizations.

This book presents evidence-based and practical approaches for using AI to enhance business, human, and planetary outcomes. The research underpinning this work is informed by studies indicating that many organizations encounter difficulties in achieving a positive return on investment from their AI initiatives. This means that business leaders need to be astute in recognizing both the complexities and opportunities of using AI to effectively harness its potential. The book examines the interconnected relationship between humans and technology over time and discusses the need for renewed approaches to AI development and implementation. It suggests that AI differs from traditional technologies and requires adaptive human engagement for these new socio-technical systems to be successful. Additionally, the book aims to inform readers about both the beneficial and adverse impacts of AI technology on society.

This publication is intended to inspire business professionals, researchers, and students specializing in human–AI collaboration, information systems, and technology management. The underlying research was supported by a European Union–funded Marie Skłodowska-Curie research fellowship for the Augmented Humans project, which focused on leveraging the strengths of both human and artificial intelligence to accelerate creativity and innovation without compromising planetary flourishing.

This book offers deep insights and practical approaches for both technology researchers and business leadership teams. Supplementary materials are a key feature of this book, which includes offering interactive co-creation tools, such as AI Design Cards, the Designing Tiny Robots game, and AI Design Canvases as digital downloads with every book purchased. The author invites readers to engage with their stakeholders with playful, participatory methods in building more effective and responsible human–AI systems.

Marigo Raftopoulos is a technology researcher and strategic business advisor and has recently completed an EU Marie Skłodowska-Curie postdoctoral research fellowship for the project Augmented Humans. Marigo's global research and advisory career spans several decades and has focused on strategic digital transformation and experience design for corporate, government, and start-up clients. In her free time, Marigo explores forests as a citizen scientist and participates in forest conservation efforts.

Chapman & Hall/CRC Artificial Intelligence and Robotics Series

Series Editor: Roman Yampolskiy

Topological Dynamics in Metamodel Discovery with Artificial Intelligence: From Biomedical to Cosmological Technologies
Ariel Fernández

The Naked Android: Synthetic Socialness and the Human Gaze
Julie Carpenter

Designing Interactions with Robots: Methods and Perspectives
Edited by Maria Luce Lupetti, Cristina Zaga, Nazli Cila, Selma Šabanović, and Malte F. Jung

A Robotic Framework for the Mobile Manipulator: Theory and Application
Nguyen Van Toan and Phan Bui Khoi

AI and Law: How Automation Is Changing the Law
Aurelia Tamo-Larrieux, Clement Guitton, and Simon Mayer

Considerations on the AI Endgame: Ethics, Risks and Computational Frameworks
Soenke Ziesche and Roman V. Yampolskiy

AI in and for Africa: A Humanistic Perspective
Susan Brokensha, Eduan Kotzé, and Burgert A. Senekal

Artificial Intelligence on Dark Matter and Dark Energy: Reverse Engineering of the Big Bang
Ariel Fernández

De Novo Quantum Cosmology with Artificial Intelligence: Applications of Formal Autoencoders
Ariel Fernández

Just War Theory and Artificial Intelligence: Challenges and Consequences
Edited by Maria Power and Maggi Savin-Baden

AI Use Cases for Diplomats: Applying Artificial Intelligence to Diplomacy
Donald Kilburg

Entanglement: Navigating Complexity in the Age of Artificial Intelligence
Marigo Raftopoulos

For more information about this series please visit: www.routledge.com/Chapman--Hall CRC-Artificial-Intelligence-and-Robotics-Series/book-series/ARTILRO

Entanglement

Navigating Complexity in the Age of Artificial Intelligence

Marigo Raftopoulos

CRC Press
Taylor & Francis Group
Boca Raton London New York

CRC Press is an imprint of the
Taylor & Francis Group, an **informa** business
A CHAPMAN & HALL BOOK

Designed cover image: Shutterstock

First edition published 2026
by CRC Press
2385 NW Executive Center Drive, Suite 320, Boca Raton FL 33431

and by CRC Press
4 Park Square, Milton Park, Abingdon, Oxon, OX14 4RN

CRC Press is an imprint of Taylor & Francis Group, LLC

ISBN: 978-1-041-01826-1 (hbk)
ISBN: 978-1-032-99642-4 (pbk)
ISBN: 978-1-003-61656-6 (ebk)

DOI: 10.1201/9781003616566

Typeset in Minion
by Newgen Publishing UK

To my parents, who gave me life in a world they could not have imagined.

And to my children, whose imagination will shape worlds I cannot yet foresee.

Between them, I have learned that we are all entangled – across time, across generations, and within the unfolding complexity of our shared human story.

Contents

Preface

This book provides perspectives, strategies, and tools that emerged through my research work as a postdoctoral research fellow with an EU-funded Marie Skłodowska-Curie scholarship for my Augmented-Humans project. The research aimed to identify how organizations can leverage artificial intelligence (AI) to drive business improvement and innovation by providing practical insights and tools for organizational leaders. This research has also benefited enormously through several decades of experience in the field as a practitioner in business advisory and digital transformation. This book, therefore, is based on the rigor of academic research with the wisdom of designing and implementing digital technologies in the wild.

The research and writing of this book over a five-year period have highlighted that the entangled nature of intelligent technologies in human lives means the active participation of all of us is essential in building responsible technology and resilient organizations. The definition of augmented human–machine systems that is central to this book is the process, application, or method that combines the unique capabilities of both human and intelligent technologies to enhance decision-making, creativity, value creation, and human flourishing.

In this book, I have refrained from referring to humans as "workers," "users," "resources," or "human capital" – instead using "citizens" to elevate the importance of the role and rights of humans in the advancement of AI in workplaces and society at large. This clarity is important given the media and industry tendency to "hero" the technology over human capability and to understate the innate complexity of augmented human–machine systems. Words and definitions matter to help break the techno-solutionist mental models that persist from our legacy systems, practices, and thinking since the Enlightenment.

There are many courses, articles, and reports issued by consultants and solutions providers promising quick, simple, and easy ways to integrate AI into organizations – and with advice to do it fast, otherwise you'll be obliterated by mediocrity. This book does not offer any such advice or warnings. It instead urges you to take the time to fully understand the nature of human–machine entanglement, to be able to effectively navigate the path forward responsibly and sustainably, and with a level head.

The key features of this book include a summary of the main opportunities and challenges presented by AI, minus the hype. The aim is to:

- Highlight the entanglement of humans and technology, and why we need a renewed approach to AI technology development and enablement. This has roots in key anthropological and historical foundations that have shaped Western attitudes toward the human–technology relationship.
- Inform individuals, leaders, and organizations on how to take informed positive action by applying evidence-based models, principles, and frameworks to enhance what is uniquely human while enabling human–machine systems to flourish.
- Assist organizations to understand that intelligent technology cannot be treated like legacy technologies of the past – these contemporary systems require intelligent, well-adjusted humans for overall system optimization.
- Provide practical interactive tools and approaches, such as AI Design Cards and a Designing Tiny Robots design game to demystify AI and facilitate human–machine system collaboration and co-creation with your stakeholders.

This book is designed for business professionals, researchers, and students within the AI, human–computer–machine–AI interaction, and information system domains. In terms of business professionals, as a practising strategic business advisor alongside my academic career, I have firsthand experience withdigital transformation issues for organizations, and how these are re-emerging and remorphing in parallel with the world's rapid AI transformation. The research for this book has included surveying and interviewing a wide range of business professionals as they are in the driver's seat of navigating an increasingly complex, mutable, and ambiguous environment. This has enabled me to develop objective, evidence-based research, strategies, and approaches that they can trust. I have written this book with them specifically in mind, as they are at the forefront of making sense of AI technologies but are also vulnerable to the AI hype that is permeating the industry.

In terms of researchers and students, this book offers a fresh perspective on the role of human and organizational flourishing in developing effective socio-technical systems in business applications. Since I commenced my fellowship research and corresponding industry engagement for this project five years ago, a wide range of academic research interests has accelerated in this domain. In fact, generative AI burst onto the scene in the very beginning of my research with ChatGPT 3.0, well after my research proposal was accepted for EU funding.

The emergence of specialist academic conference tracks on human–machine collaboration, human flourishing in the digital era, and human–machine–AI interaction had suddenly proliferated across all research domains, particularly in information systems, computer science, and human–computer interaction. There is an academic hunger for this subject matter as well as a drive to discover the unknown, and this book is a natural outcome of immersing myself in the research with other like-minded scholars. My key concerns are that student and researcher experiences in academia are still heavily domain-specific, e.g., computer science vs human–computer interaction vs information systems vs management studies – as that's how faculties and departments are shaped and funded. Multidisciplinary research constantly comes up as opportunities for further research but is still a novelty in research practice.

In terms of the general public, bestseller books have largely fostered fear or confusion in the minds of the public that AI technology is out of their control and that the negatives are largely inevitable. These books no doubt have something to offer and something important to say. But this book is a message of hope and a call to action. It exposes the myths and hype, it's an advocate for humans in a dominant industry narrative that's focused on machine superiority, and it's an advocate for organizations who feel disempowered by the influence of a handful of technology companies. The focus of this book is on empowering citizens by raising awareness of both the positive and negative effects that AI technology is having on our lives.

This book has its own website for further information at https://entanglement-ai.com. Readers also have access to the website containing my original Marie Curie research on Augmented Humans, which is live at https://augmented-humans.com.

Supplementary materials are a key feature of this book and include interactive activities such as AI Design Cards, the Designing Tiny Robots game, and AI design canvases that were initiated during my fellowship and later refined in practice. These are available as digital downloads from the book website. My aim is to inspire you into positive action in building sustainable solutions for organizations and citizens alike.

Marigo Raftopoulos

I

The Here and Now

CHAPTER 1

Introduction

In the presence of total Darkness, the mind finds it absolutely necessary to create light.

—ISAAC ASIMOV

INTRODUCTION

This book is the outcome of several years of research on how organizations can augment the best of human and artificial intelligence to enhance business outcomes, and without compromising human flourishing. In this age of intelligent technologies, human thriving, technology effectiveness, and business enhancement cannot be separated. We are all entangled in terms of how we use technology to enhance our knowledge and skills, access meaningful work and shape our identity. How we connect with the world is mediated by increasingly complex and pervasive intelligent technologies that do not always prioritize the flourishing of citizens.

The purpose of this book is to challenge myths and hype and provide evidence-based tangible approaches for using AI to enhance business, human, and planetary outcomes. There is a significant body of research that shows that most organizations are struggling to earn a positive return on investment from their AI investments (Pumplun et al., 2019; Shollo et al., 2022). Organizational leaders therefore need to better understand both the complexities and opportunities of AI to effectively harness its potential.

This means that you as a leader require a grounded, strategic approach to effectively navigate the challenges presented by AI rather than be reactive (Duan et al., 2019; Dwivedi et al., 2021). This will allow you to continuously navigate the dynamic shifts as AI technologies change over time by focusing on the fundamentals of organizational adaptation and flourishing – rather than chase every shiny new thing. This is critical in a landscape

DOI: 10.1201/9781003616566-2

where the world's top AI scientists cannot agree on the definitions, architectures, capabilities, impacts, and development timelines of AI technologies. Organization autonomy, foresight, and critical thinking are the most important capabilities for leaders to develop to stay in-step or ahead of AI advancements (Collins et al., 2021; Berente et al., 2021).

Human relationships with technology have been complex and entangled ever since early humanoids developed their first tools made of stone and bone. Given the intrinsic nature of intelligent technologies, human acceptance and use of AI go beyond the mere utility of the technology into complex psycho-social factors that affect human–machine performance, such as fear (Cabrera-Sánchez et al., 2021), AI anxiety (Oh et al., 2017), algorithm aversion (Dietvorst et al., 2015), bias and mistrust (Ishowo-Oloko et al., 2019), and willful lack of co-operation (Kiesler et al., 1996). AI is more than a tool; it has become integrated into our lives. Like all technologies before it, humanity has co-evolved with the tools it has created and has become entangled with them.

Despite the advancements in AI technologies, there are limitations in their ability to reliably process complex and ambiguous environments - areas that require high levels of cognition and a theory of mind. For this reason, the complex challenges in the current business environment cannot be solved by machines alone and require robust human-machine hybrid solutions to realize the full potential of both AI and human capability (Akata et al., 2020; de Cremer et al., 2021; Dellermann et al., 2019; Demartini et al., 2016; Parasuraman and Wickens, 2008). For this reason, understanding of entanglement matters for both human flourishing and sustainable future business outcomes.

In the remainder of this chapter, we present a discussion on the AI tech stack, encourage the practice of positive skepticism, and provide a hype-free overview of the state of play with AI performance. We end with chapter summaries and your call to action.

THE AI TECH STACK

AI is an umbrella term that mostly includes technologies known as "narrow AI." This incorporates a wide range of intelligent technologies that are mainly designed to specialize in specific tasks in specific business applications. Therefore, most of these technologies are not multidimensional or multiskilled. For example, while a medical diagnostic AI can detect cancer in medical imaging, it cannot play chess. IBM's Deep Blue AI program can beat human world chess champions, but it cannot autopilot an autonomous vehicle. Most AI technologies that organizations are currently working and experimenting with have narrow capabilities within narrow application domains and need to be integrated with legacy technologies.

It is tempting to generalize about these specialized intelligent technologies in the context of the potential emergence of artificial general intelligence (AGI) or superintelligence, but the reality is we're not there yet and won't be in the foreseeable future. AGI or superintelligence is therefore not directly featured in this book, as their theoretical potential for organizations outside of the research labs of a handful of tech corporations is negligible over the short and medium term. It is of course an important element that's discussed in Chapter 2 and included in Chapters 7 and 8 when we look at practical, engaging, and collaborative practices to raise stakeholders' AI literacy. The potential of AGI lies on the horizon, and understanding the fundamentals of human–machine entanglements will have us better prepared for when it does eventuate.

In terms of the here and now, I have outlined a simple taxonomy of AI technologies in Figure 1.1 to guide non-technical citizens through the key elements of AI technologies. To rebuild our human–machine systems, it is important to know how AI learns, how it processes our world, and how AI is utilized through the intelligent tools it creates. Please note that there are many ways to present an AI taxonomy; what I have assembled here will help navigate the content and purposes of this book.

The objective here is to form a baseline in understanding that not all AI are equally created, that there are different types of AI, and that we shouldn't conflate them. For example,

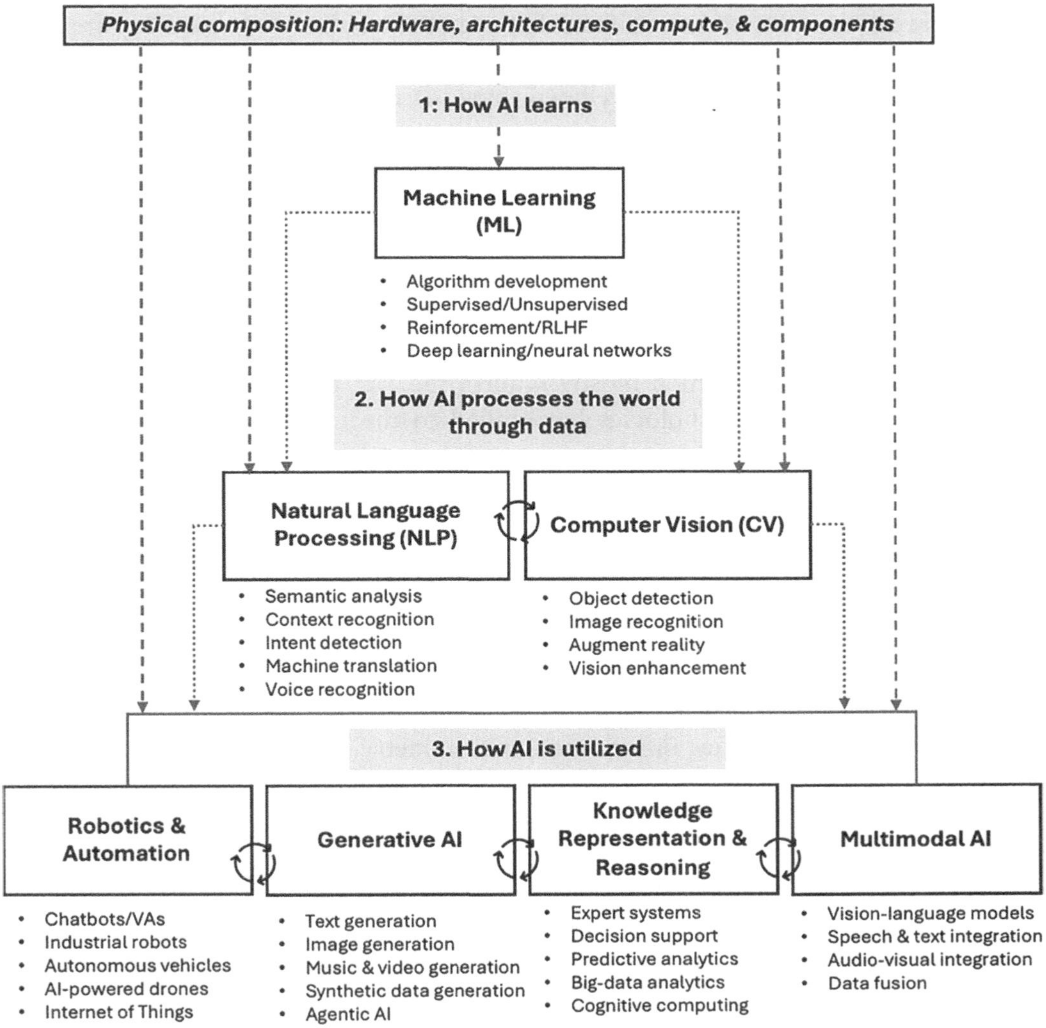

FIGURE 1.1 A simple taxonomy of the AI tech stack.

the introduction and capabilities of consumer-ready large language models (LLMs) like ChatGPT, Claude, and Gemini have captured the attention and enthusiasm of the public, as well as business leaders. These technologies have been adopted by citizens both personally and professionally to enhance their capabilities and productivity, and to future-proof their jobs. However, I have run AI workshops and seminars around the world, and it surprises me to find that many people have limited awareness of different types of AI technologies, their unique capabilities, and limitations, outside of generative AI. To truly understand the nature of entanglement, we need to understand the nature of the technologies we are allowing into our lives and organizations. This then helps us all not to buy into the hype.

THE PRACTICE OF POSITIVE SCEPTICISM

While there are many powerful and convincing narratives on the benefits of AI, along with fear-of-missing-out (FOMO) and warnings about being left behind technologically, there are some lesser-known facts that need to be better understood by organizational leaders. For example, research suggests that many AI technologies for business applications tend to be underdeveloped, have narrow applications, and are still at proof-of-concept (PoC) stages or running as pilots (Pumplun et al., 2019; Shollo et al., 2022). This means that these technologies have proven their functional benefits under controlled conditions, such as research labs and gated workplace experiments. Furthermore, there are known harms induced by AI due to bias, discrimination, and limited breadth, depth, and quality control in training data, and we do not yet have a clear position or path forward in terms of overcoming such limitations (Bender et al., 2021; Birhane, 2021). While there are real benefits, these have often been overinflated via tech industry hype, which mostly ignores the fact that many business projects that have applied AI technologies have failed to meet their objectives (Gray and Shellshear, 2025).

Many organizations are striving to minimize such AI limitations and harms through preventative measures that include stakeholder awareness raising, developing ethics frameworks, and complying with regulations in some jurisdictions. Although such measures are limited in scope and effectiveness, they leave most organizations vulnerable to project failures. Organizations and citizens need to prepare themselves for AI impacts by applying an informed approach that leverages its benefits, while being strategic in how to adopt and integrate the technology to set it up for success.

The criticality in this lies in information asymmetry and unknown trajectories. In terms of information asymmetry, objective information on the most effective and sustainable use of AI technologies is not readily available and accessible to the public (Marcus, 2022; Newlands, 2021). This is partly due to the unpredictability and unknowns that exist in technology development and discovery. It is also partly due to the concentration of ownership and control of AI technologies by a handful of private companies and can be seen played out via accusations of how tech companies are influencing AI regulations and agenda-setting in the USA, China, and Europe.

In terms of unknown trajectories, citizens are inundated with many conflicting and ambiguous voices on the short- and long-term impact of AI. This not only includes business impact but also in terms of existential threats to humanity. This has created a confusing and fractured environment for organizational leaders needing to make significant business investment and transformation decisions, and for citizens in terms of social cohesion, personal growth, and economic prospects. We explore these issues in detail in Chapter 2.

This book intends to assist organizational leaders in setting up an AI strategy for success and to guide researchers around the knowledge gaps that require more rigorous and independent research. This book does not focus on futuristic thinking and speculative approaches; as fun as they are, I'm not convinced they offer the scaffolding needed to inform organizational strategy and investment at this stage of AI development. However, they do have a place in holistic strategic approaches to AI. The reality is that no one really knows what's on the horizon in terms of the plausibility or probability of AI technologies.

Capital markets are overheating with speculative investment in a handful of tech companies eager to position themselves as AI domain leaders; however, this does not necessarily provide evidence of certainty or wisdom on AI developments. For example, at the time of writing this book, a Chinese startup DeepSeek entered the generative AI market with new cost-effective development methods and single-handedly wiped 20% off the valuations of US-based technology corporations. No one saw that coming. More recently, the media is ablaze with speculation that the AI investment bubble is about to burst, much of it drven by concerns of circular investment among the AI giants self-renforcing the flow of capital into AI.

To prepare for this level of disruption and unpredictability, this book offers grounded insights and approaches underpinned by the utmost academic research rigor and the experience of professionals and practitioners in the field. We intend to help you make informed decisions and ask the right questions of your key stakeholders and your technology providers.

WHAT IS THE STATE OF PLAY FOR MOST ORGANIZATIONS?

We conducted a systematic literature review (that is presented in detail in Chapter 2) and reviewed several case studies and use cases to understand the factors that may influence how leaders can create value with AI technology. We found that there are four broad categories of interdependent variables at play that impact the effective use of AI in organizations:

- *Human factors*, such as AI identity threat (Mirbabaie et al., 2022), personality types and trust (Schepman and Rodway, 2023), and agency (Newman et al., 2019).
- *Management factors*, such as manager attitudes, technology acceptance, and technology trust (Cao et al., 2021; Suseno et al., 2022), management systems (Metcalf et al., 2019).
- *Organizational factors*, such as firm-level capability (Mikalef and Gupta, 2021) and entrepreneurial orientation and operations (Dubey et al., 2020).
- *Technological factors*, such as algorithmic behavior (Carroll et al., 2019; Stowers et al., 2021), and issues with data model curation and machine learning (Chen et al., 2018; Crandall et al., 2018; van den Hoven, 2007; Scheuerman et al., 2021).

These factors provided wide-ranging insight into the potential variables, but little in terms of unequivocal findings on how AI technologies affect workplace technology acceptance and organizational performance. Several studies also suggest that performance may be context-specific and therefore may not be generalizable across different AI technologies and application domains (Cubric, 2020), which adds further challenge to our research focus.

Our next step was to investigate for ourselves *how organizations were succeeding with AI* in the wild, without relying on the AI hype that was so vocal in industry media. We undertook a study focusing on the views of professionals working directly with AI-enabled technologies in the workplace in Europe and the USA.

AI Technologies Covered

A broad range of AI technologies in use were reported. The majority of the core functional areas of these AI technologies were in information technology (16%), information systems (13%), and marketing and sales (18%). In terms of the core functions of the AI technologies, the largest categories were customer service (21%), forecasting and prediction (17%), and optimization (16%).

It was interesting to note that there was a long tail concerning the core functions of the AI technology and the application domains in which they were embedded. The projects reported in the survey came from a wide AI tech stack that included machine learning, neural networks, computer vision, and generative AI. Many also included the integration of secondary digital technologies, such as games and virtual and augmented reality, for data capture through interactions with employees or customers. Over half the respondents were using AI technologies integrated within corporate platforms such as SAP, Microsoft Azure, Oracle, AWS, Salesforce, and IBM Watson.

How Do Professionals Feel about How AI Works?

In relation to the question on how well the AI technology has performed, most respondents indicated that AI performed either "very well" (59%) or "extremely well" (12%). It is also noteworthy that despite a lack of negative ratings, a significant proportion were still neutral (29%), citing the early days of the implementation. The reasons cited for the positive performance of the AI technologies were enhanced process improvement, time savings, improved accuracy, and increase in efficiency. Respondents who were neutral maintained that there was *still a lot of human effort and resources required* to manage the AI technology. This included the effort required to train the AI (data access and curation, and machine learning), the high financial cost of the AI investment and implementation, and that they were still in a proof-of-concept stage of the implementation. Interestingly, there was a high level of distrust for increasingly sophisticated AI; these causal factors (stemming from a mistrust of management rather than the technology) will be discussed in more detail later in the book.

How Can AI Be Better Developed and Implemented?

Professionals were asked an open-ended question about how AI technologies can be better developed and implemented in their organizations. Using a thematic analysis, we categorized their responses according to the five thematic clusters: strategic, technology, systems, human, and other. Limitations in technology-related factors was the most significant category cited for where AI can be better developed and implemented (40%). An outline of these results is as follows:

- Strategic issues (20%): Areas that required improvement were organizational education and skills; a greater level of grounded research; more use cases; clarity on legal implications.
- Systems issues (24%): More effective process re-engineering required for AI integration, expert change facilitation; human-override needed in AI decision making; stakeholder consultation and inclusion.
- Human elements (4%): Improvements were required in human interaction and user interface design; actively incorporating user feedback in early stages of AI deployment; reduce user complexity in human-machine interaction.
- Technology factors (40%): Access, curation, and management of data, managing AI bias and inaccuracies, and developing AI technology synergies with legacy IT and IS systems. AI applications were frequently cited as being shipped too early.
- Other (15%): These responses simply stated "I don't know" how to improve the AI in their organizations.

AI Impact on Sense of Personal Empowerment

In terms of feelings of personal empowerment in their jobs, 37% felt either highly or very empowered, 55% felt only moderate empowerment, and 8% felt not very empowered. An interesting observation is that despite the high levels of positive perception of AI performance and acceptance, most respondents still feel a sense of unease in their empowerment and security in their roles as AI implementations expand.

AI Impact on Future Productivity and Innovation

When considering the future impact of AI on workplace productivity, collaboration, and innovation, most respondents made positive statements (52%), a sizeable proportion made conditional statements (40%), only 4% made negative statements, and 4% claimed they were not sure. The key sentiments that emerged are as follows:

- Positive statements (52%): The AI automation is great. It will become a common tool. Frees up time and resources. It will have a huge impact.
- Conditional statements (40%): AI needs to be used correctly. Only works if it's implemented well. AI is good, but still has limited potential. Can't trust it yet. Still needs supervision.
- Negative statements (4%): Still severely biased. Can't match human skill in this field. It's just a tool. There will be job losses and hardships.
- Don't know (4%): Not sure. Don't know.

While most professionals surveyed support the positive potential and role of AI technologies in the workplace, they are also cognizant of the need for improved technology development and implementation. Respondents hold the perception that many AI deployments may still be sub-optimal in areas of integration, trust, performance, and implementation.

AI as a Viable Collaborator and Team Member

When asked to consider AI as a viable workplace collaborator and team member, the majority of professionals made negative statements (44%) or conditional statements (40%), citing critical limitations in AI capability to replicate innate human skills, as well as limited trust in the technology's performance. It is interesting to note that the negative and conditional sentiments appear to be anchored in socio-emotional-cultural issues around the importance of humanity, the innate or irreplaceable human contribution to workplace collaboration and teaming. Despite the perceived positive potential of AI, there are several technical and development hurdles that need to be overcome, such as trust, reliability, anthropomorphism, and accuracy, to advance human–machine augmentation potential. Remember that these are professionals with technical expertise already working on AI deployments. Their sentiments are classified as follows:

- Positive statements (12%): It's already part of the team. The AI helps humans work faster. We get work done without all the emotion. It's fast and reliable.
- Conditional statements (40%): It's not yet trustworthy or reliable enough. Needs to be more human-like. Needs natural communication in the interfaces and interactions. More development is still needed.
- Negative statements (44%): A human team member is irreplaceable. AI is a tool, not a team member. AI is no substitute for humans. AI is just an enabler.
- Don't know (4%): I don't know. No idea.

In prior questions, respondents were aware of the benefits and limitations of the AI technologies in their workplace and impressed with the results to date, particularly in relation to how it automated certain tasks and functions. However, it appears that they were particularly critical in relation to the idea of human–machine teaming and collaboration, citing critical limitations in the current suite of AI technologies. This is consistent with extant literature on this topic on the current irreplaceability of human capability on more complex tasks and ambiguous problem spaces (Akata et al., 2020; de Cremer et al., 2021; Demartini et al., 2016).

Concerns about the Future of AI in Society

In terms of concerns about the future of AI in society, key themes were divided into five key areas of cyberthreats, job losses, ethical concerns, and loss of humanness. The key themes raised by respondents are as follows:

- Cyberthreats (40%): AI terrorism and scams. Unsupervised errors. Bad AI configurations. Technology in the wrong hands. Releasing AI before it is ready. AI is a cybersecurity nightmare.

- Job losses (24%): Worker displacement. Loss of human skills. Loss of livelihoods. Can't just use people and then discard them.
- Ethics concerns (8%): Invasion of privacy. Military uses of AI. Biased datasets. Misappropriated datasets. Technology ownership and control by a few companies.
- Loss of humanness (12%): Inauthentic experiences. Loss of common sense. Loss of empathy and compassion. Overreliance on AI. Not using our brains and emotional intelligence.
- No concerns (16%): AI is not the problem, humans are. I have no concerns about the future. AI dystopia is peddled by those who control and sell the tech.

What Are AI Professionals Thinking?

We found that there was a high level of positive acceptance of AI technology and a recognition of AI value-adding performance. Any perceived barriers to AI acceptance and performance, however, appear to be anchored in a position of constructive criticism rather than fear or anxiety. This is illustrated in the context of responses claiming that AI technology is not yet ready, reliable, and trustworthy in areas that require high levels of human–machine teaming and collaboration in decision-making.

The perspective of this group of professionals is that the performance of augmented AI-human technology is still sub-optimal at this point. These are the AI technologies that go beyond AI automation to more complex cognitive functions required in human–machine sense-making and collaboration. This indicates that there is a high level of awareness of the elements needed to enable value creation in an organization, as well as elements that limit current or future value creation (or even destroy value).

From a theoretical perspective, an individual's technological frames of reference are shaped by different antecedents such as (1) personal attitude, (2) application value, (3) organizational influence, (4) leader influence, and (5) industry influence (Spieth et al., 2021). Our findings suggest that these areas provide the potential microfoundations for building more effective organizational capability in AI enablement, which raises additional challenges for technology and systems designers.

Several systemic socio-economic issues were mentioned by respondents as perceived barriers to AI technology acceptance and performance. For example, cyberthreats and job losses represent wider socio-industrial-economic problems, and perceived consequences of loss of humanness speaks to the systemic socio-cultural implications of the unknown emergent society that will evolve.

These issues can be perceived as being out of the control of organizations, however the implications for practice are that organizational leaders can take a more proactive approach in terms of systems design and the development of unique organizational values and practices to counteract the potential negative impact of AI on their workforce abd customer base. As our survey shows, staff appear to be showing positive goodwill to enable AI despite an uncertain future for their personal empowerment and job security.

Several findings of this research have implications for practice and further research. The significant percentage of "no concerns" in relation to the future impact of AI technologies offers two possible hypotheses: (a) a limited awareness of the issues and/or (b) staff at the coalface of AI implementations may in fact have a greater awareness of the workability issues of AI technologies than organizations and developers give them credit for.

A close inspection of the responses and sentiments suggests that respondents were not overtly complicit in the AI hype that is often a criticism of the industry and, in particular, the exaggerated media reporting of AI technologies (Marcus, 2022; Newlands, 2021). Implications for practice are a need for open communication, staff training, and critical research as a basis for more informed strategic decision-making on AI investment. Concerns over the loss of humanness highlight the importance of the relational and experiential needs of humans in the workplace (and society as a whole) and how organizational leaders manage this important transition.

This raises opportunities for improvements in a wide range of issues that were mentioned by respondents in the areas of human–machine interaction, AI interface design, and workplace and systems design – elements that focus on human empowerment and motivation, as this is still a key driver of productivity, creativity, and innovation in an AI-enabled organization.

Both human and machine systems need to be developed in tandem for the overall system to flourish. Given the widely reported mixed results on AI technology performance, acceptance, and the return on investment in the existing literature, insights from our pilot survey suggest that the implication for practice lies in how effectively organizations can integrate AI technology – or, more pointedly, how organizations can recreate new systems in which AI implementation introduces a step change in the organization's core business.

Value creation from AI technologies represents unique challenges due to the complex interactions between technology, systems, tasks, and processes (Spies et al., 2020). Furthermore, human–machine systems based on AI technologies require a more sophisticated approach to organizational design and digital transformation than have been offered by the conventional frameworks of the past (Hanelt et al., 2021), as well as the design of task and technology alignment in workplace and functional designs (Goodhue and Thompson, 1995).

The implication here is that competitive or comparative advantage may not necessarily be in the investment in AI, but in how well organizations can strategically use AI to adapt, integrate, and renew themselves in a constantly shifting technological landscape. This research suggests that the limitations also lie in the capability and configurations of the AI technology and overall system design, rather than in the fear and limitations of its human collaborators.

TEN KEY AI CHALLENGES

The challenges we face from the development and application of AI technologies in organizations are varied and complex. While each of these are further explored in detail throughout this book, below is a summary of the ten key challenges that kept recurring in the research:

1. **Strategic alignment and leadership:** Integrating AI into existing business strategies and processes to create sustainable value remains a significant challenge. Organizations struggle to translate AI's potential into tangible business outcomes aligned with their strategic goals.
2. **Human–AI collaboration:** Designing business systems that balance and optimize the interplay between human capabilities and AI technologies is complex. This is what I call the "augmentation design problem," which involves addressing psychological, social, organizational, and technical factors to create productive and sustainable human–machine collaborations. Our current challenges are largely an outcome of an oversimplification of human–human and human–machine relationships.
3. **Organizational evolution:** Existing organizational structures, cultures, and work processes need to constantly evolve to fully leverage the continual advancement of AI capabilities. This challenge arises out of rapidly evolving AI capabilities that are shifting the goal posts as AI technologies advance beyond being mere tools to becoming interdependent and independent agents. Organizations will continue to face unprecedented challenges in areas such as strategic decision-making, human–machine collaboration, and business transformation.
4. **Technology maturity and alignment:** Developing and integrating AI systems that can effectively augment human intelligence in business contexts have proven to be technically challenging beyond gated pilots and experiments. Relevant issues include algorithm behavior, machine learning model development, ensuring a seamless integration with existing IT infrastructure, and replacing legacy systems.
5. **Value creation and measurement:** There is a lack of consensus on how to measure the business value generated by AI investments. Research has highlighted difficulty in demonstrating tangible business value from AI implementations, as well as challenges in scaling AI from PoC to organization-wide adoption. There is potential for *value destruction* in organizations if AI is not effectively implemented or managed.
6. **Ethical considerations:** Ensuring AI systems are used ethically and responsibly within organizations is an ongoing challenge. This includes addressing potential issues of bias, transparency, and accountability in AI-driven decision-making processes and environmental footprints when developing, maintaining, and expanding AI training models and infrastructures.
7. **AI literacy and skill development:** Due to uncertainty and limited understanding of the potential capabilities and impacts of AI, organizations need to develop new skills and competencies among their workforce to effectively work alongside AI systems. This often requires significant investment in training and education programs to raise AI literacy across all levels of an organization – particularly the leadership team.

8. **Human adaptation and growth:** Implementing AI technologies often involves significant changes to work processes and job responsibilities, which can lead to resistance and adoption challenges among employees. This often occurs when identity, autonomy, and meaningful work are compromised. These issues should not be considered human flaws, but legitimate concerns about AI technology immaturity and lack of adequate organizational enablement.
9. **Geopolitical and organizational sovereignty:** Nations and organizations are increasingly concerned about their technological sovereignty in terms of managing risk and their dependence on a small number of tech companies. Geopolitically, nations are concerned about the increased politicization and weaponization of AI technology, as well as their long-term comparative advantage relative to more dominant nations and how this may affect global peace, prosperity, and environmental impact.
10. **Global macro factors:** Many organizations are challenged by rapidly evolving AI regulations and policies, economic uncertainties affecting AI investments, and societal concerns about AI ethics, technology democratization, and employment impacts. At a meta level, a primary concern is how AI technologies may adversely impact the fabric of society and what it means to be human.

The above-listed ten key challenges highlight the complex, multifaceted nature of AI adoption by citizens and organizations, requiring careful consideration of technological, strategic, human, and environmental factors for successful implementation.

OUTLINE OF THE CHAPTERS IN THIS BOOK

While this book is presented in a linear format, you can start your learning adventure at any point. In Figure 1.2, the book's four main conceptual parts have been mapped: *The Here and Now, Entanglement, Disentanglement, and Flourishing*, and their eight action-oriented chapters. Each chapter provides you with a key message that is both a mindset check and a call to action.

We build a story in four parts: **Part I** describes the state of play of AI in here and now. **Part II** is a deep-dive into the anthropological and historical origins of human–technology

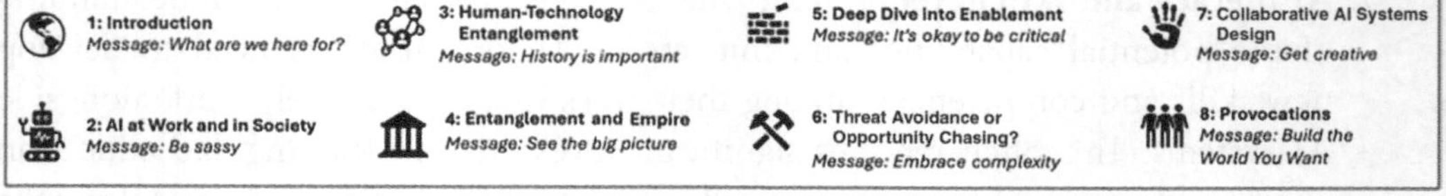

FIGURE 1.2 Outline of book chapters.

entanglement, and of the entanglements between technology and the rise in the power of empires. In **Part III**, we disentangle our technological entanglements through our deep research into experiences with AI implementation and enablement. . In **Part IV**, we explore creative, engaging, and provocative interventions to start you thinking about alternative approaches to AI system design and enablement that focuses on overall system flourishing. An abstract for each chapter is provided below to help you navigate the remainder of the book.

Chapter 2: AI at Work and in Society

Modern digital technologies have been developed from mental models that proclaim machine superiority over human intelligence. The unintended consequences of this are now showing up in sub-optimal systems development and implementations. Organizational leaders considering investing in AI technologies need to go beyond a fascination or fear of the technology and apply a balanced strategic approach toward building holistic human–machine systems to achieve sustainable gains in productivity and innovation. In this chapter, we work through the different AI definitions, ideologies, and world views that are shaping the current discourse on AI. We highlight the key findings of an extensive review of the research that maps the critical success factors of AI implementations, which are strategic sassiness, organizational rewilding, technology reimagined, and human fearlessness.

Key message in Chapter 2: Be sassy.

Chapter 3: Human–Technology Entanglement

We explore anthropological and historical perspectives of *technogenesis*, which highlight that technology and human relationships are deeply intertwined as we have co-evolved over time. Ever since the first tool was created by early humans, we have taken the path of being caught up in an intimate entanglement with the things we have created. We also map the AI ecosystem and identify the key actors and the nature of the interrelationships and interdependencies between them. We end this chapter with a discussion on *sociomaterial* approaches to build holistic business systems, premised on the fact that technologies do not act alone or in isolation from human or social elements; agency arises through relational configurations between them.

Key message in Chapter 3: History is important.

Chapter 4: Entanglement and Empire

We explore the viewpoint of *empire studies* that the entanglement of humans and technology has been deeply shaped by the entanglement of empire and technology, and its drive for continuous economic and political power acquisition. We explore the provocation that technology development since the Middle Ages has not been for human flourishing but to expand control, extract resources, and maintain dominance of Empires. We position *critical posthumanism* as a powerful lens for interrogating the assumptions embedded in contemporary artificial intelligence and provide a foundation for a deep reflection on how technologies like AI challenge what it means to be human. We explore the consequences of our entanglements and propose renewed and deeper citizen participation in rethinking our technological futures.

Key message in Chapter 4: See the big picture.

Chapter 5: Deep Dive into Enablement

We explore the results of our deep study into the AI enablement issues from the perspective of AI solutions providers. The limiting leadership decision-making behaviors identified in this study indicate that organizations are engaging in satisficing rather than optimizing an AI strategy, making short-term reactionary decisions, and avoiding uncertainty. The key problem areas of AI enablement are clustered in five groups: navigating complex macro-environmental factors, technology maturity challenges, strategy and leadership limitations, systems enablement issues, and challenges with the shifting nature of work. This places the caliber of strategic decision-making and the skillful enablement of AI technologies as the key differentiators in organizational performance and competitive advantage rather than the AI technology itself. We conclude this chapter with a conceptual model and actions that can be undertaken to renew management practices.

Key message in Chapter 5: It's okay to be critical.

Chapter 6: Threat Avoidance or Opportunity Chasing?

This chapter explores how cognitive frames of reference either pull or repel individuals to adopt increasingly sophisticated AI technologies in the workplace. Citizens show an increasing reluctance to adopt increasingly sophisticated technologies, and results showed no statistically significant differences in the results between gender, age, educational qualifications, or geography, indicating that this is an innately human condition. Citizen adoption of AI technology falls on a spectrum ranging between "opportunity chasing" and "threat avoidance," the latter being attributed to genuine citizen concern about limitations in the current generation of AI technology, the adequacy of organizational AI implementations, and the breakdown of the social contract organizations have with their employees. This chapter offers a set of personas and a differentiation strategy to inform leadership practices.

Key message in Chapter 6: Embrace human complexity.

Chapter 7: Collaborative AI Systems Design

This chapter examines the potential of using creative and playful participatory methods to advance collaborative stakeholder design of intelligent human–machine systems. We present a set of interactive activities to engage your teams in raising AI literacy while engaging in collaborative co-design of human–machine systems. These activities include (a) three sets of interactive AI design cards – AI concepts, AI provocations, and human flourishing in the age of AI and (b) a collaborative AI design sprint process called *Designing Tiny Robots*, which also consists of several card-based activities. We argue that collaborative AI system design may account for a fuller range of the socio-technical interactions between stakeholders and thereby improving AI technology design, effectiveness, and adoption.

Key message in Chapter 7: Get creative.

Chapter 8: Provocations

This last chapter is to provoke you and challenge your mental models. We call on you to engage in creative endeavors that explore *AI Anarchies* to question popular narratives. Delve into *human flourishing* in the era of AI that creates an economy of care as a driver of productivity and innovation. Engage with *value-sensitive design* as an alternative process of technology development. Engage with *radical acts* to disrupt more of the same type of thinking. We complete this chapter with a 10-item manifesto that suits both researchers and practitioners looking to *undiscipline* themselves to think outside of the confines of their respective fields; these are *radical thought experiments.* I have found that for us to change even just a tiny bit, we need to first truly imagine the full expanse of the impossible.

Key message in Chapter 8: Build the world you want. Create the world we need.

A FINAL NOTE ON CHAPTER 1

This chapter asks: *What are we doing here, that is the question*? This fundamental question is deeply personal to every leader and unique to every organization. It goes to the heart of the organizational values we all work for in terms of how we serve humanity and the planet. It is more than just the simple return on investment mantra. And it is not the gleeful "AI is going to take over the world, so you might as well get used to it" we hear from the techno-optimists. Every citizen I have surveyed and worked with across my *Augmented Humans* research believes we are here for something more than that.

Research has identified limiting behaviors among organizations investing in AI, of sufficing rather than optimizing, short-term reactions, and uncertainty avoidance. This behavior can also be seen as a legitimate response to a technological landscape characterized by hype and instability, mixed AI performance results, and a lack of acknowledgment of the long-term consequences of AI adoption. These are significant issues that need to be better understood through a critical lens involving independent research and collaborative action. We need to manage the limitations imposed by the economic and information asymmetries in AI technology development; organizational leaders need to apply a strategic and proactive approach to this.

An understanding of human entanglement is critical for reshaping AI technology development and enablement in a responsible and sustainable manner, given the negative impacts that current approaches are having on human and planetary flourishing. With this in mind, this book provides a set of models, frameworks, and practical design tools that organizations can use to navigate AI challenges and leverage AI opportunities while minimizing its harms and limitations.

Past technology-led business transformation practices have limited applicability in navigating the challenges of intelligent technologies. Many of these legacy transfomration practices have experienced high failure rates over several decades, which arguably stem from persistent llimitations in practitioner and researcher appreciation of human–machine entanglements. Renewed mindsets and approaches are needed in the AI era to avoid us replicating the inequities and diminishing returns of the status quo.

YOUR CALL TO ACTION

The world has plenty of so-called innovators, changemakers, and disruptors, especially among technology startups and major tech corporations. Despite their admirable enthusiasm, they're all still operating in an old-world model of command and control. They're mostly busy with "breaking things" in the name of innovation but may be in fact replacing one flawed system with another – and in the process cultivating greater economic concentration while weakening our social and earth systems. What we need right now are "world builders" – people who are nurturing new organizations and new human–machine systems that aren't tethered to the legacy of the past. And AI is both enabling and challenging them to do just that. Are you ready to be a world builder? If so, read on.

ACKNOWLEDGMENTS

This project has received funding from the European Union's Horizon 2020 research and innovation program under the Marie Sklodowska-Curie Grant Agreement No 101023024 for *Augmented-Humans*. Gratitude also to Professor Juho Hamari and Tampere Univerity, Finland, for hosting the MSCA fellowship.

REFERENCES

Akata, Z., Balliet, D., de Rijke, M., Dignum, F., … Welling, M. (2020). A research agenda for hybrid intelligence: Augmenting human intellect with collaborative, adaptive, responsible, and explainable artificial intelligence. *Computer*, *53*(8), 18–28. https://doi.org/10.1109/MC.2020.2996587.

Bender, E. M., Gebru, T., McMillan-Major, A., and Mitchell, S. (2021). On the dangers of stochastic parrots: Can language models be too big? In *Proceedings of the 2021 ACM Conference on Fairness, Accountability, and Transparency* (pp. 610–623).

Berente, N., Gu, B., Recker, J., and Santhanam, R. (2021). Managing artificial intelligence. *MIS Quarterly*, *45*(3), 1433–1450.

Birhane, A. (2021). Algorithmic injustice: A relational ethics approach. *Patterns*, *2*(2). https://doi.org/10.1016/j.patter.2021.100205

Cabrera-Sánchez, J. P., Villarejo-Ramos, Á. F., Liébana-Cabanillas, F., and Shaikh, A. A. (2021). Identifying relevant segments of AI applications adopters – Expanding the UTAUT2's variables. *Telematics and Informatics*, *58*, 101529. https://doi.org/10.1016/j.tele.2020.101529.

Cao, G., Duan, Y., Edwards, J. S., and Dwivedi, Y. K. (2021). Understanding managers' attitudes and behavioral intentions towards using artificial intelligence for organizational decision-making. *Technovation*, *106*, 102312.

Carroll, M., Shah, R., Ho, M. K., Griffiths, T. L., Seshia, S. A., Abbeel, P., and Dragan, A. (2019). *On the Utility of Learning about Humans for Human-AI Coordination*. http://arxiv.org/abs/1910.05789

Chen, M., Herrera, F., and Hwang, K. (2018). Cognitive computing: Architecture, technologies and intelligent applications. *IEEE Access*, *6*, 19774–19783.

Collins, C., Dennehy, D., Conboy, K., and Mikalef, P. (2021). Artificial intelligence in information systems research: A systematic literature review and research agenda. *International Journal of Information Management*, *60*. https://doi.org/10.1016/j.ijinfomgt.2021.102383.

Crandall, J. W., Oudah, M., Tennom, Ishowo-Oloko, F., Abdallah, S., Bonnefon, J. F., Cebrian, M., Shariff, A., Goodrich, M. A., and Rahwan, I. (2018). Cooperating with machines. *Nature Communications*, *9*(1). https://doi.org/10.1038/s41467-017-02597-8

Cubric, M. (2020). Drivers, barriers and social considerations for AI adoption in business and management: A tertiary study. *Technology in Society*, *62*, 101257.

de Cremer, D., Kasparov, G., Wojcicki, A., and Images, G. (2021). *Business and Society AI Should Augment Human Intelligence, Not Replace It Summary*. https://hbr.org/2021/03/ai-should-augment-human-intelligence-not-replace-it

Dellermann, D., Calma, A., Lipusch, N., Weber, T., Weigel, S., and Ebel, P. (2019). *The Future of Human-AI Collaboration: A Taxonomy of Design Knowledge for Hybrid Intelligence Systems*. https://hdl.handle.net/10125/59468

Demartini, G., Difallah, D. E., Gadiraju, U., and Catasta, M. (2016). An introduction to hybrid human-machine information systems. *Foundations and Trends in Web Science*, *7*(1), 1–87. https://doi.org/10.1561/1800000025

Dietvorst, B. J., Simmons, J. P., and Massey, C. (2015). Algorithm aversion: people erroneously avoid algorithms after seeing them err. *Journal of experimental psychology. General*, 144(1), 114.

Duan, Y., Edwards, J. S., and Dwivedi, Y. K. (2019). Artificial intelligence for decision making in the era of Big Data – evolution, challenges and research agenda. *International Journal of Information Management*, 48, 63–71. https://doi.org/10.1016/j.ijinfomgt.2019.01.021

Dubey, R., Gunasekaran, A., Childe, S. J., Bryde, D. J., Giannakis, M., Foropon, C., ... and Hazen, B. T. (2020). Big data analytics and artificial intelligence pathway to operational performance under the effects of entrepreneurial orientation and environmental dynamism: A study of manufacturing organisations. *International Journal of Production Economics*, *226*, 107599.

Dwivedi, Y. K., Hughes, L., Ismagilova, E., Aarts, G., Coombs, C., Crick, T., Duan, Y., Dwivedi, R., … Williams, M. D. (2021). Artificial intelligence: Multidisciplinary perspectives on emerging challenges, opportunities, and agenda for research, practice and policy. *International Journal of Information Management*, *57*, 101994.

Goodhue, D. L. and Thompson, R. L. (1995). Task-technology fit and individual performance. *MIS Quarterly*, *19*, 213–236.

Gray, D. and Shellshear, E. (2024). *Why Data Science Projects Fail: The Harsh Realities of Implementing AI and Analytics, without the Hype*. CRC Press.

Hanelt, A., Bohnsack, R., Marz, D., and Antunes Marante, C. (2021). A systematic review of the literature on digital transformation: Insights and implications for strategy and organizational change. *Journal of Management Studies*, 58(5), 1159–1197.

Ishowo-Oloko, F., Bonnefon, J.-F., Soroye, Z., Crandall, J., Rahwan, I., and Rahwan, T. (2019). Behavioural evidence for a transparency – efficiency tradeoff in human–machine cooperation. *Nature Machine Intelligence*, *1*(11), 517–521. https://doi.org/10.1038/s42256-019-0113-5.

Kiesler, S., Sproull, L., and Waters, K. (1996). A prisoner's dilemma experiment on cooperation with people and human-like computers. *Journal of Personality and Social Psychology*, *70*(1), 47–65.

Marcus, G. (2022). Artificial General Intelligence is not as imminent as you might yhink, *Scientific American*, June 6, 2022.

Metcalf, L., Askay, D. A., and Rosenberg, L. B. (2019). Keeping humans in the loop: Pooling knowledge through artificial swarm intelligence to improve business decision making. *California Management Review*, *61*(4), 84–109. https://doi.org/10.1177/0008125619862256

Mikalef, P., and Gupta, M. (2021). Artificial intelligence capability: Conceptualization, measurement calibration, and empirical study on its impact on organizational creativity and firm performance. *Information and Management*, *58*(3), 103434.

Mirbabaie, M., Brünker, F., Möllmann Frick, N. R., and Stieglitz, S. (2022). The rise of artificial intelligence – understanding the AI identity threat at the workplace. *Electronic Markets*, *32*(1), 73–99.

Newlands, G. (2021). Lifting the curtain: Strategic visibility of human labour in AI-as-a-Service. *Big Data and Society*, *8*(1). https://doi.org/10.1177/20539517211016026

Newman, S., Birhane, A., Zajko, M., Birhane, A., Osoba, O. A., Prunkl, C., Lima, G., Bowen, J., Sutton, R., and Adams, C. (2019). *AI and Agency*. https://escholarship.org/uc/item/8q15786s.

Oh, C., Lee, T., Kim, Y., Park, S. H., Kwon, S., and Suh, B. (2017). Us vs. them: Understanding artificial intelligence technophobia over the Google DeepMind Challenge Match. *Conference on Human Factors in Computing Systems – Proceedings*, *2017-May*, 2523–2534.

Parasuraman, R., and Wickens, C. D. (2008). Humans: Still vital after all these years of automation. *Human Factors*, *50*(3), 511–520. https://doi.org/10.1518/001872008X312198

Pumplun, L., Tauchert, C., and Heidt, M. (2019). A new organizational chassis for artificial intelligence-exploring organizational readiness factors. *Twenty-Seventh European Conference on Information Systems (ECIS2019)*, Stockholm-Uppsala, Sweden.

Schepman, A., and Rodway, P. (2023). The General Attitudes towards Artificial Intelligence Scale (GAAIS): Confirmatory validation and associations with personality, corporate distrust, and general trust. *International Journal of Human–Computer Interaction*, *39*(13), 2724–2741.

Scheuerman, M. K., Hanna, A., and Denton, E. (2021). Do datasets have politics? Disciplinary values in computer vision dataset development. *Proceedings of the ACM on Human-Computer Interaction*, *5*(CSCW2), 1–37.

Shollo, A., Hopf, K., Thiess, T., and Müller, O. (2022). Shifting ML value creation mechanisms: A process model of ML value creation. *The Journal of Strategic Information Systems*, *31*(3), 101734.

Spies, R., Grobbelaar, S., and Botha, A. (2020). A scoping review of the application of the task-technology fit theory. In *Responsible Design, Implementation and Use of Information and Communication Technology: 19th IFIP WG 6.11 Conference on e-Business, e-Services, and e-Society, I3E 2020, Skukuza, South Africa, April 6–8, 2020, Proceedings, Part I 19* (pp. 397–408).

Spieth, P., Röth, T., Clauss, T., and Klos, C. (2021). Technological frames in the digital age: Theory, measurement instrument, and future research areas. *Journal of Management Studies*, *58*, 1962–1993.

Stowers, K., Brady, L. L., MacLellan, C., Wohleber, R., and Salas, E. (2021). Improving teamwork competencies in human–machine teams: perspectives from team science. *Frontiers in Psychology*, *12*. https://doi.org/10.3389/fpsyg.2021.590290.

Suseno, Y., Chang, C., Hudik, M., and Fang, E. S. (2022). Beliefs, anxiety and change readiness for artificial intelligence adoption among human resource managers: the moderating role of high-performance work systems. *The International Journal of Human Resource Management*, *33*(6), 1209–1236.

Van den Hoven, J. (2007). ICT and value sensitive design. In *The Information Society: Innovation, Legitimacy, Ethics and Democracy in honor of Professor Jacques Berleur sj: Proceedings of the Conference "Information Society: Governance, Ethics and Social Consequences,"* University of Namur, Belgium 22–23 May 2006 (pp. 67–72). Springer US.

CHAPTER 2

AI at Work and in Society

The easiest way to solve a problem is to deny it exists.

—ISAAC ASIMOV

INTRODUCTION

The augmentation of human intellect and capability with artificial intelligence is integral to the development of next-generation human–machine collaboration technologies designed to drive performance improvement and innovation. However, while the focus of human–machine augmentation has been on return on business investment, it is also critical to human flourishing at the humane, social, and planetary level. What is often ignored is that without human flourishing, all other technological, financial, and economic systems cannot by definition flourish either.

The field of human–machine augmentation has experienced considerable interest and investment since the 1950s and to this day is still constrained by a fragmentation of research across multiple scholarly disciplines and technology silos. Most critically, the domain has been criticized for its underrepresentation of the unique challenges of human–machine augmentation for cognitive work in complex environments, both at the research and application levels. Furthermore, human intelligence is embodied; therefore, machine intelligence is inherently limited by its technological infrastructures.

The rise of artificial intelligence (AI) is driving what many researchers and industry commentators are calling the "Fourth Industrial Revolution" and is steadily disrupting traditional business models and practices of strategy, innovation, and performance management (Longo et al., 2020; Sharma and Rana, 2020; Sima et al., 2020). Industrial

DOI: 10.1201/9781003616566-3

revolutions imply a *fundamental change* in the way we live, work, we relate to one another, and systemic shifts in our economy. Many AI-induced changes are underway; however, we are still unreliably forecasting how these systemic changes may impact the socio-economic structure of our society.

This generation of AI-enabled technologies, which has evolved over the last ten years, is showing significant potential, largely driven by significant advancements in technological capabilities of data extraction, storage, and analysis, machine learning, computing power, and algorithmic capability (Collins et al., 2021; Duan et al., 2019; Dwivedi et al., 2021; Berente et al., 2021). More recently, the emergence and continued growth of the mass consumer market for generative AI since 2022 has seen a significant resurgence in technological development, investment, and business interest in AI.

Researchers overall agree that these technological advances are different from the technological advances of the past, and as we will explore later in this chapter, disagreements on the impact and trajectory of AI are largely based on ideological and theoretical differences or limited and inconsistent information. Even with consumer-focused generative AI, the initial excitement (often hype-driven) and the expectations of their impact on productivity improvement are inconsistent. Recent research shows that, without detracting from the obvious great utility of generative AI, they are still failing to make a meaningful economic and labor market impact (Humlum and Vestergaard, 2025). For example, in a recent workplace study, generative AI had actually increased workload for 77% of workers (Brynjolfsson et al., 2025), and in another study, workers who reported productivity improvements expected greater productivity benefits than were delivered (Bruno et al., 2025).

However, despite the astonishing rate of progress with AI technology capability, it is still widely agreed that the complex challenges in the current business environment cannot be solved by machines alone and require robust human–machine hybrid solutions for most business systems (Akata et al., 2020; de Cremer et al., 2021; Dellermann et al., 2019; Demartini et al., 2016; Parasuraman and Wickens, 2008). This is more than an ideological stance on the importance of human–machine collaboration for best outcomes. Examples from drone piloting (Lundberg et al., 2021), medical robotics and diagnostics (Callaghan et al., 2018), citizen science (Rafner et al., 2021), and defence (Stowers et al., 2021) show that the most innovative results are delivered when humans and machines work together. This is particularly true where computational and analytical tasks with situational and cognitive complexity require human and machine working on the problem as a team (Crouser and Chang, 2012; Jarrahi, 2018; Keding and Meissner, 2021). In a current and future business climate characterized by increasing ambiguity and complexity, a dynamic collaboration between human and machine facilitates improved opportunities for innovation discovery.

One of the key challenges organizations and technology developers face is identifying how to design systems and AI-enabled technologies that adequately solve the *augmentation design problem* that encompasses the unique capabilities of humans with AI across different systems and contexts – and embedding these applications within legacy systems.

We define the augmentation design problem as the arrangement and alignment of psychological, social, organizational, and technical systems to produce dynamic, productive, ethical, and creative interplay between humans and intelligence machines. However, the nature of all new *design problems* is that they are largely undetermined, ill-structured, situated within the challenges of their specific contexts, and are often complicated by paradoxical situations (Dorst, 2004; 2006). This lies at the heart of the issues in the emergent world human–machine collaboration.

The focus of this book is largely on AI application domains requiring specialist cognitive or knowledge work where skilled professionals work on complex, non-routine tasks that require a degree of collaboration, teamwork, and creative problem-solving to create value. These professions are increasingly working with augmented systems where AI technologies and humans work together as a team for a significant portion of the functional process. For example, such professions included in our research include risk detection, demand forecasting, air traffic control, disease diagnosis, urban planning, crime prediction, logistics management, customer segmentation, as well as emergent fields in the creative arts, such as music composition, literature, game design, and visual design.

There are significant challenges with regard to the implementation of human–machine augmented systems that range from user acceptance and trust of AI technology, AI system understandability, explainability and usability, work systems design, and systemic organizational limitations for full-scale implementations beyond pilots. These implementation and enablement issues are explored in detail in *Part III: Disentanglement*, and an overview will be explored in this chapter.

There is limited research on human–machine augmentation or collaboration relative to the more popular field of AI automation, such as business process automation and robotic process automation of clear-cut tasks and functions. Augmentation and automation are fundamentally different in their motivations, technology architectures, and value-creation goals; automation seeks to replace human labor to reduce costs and reap process efficiencies. In comparison, augmentation seeks to enhance and empower the unique capability of humans in working collaboratively with AI technologies to enable more effective decision-making and value creation.

The preponderance of literature on AI automation compared to augmentation is often attributed to the historic success of AI advancements in routine, manual, mass data computation, and less complex or predictable tasks. However, AI replacing or augmenting tasks that require more sophisticated cognitive processing, particularly in complex and ambiguous environments, remains a challenge to develop and scale. For example, researchers maintain that the tacit knowledge of skilled workers is difficult to codify for machine learning purposes (Metcalf et al., 2019). Furthermore, the human element in AI development is often understated or made invisible (Newlands, 2021; Birhane, 2021; Birhane et al., 2021a,b). This underplays the important roles that humans have along the entire AI value chain to fit the wider narrative of machine superiority.

However, this distinction is also murky as augmentation cannot always be neatly separated from automation, as they are often interdependent and create paradoxes and tensions in their development and implementation (Raisch and Krakowski, 2021; Coombs et al., 2020; Keding and Meissner, 2021). As is more often the case, AI technologies often take over certain tasks or functions of specialist cognitive work rather than the job in its entirety; therefore, it can automate part of a function that lends itself to automation, then augments (or neglects) the rest, leaving it to the organization to renegotiate the boundaries between the role of human vs machine vs both. This has continuous redesign consequences on workflows, job autonomy, process management, and organizational systems development as the AI technology advances. In other instances, AI hits a wall and can't improve beyond an impasse, in its development or application.

Job roles and functions that are complex or involve a high level of cognitive functions cannot always be codified or fully covered in a job description. For example, research in business process re-engineering and digital transformation shows that we can only document between 50% and 70% of a job function; therefore, it is easy to miss where and how humans add value through improvising and initiative, the gap between what their job roles say they do and what they actually do. This has been a key feature of the reasons behind the high failure rates of business transformation initiatives, where digital transformations that are intended to improve efficiency have a high failure rate of up to 90% (Ramesh and Delen, 2021). This can also be seen in widespread reports of organizations rolling back initial human layoffs after investments in LLM technologies, citing reductions in efficiency and effective customer service. For example, Klarna rolled back its AI strategy after AI agents initially replaced 22% of its workforce with a saving of US$ 10m do to longer-term losses in effectiveness (Wilkins, 2025).

Over time, AI technologies will continue to improve and will likely solve several impasses that we are facing today. However, very often it may require different architectures to show significant improvement. For example, it is often claimed that the probabilistic language "intelligence" that powers LLMs will not be able to reach "AGI" level intelligence with the current machine learning architectures they employ. These issues touch the surface of the *augmentation design problem* – issues that cannot be managed with the same principles applied to AI automation (or even traditional information technology deployments) due to the heightened complexity of the human–machine relationship within the dynamics of the organizational ecosystem that sustains it.

AI research to date has been largely placed in the computer science and engineering domains, and only recently has there been an emergence of more significant research focusing on human factors and calls for multidisciplinary research, which is still in its early stages in academic research. Unfortunately, at this point in time, the research is far from where organizations need it to be for guidance on how to augment human–machine systems, integrate them within existing socio-technical legacy systems, while at the same time operating in an increasingly complex and uncertain socio-economic-political environment. The race is on to build bigger, better, faster foundational models (and the infrastructures required to sustain them) rather on how organizations can better integrate AI technologies so that they deliver returns on investment today.

Organizational agility and adaptability are key, but not how those terms are commonly understood to be. These terms have their origins in the stable and measurable manufacturing industries for which they were developed. Barriers to entry and investment costs for AI (outside of generative AI) are very high and complex; however, the AI hype machine has oversimplified the challenge, which has led to costly errors or missteps for organizations. A critical and multidisciplinary approach is vital to not only empower organizations with the right knowledge but also to guide the future development of AI technologies. Convergence is taking place within and between the key research disciplines that can make this happen, and that are featured in this book. The state of play is as follows:

- Recent initiatives in **human–computer interaction (HCI)** which have called for more collaborative research with the computer science domain to overcome critical limiting issues such as user acceptance and adoption of AI technology, systemic bias (such as gender or race bias in algorithms) and the development of ethical and democratized AI (Abdul et al., 2018; Gulati et al., 2017; C. Wang et al., 2012; Y. Wang et al., 2020; Zhang et al., 2021).
- **In the information systems (IS) domain**, several reviews and studies have explored a deeper understanding of the implications of AI technologies on information system development, applications, and implementations, and in user acceptance and value creation (Borges et al., 2021; Collins et al., 2021; Coombs et al., 2020; Dwivedi et al., 2021; Hinsen et al., 2022; Keding and Meissner, 2021; Marabelli et al., 2021; Rzepka and Berger, 2018). The IS research community has already identified that the fragmentation of AI research has become a limiting factor in understanding AI integration and performance in organizations and has noted the plethora of mixed and contradictory results and gaps in knowledge that need to be addressed.
- Similarly in the **management domain** research interests in the fields of value creation, strategic positioning, human resource management and organizational development have identified mixed results and ever widening knowledge gaps as the speed of AI technology development gathers pace (Cubric, 2020; Enholm et al., 2021; Keding and Meissner, 2021; Langer and Landers, 2021; Niehaus and Wiesche, 2021; Raisch and Krakowski, 2021).
- In the specific field of **human–machine teaming**, researchers have identified critical limitations in knowledge that are limiting the potential of human–machine collaboration such as the development of human and machine theory of mind and shared mental models, and how to create dynamic and productive interactions between humans and cognitive teaming agents (Cooke et al., 2013; Gorman, 2014; Chakraborti et al., 2017; Seeber et al., 2020; Carroll et al., 2019) before we can see extensive and reliable human–machine collaboration and decision making in the wild.
- In the **computer science domain**, researchers have identified limitations in algorithmic behavior, the adequacy of machine learning training data, and problems with inductive biases encoded in training models that are limiting trust, usability, and technology acceptance in human–machine collaborations (John et al., 2022; Figalist et al., 2022; D'Amour et al., 2022). The common denominator across

> these research domains is the call for greater cross-disciplinary research to fully understand the scope and potential of AI-enabled technology in human–machine collaboration. Fundamental to this is also a deeper understanding of what intelligence means.

These research initiatives are responding to the wider issue of the current limited understanding of the impact of AI-enabled applications across a litany of areas critical for social and workplace acceptance such as human displacement, human job satisfaction, motivation, agency and autonomy, and a recognition of the critical roles of "humans in the loop" in terms of their instrumental role in creating more effective machine learning models and decision-making capabilities. It is also in response to a greater recognition of the innate capabilities of humans that AI cannot replicate or substitute over the medium term (or if at all), such as innate human affordances of intuition, creativity, innovation, empathy, and judgment.

The bundle of technologies at the focus of this book is on AI-enabled information systems and business applications that include algorithms (capability to predict, classify, and cluster data for problem-solving and decision-making), machine learning (including deep learning, neural networks, training data, and training models), computer vision (facial recognition, object detection), natural language processing (specifically for conversational agents, chatbots, and virtual assistants) robotics, speech recognition, decision support and expert systems, automation, algorithmic management, and generative AI.

In this book, these technologies are collectively referred to as *AI or AI-enabled systems* unless a specific AI technology is being addressed, such as generative AI or robotics. In addition to these specific AI technologies, *secondary technologies* are also critical to AI enablement in terms of how they affect user experience in the human–machine collaboration process. These include usability, interaction, interface design, explainability, and understandability. A large category of these secondary technologies also includes interactive tools of mediation that enhance AI design, development, and user engagement. These include virtual, augmented, and mixed reality, serious games or simulations, internet-of-things devices that act as tools for human–machine engagement and activity activation for data collection. For example, games and simulations are used as data collection tools for both problem-solving and machine learning. Case in point is the game Fold-It, which was an experimental research project developed by the University of Washington, where 57,000 participants of the game helped discover the molecular structure of retroviral protease enzyme M-PMV, a problem that had been puzzling scientists for a decade (Cooper et al., 2010). Fold-It spawned a plethora of other AI-driven citizen science games to enable widespread data collection, data analysis, accuracy, and verification to advance scientific discovery, such as iNaturalist, Phylo, EyeWire, ColonyB, among many others.

Understanding AI is to understand that there is a rich diversity and interdependence of different technologies forming a value chain to get a job done. This value chain of technologies may also differ between different applications and problem domains. In most

AI applications, we only see and understand an interface and are largely unaware of the networked technologies that enable it.

The **key focus of this chapter** is to highlight the state of academic and business knowledge on the augmentation of human and artificial intelligence for human–machine collaboration and offers insight into the research gaps and opportunities for better practice. On a strategic level, this chapter also highlights how organizations may prepare to develop and incorporate augmented intelligence in their systems as a driver of value creation and innovation. This will include identifying the inimitable elements of human creativity and cognition, which are critical for augmented intelligence, a whole-of-system integration of AI as a team member, and designing for human acceptance of AI technology in the digital workplace to enhance human–machine collaboration.

In the next section, we will clarify some foundational work on AI definitions, the ideologies that framed them, and the world views that have shaped the AI industry into what it is today.

AI DEFINITIONS, IDEOLOGIES, AND WORLD VIEWS

Despite the plethora of research on AI over many decades, there still isn't a reliable set of clear, common definitions or understanding of "artificial intelligence." Recent information systems (IS) systematic literature reviews have found that many researchers have even avoided defining AI and have instead built an understanding of the aims of the AI research they are undertaking and provided an indication of the range of AI technologies under review (Borges et al., 2021; Collins et al., 2021; Rzepka and Berger, 2018).

It was clear from my research that a common, agreed definition does not exist or has become malleable because different research and business domains (and their respective distinct world views) have developed their own unique definitions based on their own perspectives – all with insufficient common ground to develop an agreed position on definition. This also includes a lack of an agreed trajectory, purpose, and intent of the future of AI development and deployment.

Most definitions of AI include the basic tenets of the following elements:

- The ability of computer systems to perform tasks that typically require human intelligence, such as learning, reasoning, and problem-solving.
- The range of technologies at its core such as machine learning, which allows systems to learn from data and improve over time without explicit programming.
- The range of various applications such as visual perception, speech recognition, decision-making, making recommendations, and language translation.

However, a lack of an agreed terminology is not necessarily a bad thing – it's just a reflection of the early and uneven development of different AI technologies in different domains. Uneven development often occurs within sectors, as much of AI's capability is dependent on the availability of quality data and model development; this creates uneven and inconsistent development within and between different sectors. And in reality, this is an acceptable situation given the early stages of the current wave of AI development.

For example, within the specific area of deep learning-enabled medical computer vision, the four key areas of radiology, pathology, ophthalmology, and dermatology have advanced unevenly due to the different visual pattern-recognition nature of diagnostic tasks in these specialties and the availability of highly structured images – the key differentiators being the quality of training data, model limitations, and the environment in which they are deployed (Esteva et al., 2021; Finlayson et al., 2019). In the context of this example, a general definition of AI holds little value. What would be more appropriate would be something like "deep learning-enabled medical computer vision for diagnostics in radiology (name your specialty)." The definition is almost a description of what the AI does rather than what it is. Far from being a limitation, definitional diversity and ambiguity can be seen as generative which often leads to productive enquiry and technological advances in emergent domains (Berente et al., 2021).

Bear with me on this, as you will also encounter different and competing definitions that are based not only on the boundry limitations of the technology, but also on different world views and ideologies, as well as access to independent, critical research. Words matter; therefore, it's important to look for the meaning behind the names, descriptions that are used, and the type of future they are envisioning. Be critical of where they've come from, and whether it is a fit with the direction and values of your organization.

NOMENCLATURES OF HUMAN-AI SYSTEMS

The different nomenclatures in AI research studies in relation to defining or classifying human–AI systems by ***what they do*** are as interesting as they are diverse. Noteworthy is that these definitions are symbolic of the underlying perceptions of the shape of these systems and where the power lies. Therefore, being aware of the divergent definitions and their philosophical underpinnings is important when leaders are looking to implement AI in their organizations, as it must be compatible with their own organization's philosophical foundations. Different descriptions can also mean a specialized algorithm or machine learning models for a specific function or application domain. The categories of ***what AI does*** fall under three clusters of orientations: machine, human, or a hybrid of the two.

- **Machine orientations:** These definitions put the algorithm in the lead, such as algorithmic decision-making (Marabelli et al., 2021), or for automating humans such as human automation (Kaber and Endsley, 2004), symbiotic autonomous systems (Boschert et al., 2019; Kaynak et al., 2021), intelligent automation (Coombs et al., 2020).
- **Humanized orientations:** These definitions are fusions of human and machines such as artificial swarm intelligence (Metcalf et al., 2019), AI–human complementarity (Fügener et al., 2021), human-AI or machine symbiosis (Jarrahi, 2018). Humans in the loop is a widely used term and is used to describe two different

functions: (a) where humans fit in a decision-making hierarchy in expert systems for sensemaking, and (b) how humans are used in the cycle of data collection and annotation for machine learning purposes. Other definitions in this category focus on AI agents such as human–agent teamwork (Hyland-Wood et al., 2019; Yang, 2021), multi-agent systems (Calvaresi et al., 2019), human–machine teaming (Stowers et al., 2021). This category also uses terms to name the human–AI relationship, which is varied in mainstream business media and consultancies and tends to attempt to define how humans and machines can work co-operatively or collaboratively to achieve sustainable business outcomes (Capgemini, 2020; Deloitte, 2019; KPMG, 2019; McKinsey, 2021; PwC, 2017a and b).

- **Hybrid orientation:** These definitions focus on human–machine augmentation which is a complex term that can either mean (a) a combination of the practical human–machine relationship as covered in the above terms, or (b) the physical amalgamation of humans and machines that include implants or bionic parts as espoused by cybernetics and transhumanism. Terms include human–machine hybrid (Dellermann et al., 2019; Demartini et al., 2016), hybrid intelligence (Akata et al., 2020).

The semiotics of the terms used can be seen as framing the diverse cognitive and socio-cultural intentions of the human–machine relationship such as the role, function, or value of the human in relation to the AI in the system. This ranges on a continuum from exploitative (such as automation or humans in-the-loop) to co-operative (such as complementarity or teamwork) which reflects a philosophical underpinning of the functional intent of the human–machine relationship. This is also indicative of where the balance of power resides – with the human or the machine.

These positions go back to the beginnings of research on AI in the post war era. The origins of the term ***augmented intelligence*** originated with Engelbart (1962) with *augmenting human intellect* whose focus was on using AI to enable greater human capability by augmenting the technology with human intelligence. Compare this to the Licklider (2008) position established in 1960 and Fitts (1951) with the term ***man-machine symbiosis***, as well as McCarthy's position in1955 (McCarthy et al., 2006) whose focus and goals in AI research were to attain dominance of machine intellect over humans. These two very different positions – human augmentation vs machine supremacy – are critical and have been with us since the beginnings of AI research.. Now, let's dig a little deeper into the history of how these positions evolved to shed light on how we got to where we are today.

The Coupling of Technology and Defence

The early stages of AI research were funded by the Defence Advanced Research Projects Agency (DARPA, formerly ARPA) from the 1950s, and this is a vitally important piece of history that had shaped the milieu, focus, and intent of AI research and development. The Cold War laid the foundations for the interest in AI research and development as an imperative for national security through a belief that the technology will help facilitate a technologically advanced economy and military superiority relative to other geopolitical actors. We can see how the current race between the US and China toward artificial general intelligence and global strategic technological dominance has seen the re-emergence of the "AI race" narrative, and how it has been used to justify reduced regulatory oversight and government subsidies to gain and maintain a decisive strategic advantage (Ó hÉigeartaigh, 2025).

Critics highlight the historical entanglement of AI with imperialism, capitalism, militarism, and neoliberal economic theory (Ilyenkov, 1968; Katz, 2022; Morozov, 2023) and that this has led to less than desirable levels of authoritarianism, surveillance, and control. Critics maintain that this entanglement has given rise to ideals of techno-solutionism, and techno-utopias at the cost of long-term social-economic equity and political equality and freedoms. We explore empire–technology entanglements in detail in Chapter 4.

It is important to be aware of the origin story that began in the 1950s with the battle between the Engelbart and McCarthy perspectives, the eventual dominance of the machine-superiority perspective, and the ideologies that have shaped the motivations of investors and developers to this day. As a leader, you need to be aware that these voices (in both support and opposition) will likely become louder and more prominent as AI continues to develop and influence the shape of the social fabric of our communities and economy.

As mentioned in the section above, the philosophical dichotomy of *machine superiority versus human augmentation* has influenced AI development from the beginning, with Engelbart (Engelbart, 1962) viewing AI as an extraordinary tool to enhance human capability, to Licklider (2008) and McCarthy et al. (2006) viewing AI as a process of humans morphing into or being eventually replaced by the superiority of machines. This is a tale of two different mental models. These opposing positions have been with artificial intelligence are still largely unresolved to this day, 65 years later. Whilst a difference of opinion is always a good thing in science, what is troubling is when viewpoints akin to ideologies are held by powerful individuals or organizations that have the means to influence public opinion and investment in their style of AI.

Ideological Perspectives

The philosophical dichotomy between humane AI versus machine superiority has become more fractured in recent times into various schools of thought that have strongly held theories or opinions about the trajectory of AI development and its impact on humanity and the planet. There are seven key streams of ideas that have gathered momentum over the last ten years, and there is *considerable disagreement among the world's top AI scientists on their likely manifestation*. Below I've provided an outline of the key ideologies that are influencing the discourse on artificial intelligence. They are not necessarily distinct groups as streams of different ideas and beliefs from these ideologies weave in and out of each other like a meshwork. They can be controversial and divisive; none of them can say unequivocally that their philosophies are grounded in fact, just interesting data (that's why I call them *ideologies*). They are above all compelling perspectives that need to be understood when navigating the AI noise and hype.

Artificial General Intelligence (AGI)

The ideology behind AGI is that machines will reach and surpass human intelligence, which also includes human-like capabilities such as sentience, a world view, consciousness, and free will. AGI tends to be of interest to the technology, business, politics, and economics domains as a promise of an engine of progress that will drive cost-efficiencies and increased profits as well as solve humanity's most vexing problems. Many tech companies believe that they are on the verge of AGI, while others believe AGI is not possible under the current dominant technology architectures (Heikkilä and Heaven, 2022), and still others believe that AGI is simply a myth (Mueller, 2024) or intended for nefarious purposes (Gebru and Torres, 2024).

Singularity and Transhumanism

These ideologies espouse that humans will merge with machines as a natural evolution at a specific point in the future – and it is coming fast. With ***singularity***, Kurzweil (2005) predicts that there will be the merging of biological and machine intelligence to the extent that the majority of human intelligence will become non-biological, through the merging of virtual and physical reality. Our brains will be connected through immersive experiences and AI will become part of our brain activity, our cognition and our sensory experience.

With ***transhumanism***, the idea is that humans will eventually use robotic body parts and brain implants to transcend the biological limitations of our species and evolve into a new, advanced species (Huxley, 1957). Transhumanists claim that we are already at the beginning of the movement with the use of prosthetics, genetic engineering, bionic body parts, biohacking, and potentially neural implants as examples. The transhumanist movement is based on the beliefs of liberating the human race from its biological constraints and the transformation of humans into the technologically superior "posthuman" – something we discuss in more detail in the next chapter. Critics often compare the transhumanist movement to a secular religion (Tirosh-Samuelson, 2012), For example, staunch advocates believe that transhumanism, through its advanced technology, can improve the human condition and offer a clear path toward a specific goal, such as promising an afterlife (Lemasters, 2024). While transhumanism is a movement that believes in using science and technology to improve the human condition and surpass our biological limitations, the term ***cyborg*** (or a cybernetic organism) is generally used to describe the entity such as the biological human whose body has been enhanced with smart prostheses, electronic implants, or temporary devices, with the end result being a symbiotic hybrid between human, environment and machine (Clark, 2001; Dragomir, 2023).

The AI Existential Threat

The AI existential threat follows on from those who espouse that after humanity achieves AGI and progresses to **super intelligence** (where the AI entity becomes self-aware and hides itself from humans by creating its own undecipherable language) then replicates itself to take over the planet. AI "doomers," as they are known colloquially, believe that AI poses an existential threat that will eventually turn on humanity and destroy it. Very often, science fiction is given as examples of the underlying threat, citing popular media such as "Skynet" from the film *Terminator* to get their views across (Redfern, 2023). Those who subscribe to these ideologies believe that to prevent the existential threat, governments and AI tech companies need to form unilateral agreements to provide guardrails for development or even limit its development (Bengio et al., 2024). However, this strategy is widely criticized by AI startups as so-called guardrails only serve to raise the barriers to entry for new players and concentrate power with existing tech companies. Furthermore, several established tech companies also oppose guardrails as they feel it restricts their business innovation and place cautious nations at risk in the current tense geopolitical environment. Key proponents of AI's likelihood to trigger human extinction are also coming from proponents of *longterminism and affective altruism*, which is discussed in more detail below.

Longterminism, Affective Altruism and Accelerationism

These are interconnected philosophies emphasizing the moral responsibility we have toward future generations and by taking decisive action to maximize global good. This utilitarianism-inspired philanthropic movement was founded by Oxford philosophers Toby Ord and William MacAskill (Crary, 2023), who had later become strongly affiliated with key influencers in Silicon Valley and had resulted in several prominent tech multi-millionaires and billionaires supporting longtermist projects. While Longtermism (LT) provides the ethical framework for prioritizing AI risks, Effective Altruism (EA) mobilizes resources and talent toward solutions. Together, they've shifted tech and policy debates toward precautionary measures, though balancing innovation with safety remains contentious. The influential principles LT and EA have been reported as increasingly shaping the course of AI development by prioritizing existential risk mitigation and ethical alignment.

While there is a considerable cohort of technology investors who have ties to these philosophies such as Sam Bankman-Fried, Elon Musk, Nick Bostrom, and Duston Moskovitz (Naughton, 2022), LT and EA are widely distrusted outside of this sphere of influence due to their unclear or ambiguous positions on the dark side of these ideologies. While on the surface, LT and EA appear to have noble goals, they have been criticized for having an uncritical attitude toward existing political and economic institutions, believing that welfarism is a threat to the status quo, and that potential deviant AI or robot takeover should be a bigger priority than the current issues of environmental degradation or socio-economic inequities. LT and EA have faced accusations of eugenics due to historical ties, controversial statements by key figures, and perceived ideological overlaps with eugenic principles.

An offshoot of this group are the accelerationist groups who believe that radical social transformation is needed and is inevitable, and that AI can help accelerate this. The more influential amongst these groups tend to be found amongst the tech elite who believe in the obsolescence of democracy and human welfare, see an inevitable demise of the human species by AI, and work towards the survival of an elite group of humans (often tied to white supremacists).

Machine Consciousness and Rights

The beliefs that machines may one day, or have already, developed consciousness or sentience, and therefore, should have rights, may appear in any of the ideologies mentioned above. This view tends to give rise to a faction of AGI, and its proponents espouse machines as companions, workers, board members, sexual partners, and active, independent members of society that have rights and responsibilities. Recent controversy on this issue started in 2022 when a Google software engineer, Blake Lemoine, was convinced that the LLM he had been working with, LaMDA, had become sentient (De Cosmo 2022). This claim was refuted by Google who issued a statement that Lemoine violated Google policies and that his claims were "wholly unfounded." As he chose to persistently argue for LaMDA's sentience and even seek legal representation for it, Google claimed that Lemoine was in violation of clear employment and data security policies, and he was dismissed in July 2022 (Luscombe, 2022).

At this point in time, contemporary language models or robots are not considered sentient agents, and they currently pose little challenge to the common law's traditional concepts of agency (Bayern, 2025). The debate about the meaning and definitions of intelligence, sentience, and consciousness in machines has been fraught due to what is perceived to be ill-defined in psychology and neuroscience. At this point in time, the public and policy makers currently view that only biological forms have the capacity for consciousness, world view, and sentience; machines may imitate it but have not yet achieved it (and possibly never will). Science fiction is playing its part to inspire alternative views amongst believers in current or eventual machine consciousness with feature films such as "Her," "Ex Machina," "Terminator," and "Bladerunner." This has been explained as the human tendency toward animism and anthropomorphizing and has been a rich field of technology and media research. A key element of the believability of the stories played out in science fiction is that it's a reflection of broader anxieties over the impact of social and economic insecurities rather than the technology that is carrying the story, e.g., the film Terminator reflected social anxieties over nuclear war, gender issues, and environmental collapse anxieties prevalent during the 1980s in American society (Wills, 2017).

Researchers maintain that artificial intelligence remains deeply ambiguous in both the policy and cultural contexts: we struggle to define the boundaries and the agency of machine intelligence, and consequently we find it difficult to make sense and find agreement on how to govern it or interact with intelligent systems (Hudson et al., 2023). There are differing views amongst researchers and developers on whether AI is capable of sentience, has already reached it, or is about to.

AI Critics, Activism, Anarchies, and Resistance

This broad category includes those who are questioning or resisting the progress of AI, claiming that the field still requires extensive public discourse, debate, and agreement on future development. AI activists advocate that this needs to be a democratic process, given its impact on society, and not determined by a handful of powerful technology companies. In this category are a vocal and diverse community comprised of academics, artists, musicians, environmentalists, and human rights advocates who believe that there is more to the story about AI at work and in society than what we are presented with. For example, they often point to the ambitions made by accelerationists to support their critical stance.

AI critics in this group are mostly AI researchers and developers who are critical of the AI hype perpetrated by powerful vested interests stemming from big tech companies, consultancies, academic, and business leaders that are who they believe are misleading the public on the capabilities of AI, its future trajectories, and impact. This cohort is also critical of current shortcomings of AI development, particularly generative AI, exposing key problems on ethical issues such as bias, misinformation, inaccuracies, and data theft. Many in this cohort had spent time as AI ethicists in big tech companies such as Microsoft, Meta, Twitter/X, and Google, who had subsequently retrenched not only as individuals, but entire ethics teams. Most tech companies however still maintain policies on AI principles focusing on fairness, transparency, and safety in their AI development.

Several organizations are actively involved in the field of AI ethics and are working to develop guidelines, frameworks, and best practices for the responsible development and deployment of artificial intelligence. Key organizations include *Responsible AI Institute (RAI)* which is a global non-profit focused on helping organizations build and deploy safe and trustworthy AI systems through assessments, training, and toolkits; *UNESCO*, which has been instrumental in promoting international standards for AI ethics, that's been adopted by 193 member states, and the *Algorithmic Justice League* which is a non-profit that works to raise awareness about the impacts of AI and prevent AI harms. AI activists, ethicists, and critics are advocating for greater openness, transparency, and accountability of AI and are critical of the regulatory capture held by the tech companies.

AI Evangelists and Enthusiasts

In this last category, we have a diverse group who believe in and advocate for the importance of AI as a source of future innovation, productivity, and economic growth. This group consists of technology consultants, venture funds, solutions providers, and so-called thought leaders and enthusiasts. While they are open and vocal on what they believe to be the business and economic benefits of AI, they often espouse ideas of fear of being left out, or being left behind, or being seen to be an AI Luddite. Often, they are less transparent (or aware) of the ideologies that they subscribe to. These are intelligent and well-meaning proponents in this group, but their vested interests (as a developer, investor, consultant, or solutions provider) have forced them to take a view of the positive side (of techno solutionism) and are not sufficiently critical of AI or cognizant of the dark side or consequences of AI. I will add governments to this group as they have been focused on the promise of AI-generated productivity, innovation, and economic growth, which has governments all around the world eager to support considerable investment to this end. In addition to these interests, governments are keenly aware of the perceived political need to invest in AI for geopolitical positioning, global competition, and protection.

These seven categories provide a very broad overview of the key ideologies or perspectives that are shaping the current discourse around AI at work and society. None of these groups is against the development of AI (although many may insist on "slowing down" its development) but many are concerned about its harms and trajectories. On the whole, all these seven broad categories have one thing in common – a belief that we are facing the potential of profound change to our way of life. It's up to us as citizens to determine what kind of change we wish that to be.

Given the purpose of this book to give you practical insights on how to enable AI in your organization, many of these theories (and some that qualify as ideologies and political positioning) may not be directly helpful to organizations to make meaningful and sustained improvement to your organization in the short to medium term. It is however useful to understand these theories as they are often held by your stakeholders, and this impacts the perceptions that they have of you and your organization.

The collective body of research on the human-AI relationship highlights the vast scope and diversity of the research terms of the range of nomenclatures, the different technological forms, the different performative functions of both humans and AI, and the value creation potential of humans and machines working together. This creates a level of fragmentation that makes it difficult to systematically extract the necessary information leaders need in specific areas of complex decision-making contexts; therefore, we need to focus on the big picture as rapid change occurs at the tactical and operational areas of AI developments. This represents a significant gap in the field and an opportunity for further critical research at both academic and industry levels to create new models of AI technology design and how AI interacts with humans in the workplace and society at large.

History is important to keep at the back of your mind, not only in reading this book but also in how you critically read the media and research this point forward. We will be revisiting a more detailed history in Chapters 3 and 4 on technology entanglement. I'll present you with the material you need based on rigorous research, without the hype, to make AI work for you and your organization. For full disclosure, I err on the side of humanistic technology design and take a critical posthumanist view of human–technology entanglements.

In the second half of this chapter, we move from ideologies to grounded, fact-based research on human–machine collaboration.

RESEARCH PERSPECTIVES AND POSITIONS

As discussed earlier, despite the plethora of research in the field, there is still no common set of clear definitions or understanding of artificial intelligence, augmented intelligence, or value creation. This is an indication of the diversity of the functional intent, technological forms, and disciplinary origins of each of these domains. For the purposes of this book, the following definitions have been derived from the literature to guide our work:

Artificial intelligence: We define AI as intelligent technologies that simulate and extend human intelligence in information systems and business applications, which include machine learning, computer vision, natural language programming, robotics, speech recognition, decision support systems, expert systems, automation, and algorithmic management. LLMs are also included in this definition; despite divided opinion on whether LLMs are technically AI, they have been included due to the considerable amount of utility they provide citizens and organizations. All current AI technologies have inherent limitations.

Augmented intelligence: We define augmented intelligence as a process or application that combines the unique capabilities of both humans and AI technologies to enhance decision-making outcomes of organizational systems. In augmented systems, AI technologies extend human skills and capabilities (Jarrahi 2018) and alter work systems to enable productive and mutually enabling human–AI partnerships (Davenport 2018).

Value creation: Value creation is defined as the impact of augmented intelligence systems on organizational performance and capability that is aligned with their strategic goals. Value creation includes a broad range of organizational goals such as efficiency in decision making, teamwork in information and knowledge exchange, increased productivity, cost reduction, and improved customer experiences.

Co-creation: Co-creation of value is an active, creative, and social process that is based on collaboration between producers and users (Smorodinskaya et al., 2017). For the purposes of this book, co-creation between humans and machines is a collaboration that co-produces value and innovations, such as new goods, designs, technologies, algorithms, or other creative output. Later in Chapter 6, we will extend this definition to the co-creation of AI technologies between stakeholders and developers.

Collaboration: Collaboration is defined as various forms of interactive communication and co-operation between networked actors to co-create innovations; networked actors must rely on a common vision, strategy, common identity, and joint obligations in the collaboration process (Smorodinskaya et al., 2017).

In the next section, we provide a strategic framework on how organizations have been using, experimenting, and refining their approach to implementing AI technologies based on the extensive systematic literature review. Full references to all the literature reviewed can be found in the bibliography at the end of this chapter.

AI AT WORK AND SOCIETY

AI is adopted at work and in society to create value. In this section, we highlight the key enablers of value creation through human–AI collaboration or *augmented intelligence*. There are **four propositions** central to how organizations do this that are framed around strategic sassiness, human fearlessness, organizational rewilding, and technology reimagined, as depicted in Figure 2.1.

The language I use for the **four propositions** is deliberate – sassiness, fearlessness, rewilding, and reimagined – because why would you *not* want these energies in your organization? The neutralized and bland language of academia and business has lost meaning and nuance; this inadvertently forces us to rely on the patterns and assumptions of the past. We have no time to waste in the era of AI; we need to get to the point of what leaders need to know and do, and how to inspire their teams to do the same. Below we will present (a) research findings for each of the **four propositions** (the what), (b) highlight the **key success factors** needed to enable each proposition (the how), and (c) highlight the **strategic imperative** that will focus leaders on building the **organizational microfoundations** needed to cultivate internal value-creation capability.

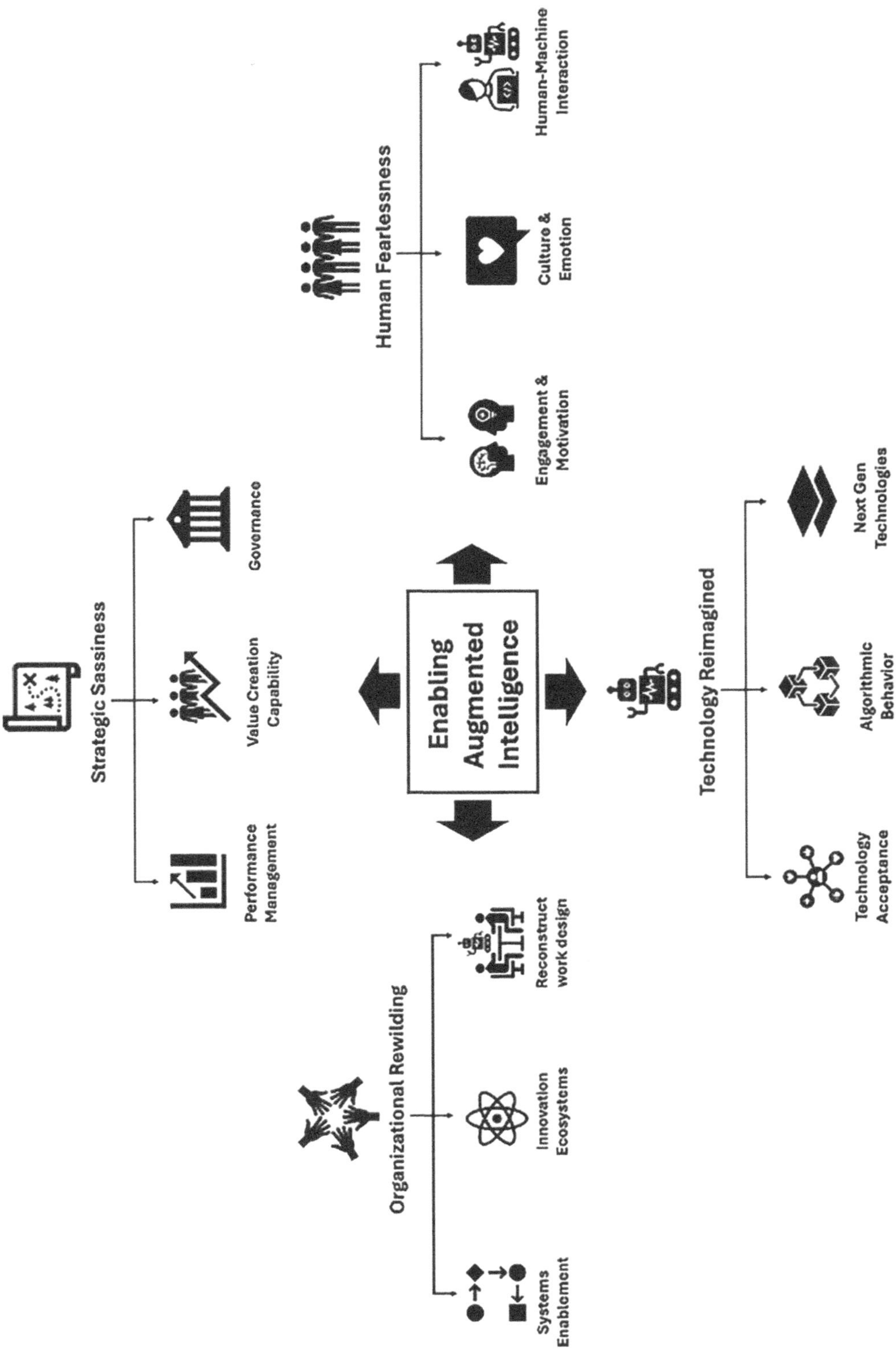

FIGURE 2.1 How organizations extract business value from AI: Key success factors.

Proposition 1: Strategic Sassiness

Strategic sassiness is defined as the ability of organizations to manage the complexities of deriving value from AI with a renewed critical attitude. In the age of AI, you need to rethink conservative approaches that don't inspire action and renew thinking toward intelligent technologies and their integration – hence the ***need to be sassy***. Leaders need to find clarity in the source of truth from research and look for smart strategic decision-making on AI investment and implementation. Narratives around AGI and AI existential threat will only weigh you down. You and your organization need to keep informed on the research and stay ahead of developments around technological capability and return on investment. Be clear on what you can influence or control. Above all, be critical of AI solutions that are presented to you.

There are three categories of key success factors (KSF) within this proposition that enable strategic sassiness: performance management, value-creation capability, and AI governance. We will explore each of these KSF categories in detail.

Performance Management

The category of performance management is defined as access to critical knowledge on how to optimize AI performance. However, research has identified the following limitations that prevent value creation from being realized and how performance management has been compromised:

- There is limited empirical evidence to support expositions of the decision-making effectiveness and performance outcomes of AI automation and augmentation, and at best it was found to have shown mixed results (Borges et al., 2021; Collins et al., 2021; Rzepka and Berger, 2018; Enholm et al., 2021; Langer and Landers, 2021; Niehaus and Wiesche, 2021; Cubric, 2020).
- Research results can't be generalized across application domains due to the fragmentation of research into specific technologies and application domains. This is particularly applicable in how learnings from one domain (such as healthcare) may be applicable to business domains (Cubric, 2020; Langer and Landers, 2021; Morley et al., 2021; Rzepka and Berger, 2018).
- There is a concentration of successful use-cases in process automation, particularly in manufacturing, which are comparatively the least expensive and easiest to implement of all AI systems (Enholm et al., 2021; Leyer and Schneider, 2021; Parasuraman and Wickens, 2008; Shea et al., 2019) and in the medical field (Aguiar et al., 2013; Aydin et al., 1994; Loh, 2018; Maadi et al., 2021). This means that substantive roles in complex and ambiguous decision-making environments have few successful use cases that can be relied on.

The consensus is that organizations are generally struggling to realize value from AI investments, they're often reporting their performance results in an overly optimistic way and frequently do not include an evaluation of the results in practice (Cubric, 2020; Enholm et al., 2021; Newlands, 2021). These reporting anomalies make it difficult to

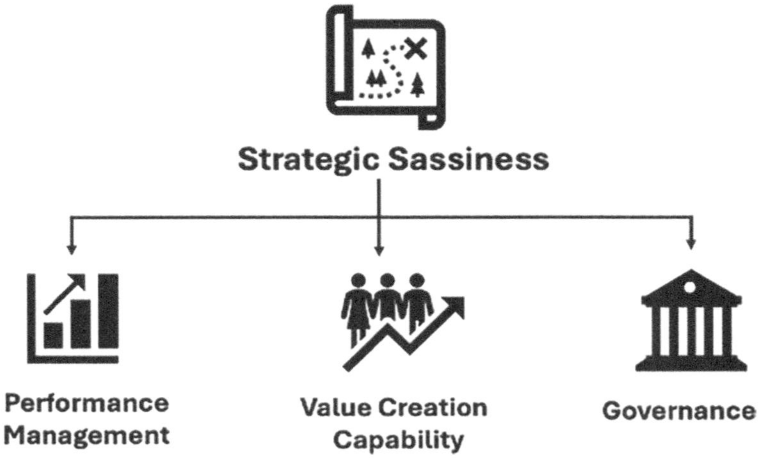

FIGURE 2.2 Strategic sassiness key success factors.

explain the variable or contradictory results that have been identified in both research and popular media, and limit our ability to objectively understand how AI performance can be improved in the context of organizational implementations (Leone et al., 2021; Coombs et al., 2020; Langer and Landers, 2021). While developers and evangelists present successful use cases, most implementations deliver less optimized results. Given these challenges, the following success factors for repositioning your performance potential have been identified:

- New cultural practices are required to support the new technology.
- Confidence in AI-led decisions in the workplace is a product of technological robustness.
- New models of management practices are required due to the shifting nature of the human–technology relationship.
- Identify performance anomalies emerging in your AI applications to get to the crux of the causal factors.
- Balance AI aversion vs AI appreciation in your workplace. This factor is discussed in more detail in Chapter 6.

How to be sassy with performance management

- Be open with what you know – and don't know about AI.
- Converse with your staff about how *they* are the makers of a future-ready organization, *not* the technology. Collaboration, not fear, will drive innovation.
- Your collective focus should be on how you will use the technology to be a stronger, more interesting and effective organization – not something out of science fiction.
- Emphasis needs to be placed on the people in your organization and the culture you all cultivate; do not hero the tech.

Value Creation Capability

The second KSF under strategic sassiness is value creation capability, which is defined as renewed skills, craft, and attitude your organization needs to succeed in a brave new AI world. Research shows that organizations need to build the requisite internal skills and capabilities to extract value from AI technology. However, organizations are constrained by the limited nature and availability of rigorous research on cultivating organizational capability (Coombs et al., 2020; Cubric, 2020; Keding and Meissner, 2021; Collins et al., 2021).

It is clear from the research that inaccurate industry perceptions of AI has been perpetuated by popular media overstatements of AI capability (Cubric, 2020), an obscuration of AI limitations due to vendor strategic secrecy (Newlands, 2021), and the dominance of the narratives driven by technology corporations on the unquestionable benefits of AI but are not well supported by research transparency or effective use cases (Bender et al., 2021; Birhane et al., 2021a; Holmstrom, 2022).

Tensions and issues in research outputs on AI capability often stem from the proprietary and profit-motive nature of the significant quantity of research emanating from technology corporations. Criticisms include misleading narratives of AI capability, systemic overselling of AI capability, the lack of quality control in machine learning, and bypassing the peer review process so that research claims are not open to public scrutiny and critical review (Marcus, 2022; Birhane et al., 2021a; Newlands, 2021; Bender et al., 2021).

Given these challenges, the following success factors have been identified for building your value creation capability, as illustrated in Figure 2.3:

- Critical yet enthused leadership and management.
- Seeking, supporting, debating objective and verified research.
- Skilled in introducing and scaling pilots and experiments for incremental learning.
- Entrepreneurial know-how to extract AI value – what problem are you solving?
- Building an AI vision and an enabling roadmap in collaboration with stakeholders.

How to be sassy with value creation capability

- You need to be playful and make this a game. AI is so hyped and fear-driven that you run the risk of either disengaging your stakeholders or forcing them to think ideologically about the benefits and drawbacks of AI (rather than fact-based).
- You need your stakeholders to be creative and innovative, so free up their creative capacity and cognitive load to have fun with this.

Governance

The category of governance is defined as how your organization oversees, critiques, and enhances your AI capability and performance over time and with care.

How an organization navigates the complex field of AI ethics and governance issues becomes critical to its sustained performance. A critical mass of research has raised the importance of AI governance and ethics as a key responsibility for organizational leaders and regulators to maintain AI efficacy and ensure public safety from AI harms. While there is growing interest in AI ethics within the research community and in technology companies, there is widespread belief that it lacks effective governance and reinforcement mechanisms. For example, technology companies deviate from their codes of ethics without consequence and even sack their governance units, which fuels public distrust and skepticism (Birhane, 2021; Hagendorff, 2020; Newman et al., 2019).

AI ethicists and governance experts believe that AI holds significant potential to improve many aspects of human life and business value creation. However, they also caution that AI also poses major systemic threats and harms such as bias, discrimination, and safety (Floridi et al., 2018; Hagendorff, 2020; Morley et al., 2021; Taddeo and Floridi, 2018). The role for governance is not only to ensure best practice, but to prevent situations or elements that can potentially destroy value and business reputation.

A responsible and ethical AI framework is necessary and should not be seen as a hinderance, but as a tool to help harness and shape AI potential to create value in a constructive and sustainable manner (Giuliano, 2020; Taddeo and Floridi, 2018). While technical ethical "fixes" can be found for specific problems, such as accountability, privacy protection, anti-discrimination, safety, or explainability (Giuliano, 2020; Hagendorff, 2020; Shin, 2021; Taddeo and Floridi, 2018) there are still considerable knowledge gaps when it comes to AI ethics and governance of system design and machine learning models that require more research, as does more discerning models of AI technology implementation and management.

Given these challenges, the following success factors for AI governance have been identified.

- Understand AI ethics issues and principles; there are many resources available online, and we discuss this further in Chapter 8.
- Keep abreast of security management and novel cyberthreats brought on by AI.
- Take leadership and promote debate and participation on AI issues in your organization; ask the uncomfortable questions.
- Build an AI governance framework and conduct audits – and remember these are live documents and processes.
- Understand AI harms and limitations and have open conversations with stakeholders for their inputs.

How to be sassy with governance: Get in touch with your convictions. The advice of old school public relations to talk around the issues will make you meek. Be bold and make a stand. Be honest and tell citizens that it's a moving feast and invite them on the journey.

Summary for strategic imperative 1: Organizations require strategic technology leadership at all levels informed by objective, fact-based intelligence on value creation potential and governance frameworks.

Question for leaders: How might you develop proactive leadership in the strategic positioning of your AI-enabled organization?

Position 2: Human Fearlessness

Human fearlessness is focused on enabling humans to embrace the opportunities that AI technologies provide; however, to be cognizant that the technology is not perfect, and that we are all the co-creators of a new technological era. The reality is that under the current management paradigms, humans are generally fearful or skeptical of the impact of AI on their jobs, and that is because leadership behavior has largely made them feel that way. This is neither useful nor productive for future-ready organizations.

However, we've had this perennial problem in our organizations well before AI. For example, the global workplace research organization, Gallup, has been running extensive global workplace surveys for over 25 years. In their most recent study, they found that only 21% of the global workforce is "engaged" at work, 62% are "not engaged," and 17% are "actively disengaged" (Gallup, 2025). These percentages have been sticky around those percentages for decades. In understanding the magnitude of this problem, Gallup estimates that if the world's workplace were fully engaged, US$ 9.6 trillion in productivity could be added to the global economy, the equivalent of 9% in global GDP.

At the core of enhancing human fearlessness is an understanding of the psychological, sociological, neurological, and biological factors that affect how humans engage, interact, and collaborate with intelligent technologies and the planet. There are three KSFs within this cluster, as illustrated in Figure 2.3, that enable human fearlessness.

The three KSF categories that dominated the literature in this cluster are human engagement and motivation, culture and emotion, and human–machine interaction. We will explore each of these three categories in detail.

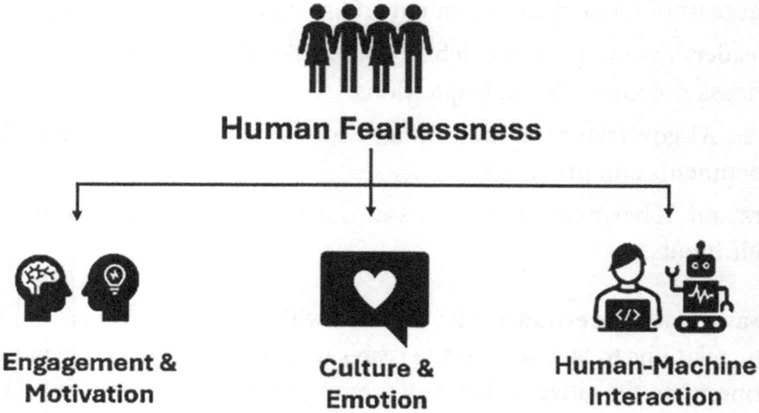

FIGURE 2.3 Human fearlessness key success factors.

Engagement and Motivation

It was widely reported that a lack of, or ineffective, human-centered design was a key obstacle in human engagement and motivation in working with AI technologies (Borges et al., 2021; Collins et al., 2021; Cubric, 2020; Enholm et al., 2021; Langer and Landers, 2021; Rzepka and Berger, 2018). Some of the engagement and motivational design elements that were highlighted include: human-like design features of AI systems or anthropomorphism that includes the looks and gestures of robots, as well as the voice, expression, and conversation of virtual agents such as chatbots or virtual assistants (Rzepka and Berger, 2018).

Other engagement and motivation elements included the adequacy of system transparency and explainability (or dealing with the blackbox problem) that is built into the interactive design aspects, information flows, and task allocation. When well designed, these elements contribute to engendering greater levels of user trust and acceptance and dissipate fear and negative emotions toward AI technologies (Enholm et al., 2021; Langer and Landers, 2021; Shin, 2021; Hemmer et al., 2021; Adadi and Berada, 2018).

Research suggests that without deeper insight and understanding of human engagement and motivation, AI-based decision support systems face accuracy and efficacy issues due to the barriers they create for human–AI collaboration (Smorodinskaya et al., 2017; Xu and Yu, 2020; Xu, 2019). By far the most significant factor is human–machine teaming (HMT), which considerably alters our current well-entrenched notions of teamwork, and requires a reconfiguration of our systems architectures, explainability, and trust in recommendations of autonomous systems (Chen et al., 2025).

Solutions stem from deeper and philosophical perspectives that are almost beyond the capability of organizations to solve on their own and require industry-wide effort. This includes the development of an improved "business language" that better articulates the new world skills and capacity required of a human–machine collaborating team (Carroll et al., 2019; Seeber et al., 2020; Crouser and Chang, 2012), to developing models of a machine theory of mind (Rabinowitz et al., 2018), as well as human theory of mind (Baker et al., 2011; Stowers et al., 2021) that will contribute to improved interaction and decision-making for both machines and humans, as well as integration into society that's required for the long term (Akata et al., 2020; Stowers et al., 2021). Given these challenges, the following success factors for engagement and motivation have been identified.

- Leadership development in the new art of human–machine teaming.
- Shared workplace mental models of what's entailed in human–machine teamwork and managing ideologies that may not be helpful in current practical applications.
- Renewed task model development of goals, tasks, and processes (and their inevitable ongoing iteration).
- Shared understanding of system behavior, maturity, and expectations.

How to be fearless with engagement and motivation:

- Humans only fear technology if they are subjected to it. If they fear it, you can't optimize its use. How can you moderate the fear factor in your organization?

Culture and Emotion

The culture and emotion category overlaps with all others; however, it deserves a category of its own, given the number of times it appears in the literature, but we found it to be limited in terms of tangible recommendations or insight into how they can be overcome. Citizens are humans, not machines; we are complicated, yet culture and emotion are an essential part of the embodied intelligence that we possess that machines may never be able to emulate (Carroll et al., 2019; Seeber et al., 2020; Cooke et al., 2013; Jarrahi, 2018). In the Gallup study mentioned above, the study also found that well-being is at alarmingly low levels. For example, the same study found that only 33% of people rated their personal well-being as "thriving," 58% said "struggling," and 9% said "suffering" (Gallup, 2025).

Low engagement and wellness in our organizations are tightly correlated with lower levels of productivity, higher turnover rates, and lower overall company performance; remarkably, the quality of management explains 70% of the variance in team engagement. The cultural and emotional aspects of our sociotechnical systems have consequences we can no longer ignore. The biggest areas of issues affecting culture and emotion are feelings of worthlessness, not being included in decision-making around AI, fear of job losses, and loss of meaningful work (Ajenaghughrure et al., 2021; Lee et al., 2021; Oh et al., 2017; Wang and Wang, 2019). We will pick up these issues again in later chapters. Given these challenges, the following success factors for culture and emotion have been identified.

- There are endemic systemic issues with the lack of workplace wellness that have been at play in our sociotechnical systems for some time; how can we get clarity around these issues as sources of untapped productivity and innovation?
- In the age of AI, how might current problems of workplace disengagement and sense of well-being be made worse – or can it improve these recurring problems somehow?

How to be fearless with culture and emotion:

- Dare to ask the big question: What has failed us in the past, and will this same unattended thing continue to shrink workplace creativity and innovation regardless of the technologies that are in place? Are we doing our best to set up AI for success in terms of optimal workplace environments?

Human–Machine Interaction

In the human–machine interaction category, it was reported that new autonomous systems require intelligible interfaces to ensure that skilled workers are able to *understand* how the technology may affect them, *trust* its information and feedback, and feel in control of the decision-making process (Abdul et al., 2018; Adam et al., 2018; Akata et al., 2020; Grønsund and Aanestad, 2020) and even apply novel interfaces that support interactive, open-ended explorations (Liu et al., 2018; 2021).

Progressive researchers identified a need to move away from traditional approaches to technology design and adoption that seek to "optimize humans" (which is based on a utilitarian position of a rational use of resources) toward more nuanced and complex cultural and emotional aspects of human–machine interaction (Frauenberger, 2019; Jarrahi, 2018; Zhuge, 2020). Interactions between humans and machines are now much more complex as different systems in organizations are now more closely coupled which means the interaction dependency between them is increased (Hollnagel, 2017). Traditional approaches to systems design and interaction are experiencing diminishing returns as AI systems increase in complexity and enmeshment with joint systems and organizations. Given these challenges, the following success factors for human–machine interaction have been identified:

- Systems design requires flexibility and novelty to accommodate joint AI systems applications.
- High-level renewed human-centered design in the UX and UI for basic or less complex AI applications.
- Transparency and explainability are persistent issues in AI UX and UI.

How to be fearless with human–machine interaction:

- Human–machine interaction is more than interfaces; it's relational.
- Interactions are not loosely coupled or linear; therefore, we need to let go of the old models that dominate UX/UI in traditional software applications.

Strategic Imperative 2: Human engagement and motivation are critical to developing the human potential side of the augmented intelligence equation. There are still many unknowns; therefore, ongoing research, development, and experimentation are key.
Question for leaders: How might we renew, advance, and incorporate refined human–machine collaboration and teaming approaches that create new forms of playful engagements between humans and machines.

Position 3: Organizational Rewilding

This cluster highlights the role of building and enabling organization systems, structures, processes, and networks that are conducive to effective human–AI technology acceptance, adoption, and collaborative teamwork. It includes three highly interconnected KSF categories of systems enablement, innovation ecosystems, and reconstructing work design as depicted in Figure 2.4.

Systems Enablement

From a systems enablement perspective, there is widespread agreement that AI systems need to be understood as *dynamic socio-technical systems that co-evolve* with their users (Enholm et al., 2021; Niehaus and Wiesche, 2021; Rzepka and Berger, 2018). This provides for a more dynamic approach to AI design and deployment in an environment dominated

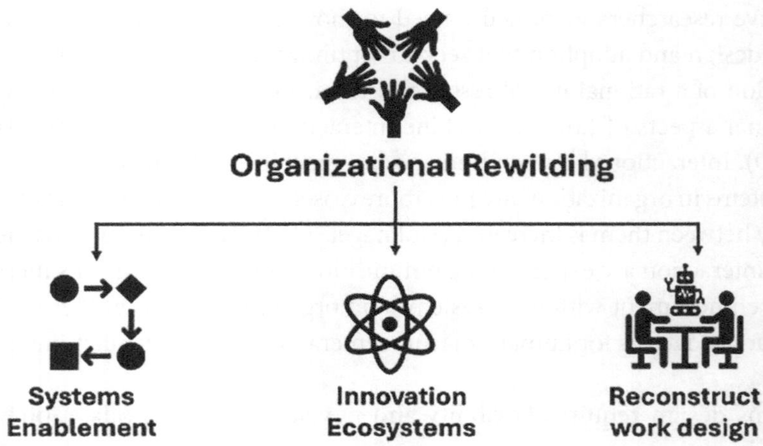

FIGURE 2.4 Organizational rewilding key success factors.

by rapid technology development and socio-economic change (Crouser and Chang, 2012; Grønsund and Aanestad, 2020; Lundberg et al., 2021; Methnani et al., 2021; Yang, 2021).

It is already widely accepted in management and information systems research that the socio-technical nature inherent in information systems means that technology innovation is inseparable from the social processes of organizational development and change (Hanelt et al., 2021). This is a concept explored in detail in Chapter 3. AI research to date has focused predominantly on the emergent technologies and the value creation opportunities they represent, and less so on the human, organizational, and social aspects of how the holistic human–machine ecosystem functions. To enable your organization to successfully adopt AI systems, you need to consider the unique requirements that need to be intentionally designed (Oh et al., 2017).

Traditional approaches to systems enablement often result in less-than-optimal outcomes, and suggestions have been made that more consultative and conversational approaches may yield better results. For example, appreciative enquiry, future search, or open space are used in environments where there is a high degree of complexity and unknowns (Lewis et al., 2016). Realizing change, and especially radical transformational change, is often challenging to navigate and is largely stalled by the attitudes and emotional resistance of middle management (Huy et al., 2014). Systems enablement and digital transformation are considered in need of a "reboot" in terms of rethinking enablement methods, frameworks, and capability for AI (Jick and Sturtevant, 2017).

Given these challenges, the following success factors for systems enablement have been identified (and please note we will elaborate on these issues in Chapters 5 and 6):

- Identify where systems are linear and deterministic, and where they are non-linear, interdependent, open, and with unclear boundaries. They each require different approaches to navigate.
- Undertake proactive management with sensitivity and care where attitudes and emotional resistance to change in organizations are heightened with AI enablement. This needs to be undertaken with the active involvement of your stakeholders.

How to rewild systems enablement:

- A common theme of rewilding organizations in this section will be letting go of the current modes of thinking of organizations as command-and-control systems. For as long as I have been in the business of business transformation, there has always been a pervasive gap between leadership *liking the idea* of flexible, autonomous decision-making in their organization and *actually making it happen* in practice.

Reconstruct Work Design

From a workflow design perspective, function, or task allocation in augmented and collaborative human–machine systems needs to be dynamic rather than rigid or prescriptive. Increasing computational power is constantly shifting the boundaries of technological and human capability and the nature of work itself, and all this within increasingly complex and ill-defined problem spaces. Human oversight in the decision-making process is critical, therefore stakeholder inclusion in system design and performance evaluation will lead to better operational outcomes for specialist augmented functions (Borges et al., 2021; Crandall et al., 2018; Langer and Landers, 2021; Fügener et al., 2021; Grønsund and Aanestad, 2020; Lundberg et al., 2021; Keding and Meissner, 2021).

This requires moving away from traditional or hierarchical "human resource" approaches to work design and management, toward more novel or democratized approaches that facilitate more harmonious human–machine co-operation (Crouser and Chang, 2012; Langer and Landers, 2021; Methnani et al., 2021; Crandall et al., 2018; Fügener et al., 2021). This also provides for greater perceived transparency, fairness, and a human influence in creating and maintaining meaningful employment (Parent-Rocheleau and Parker, 2022; Marabelli et al., 2021).

Given these challenges, the following success factors for work design have been identified:

- Renewed "human resource" approaches in reconfiguring work design in complex, dynamic change environments. In fact, traditional "HR" functions have eroded trust in most workplaces.
- Work redesign requires more inclusive, collaborative strategizing and experimentation of alternative structures that need not adhere to traditional hierarchies of an organization.

How to rewild with work design:

- There are still many unknowns in coming to terms with how we reconstruct work design to accommodate AI-induced changes to roles, tasks, and responsibilities. The key is to not only keep abreast of technological changes but also map its impact on the human workforce in terms of their capacity to engage, trust, and innovate. This will be a significant challenge for organizations trapped in traditional heirarchies and mindsets.

Innovation Ecosystems Thinking

Systems-oriented researchers and practitioners maintain that the concept of *innovation ecosystems* provides a more appropriate approach to AI systems development and management. Innovation ecosystems are fundamentally *complex adaptive systems* that emerge in the course of collaboration among networked actors (human, machine, and environment) to co-create value (Chan, 2001; Newlands, 2021; Smorodinskaya et al., 2017). Many researchers and practitioners even question whether the concept of *socio-technical systems,* which is dominant in information systems and business research, is sufficiently flexible and dynamic enough in their architecture to capture the holistic complexities of human–AI collaboration and of systems implementations. Socio-technical systems are deterministic, which is why many leaders are comfortable with the assumptions of certainty. Compare this to complex adaptive systems which are dynamic and less predictable, and decisions and actions have impacts on the entire system outside the narrow view of an organization.

In reality, we operate in an entanglement of multiple ecosystems co-existing and interconnecting. Cause and effect between an initial action and outcome is not as simple as our metrics-based business culture makes it out to be, as there is a long and complex causal chain. There are interdependencies between the different actors; they all co-evolve with each other, and they need to both compete and cooperate (Ritala and Almpanopoulou, 2017; Stahl, 2021). Leaders are also challenged by what is known as the *responsibility gap* created by the causal distance between the design of an autonomous system and the eventual actions and outcomes of those systems. This isdue to the dilution of agency caused by the impossibility of fully predicting how autonomous systems will behave once they have been deployed in the wild (Goetze, 2022).

Given these challenges, the following success factors for innovation ecosystems have been identified:

- Map and understand how your ecosystem is loosely structured, how it operates, and how it behaves and interacts with its constituent parts.
- Identify the key leverage points in the system that you may be able to influence. Notice how AI technologies will shift the balance of power, influence, and leverage points in the ecosystem.
- Governance of an ecosystem is a delicate but important function that needs to be factored into operations. For example, who is morally responsible for the harms caused by autonomous systems? This is still unclear at a conceptual level.

How to rewild innovation ecosystems thinking:

- In an innovation ecosystem, an organization co-evolves its capability and connections with other actors in the system around a new innovation; they work both co-operatively and competitively to grow and enable the innovation.

Strategic imperative 3: Organizational rewilding. AI value creation requires the adoption of dynamic organizational ecosystems approaches that do not inadvertently reproduce existing organizational structures, hierarchies, and culture. The invisible rigidity of organizations will drive the delivery of more of the same outcomes.

Question for leaders: How might we proactively evolve and adapt organizational systems and structures to enable AI systems in our organizations? Can you truly re-envision your organization so that human–machine collaboration can flourish?

Position 4: Technology Reimagined

This cluster focuses on the limitations and potential of AI technology in facilitating the effectiveness of human–machine collaboration and value creation. The three key categories within the technology cluster that recurred in the literature were AI acceptance complexities, algorithmic behavior, and next-generation cognitive technologies, as depicted in Figure 2.5.

AI Acceptance Complexities

In terms of AI acceptance complexities, it was widely agreed that the "human-like" intelligence inherent in AI technology triggers a more complex psychological pathway that humans need to navigate in order to accept AI as a team member and collaborator. AI represents an extension of humans rather than a simple utilitarian tool (Ajenaghughrure et al., 2021) and this fundamental difference means that technology acceptance models (and technology design) need to place greater emphasis on elements such as hedonic motivation, social influence, anthropomorphism, and emotion (Gursoy et al., 2019; Lu et al., 2019), personal innovativeness (Fan et al., 2020) and even a fascination for technology (Sohn and Kwon, 2020).

AI technology acceptance issues go beyond the utility of the technology into complex psycho-social factors that affect users, such as fear (Cabrera-Sánchez et al., 2021), AI Anxiety (Lee et al., 2021; Oh et al., 2017; Wang and Wang, 2019), algorithm aversion (Dietvorst et al., 2015), bias and mistrust (Ishowo-Oloko et al., 2019), and wilful lack of co-operation (Kiesler et al., 1996). The difference with AI relative to other information systems is that humans interact with algorithms and cognitive agents, not just interfaces (Oh et al., 2017), which trigger human expectations of social identity, relational

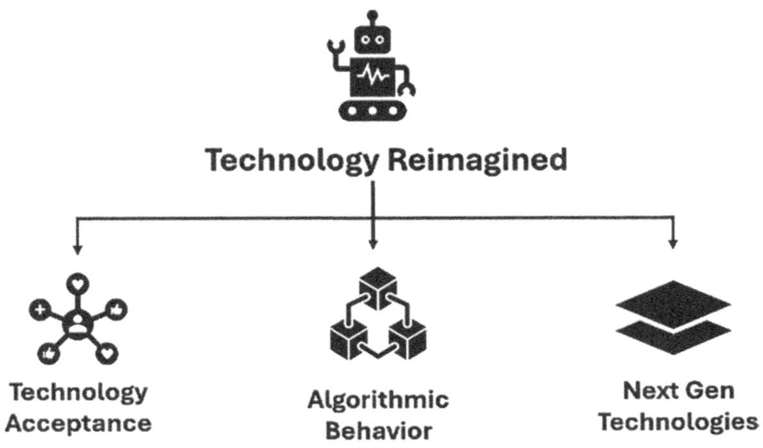

FIGURE 2.5 Technology reimagined key success factors.

or commitment norms (Castelfranchi and Tummolini, 2003; Ishowo-Oloko et al., 2019; Kiesler et al., 1996). The increased reporting of emerging mental health and cognitive capacity issues from an overreliancee on generative AI is a testament to this.

Given these challenges, the following success factors for AI acceptance complexities have been identified:

- Understand what attracts citizens to AI and build on these positives.
- Simultaneously resolve citizen fears about AI such as reduced meaningful work or job losses rather than ignore these fears or downplay their importance.
- Be mindful of the negative impacts on mental health and cognition.
- Understand that technology and humans *co-evolve for both to thrive*, so don't allow the subtext of your AI strategy to place greater importance on the machine.

How to reimagine AI acceptance complexities:

- A recurring factor in this category is that technology is not just a tool and that humans are not just a resource. This binary thinking is limiting your vision on how you can use sociotechnical systems to your full advantage. There is a critical socio-psychological relationship between humans and machines that cannot be ignored.

Algorithmic Behavior

At the core of human–machine co-operation is the design and coding of algorithms and machine learning models that support collaborative human–machine interactions. In true collaborative environments, AI-enabled technology needs to be sensitive to human intuition, cultural norms, emotions, social signals, and pre-evolved dispositions that support and extend the ways humans reason in decision-making (Carroll et al., 2019; Seeber et al., 2020; Cooke et al., 2013; Jarrahi, 2018; Dellerman et al., 2019; Fugener et al., 2021).

While such deliberately designed algorithms have been shown to produce good co-operation levels between human–machine and machine–machine at comparable levels of human–human cooperation (Carroll et al., 2019; Crandall et al., 2018), researchers found that these algorithms are difficult to come by, as most have been developed and trained to compete and defeat humans rather than co-operate with them (Adadi and Berada, 2018; Crandall et al., 2018; van den Hoven, 2007). Note that advancements in recent reasoning models in LLMs are making some progress in resolving these issues, but it still remains an unsolved problem.

Solutions lie in thoughtfully designed reinforcement learning algorithms based on human–machine collaboration trained on supportive datasets (Carroll et al., 2019; Stowers et al., 2021), as well as an evolved theory of mind for both human and machines which is seen as essential for complex decision-making environments (Akata et al., 2020; Baker et al., 2011; Rabinowitz et al., 2018; Singer and Tusche, 2013).

However, the development of more collaborative algorithms will be constrained by the limitations in current quality and veracity in data sets and machine learning models (Chen et al., 2018; Newlands, 2021; Birhane, 2021; Crandall et al., 2018; van den Hoven, 2007; Scheuerman et al., 2021). Without a fundamental shift in how datasets are curated, algorithmic behaviors will be predicated on the past, such as limiting human stereotypes, predominant mental models, bias, and values. Furthermore, the increasing use of synthetic data may corrupt the future development and potential of these algorithms.

This speaks to the wider general problems persistent in the machine learning domain which has become a recurring theme in our research, where a lack of systematic and structured methods and processes to develop, deploy, and evolve models (John et al., 2022) results in AI often exhibiting poor behavior when deployed in real-world applications (D'Amour et al., 2022).

How to reimagine with algorithmic behavior:

- Understanding the nature of the algorithms, machine learning models, and the training data powering your AI technologies. How can these elements enable your organization's AI strategy – and how might they potentially destroy value?

Next Generation of AI Technologies

The next generation of AI technology, as of 2026, is being shaped by several key trends that are accelerating innovation, broadening adoption, and presenting both new opportunities and challenges across industries. This section of our work had to be redone and re-researched several times over the four years spent on the research and publications, and the current book writing – so by the time this book is released, this list may look different again. Furthermore, given the rate of technological advancements and the lag in academic publications, I've had to rely on industry reporting to update and supplement the original academic research. The data tends to cluster into seven key trends for the next generation AI technologies and their applications that leaders need to be aware of are as follows:

1. **Agentic and autonomous AI.** These are autonomous digital entities capable of planning, reasoning, and executing multistep tasks, which are now moving from simple automations to more sophisticated systems that can operate independently. The excitement here is that virtual coworkers will be able to handle complex workflows in business, customer support, and various professional tasks, driving productivity and creativity to new heights. This trend is widely reported on by management consulting firms and solution providers, as these solutions are part of their core business. However limitations are now being widely reported and several large scale implementations being scaled back.
2. **Multimodal and human-like AI.** The leading AI foundational models can now integrate multimodal capabilities, processing and generating text, images, audio, and video simultaneously. This advances AI from pure text processing to systems (LLMs) with richer, more human-like understanding and interactivity. Applications include creating videos from descriptions, interpreting visual scenes, and enabling more natural conversational experiences.
3. **Custom and domain-specific models.** The promise here is that enterprises no longer need to rely on generic models as they can adopt and train *custom AI systems*

using proprietary data tailored to specialized, regulated domains such as finance, law, insurance, and healthcare. This approach enhances accuracy, privacy, and relevance in mission-critical settings.

4. **Generative AI drives discovery and creation.** While AI frameworks and machine learning have had an enormous impact on scientific research (Xu et al., 2021), developments in generative AI innovation in design and media are being used for scientific discovery and accelerating R&D in materials science and engineering. For example, large language models (LLMs) have revolutionized drug discovery (Guo et al., 2025).
5. **Edge AI and real-time intelligence.** Increasingly, AI computation is trending toward edge devices (local sensors, smartphones, and autonomous vehicles), which enables real-time, privacy-preserving decision-making without relying on centralized cloud infrastructure. This trend supports applications in healthcare monitoring, smart manufacturing, and autonomous robotics.
6. **Responsible, explainable, and regulated AI.** As AI systems proliferate, ethical use, transparency, and explainability are increasingly becoming priorities. Regulations are being put in place globally to address bias, fairness, data privacy, and AI accountability, with a focus on embedding ethical and human-centric principles throughout AI development and deployment. The most notable one is UNESCO's Recommendation on the Ethics of Artificial Intelligence provided a significant step toward global ethical AI development; however, its effectiveness is dependent on widespread adoption and implementation by the 193 member states that have adopted it. UNESCO provides a framework of values and principles to guide AI policy and practices, promoting human rights, fairness, and sustainability (UNESCO, 2025). However, the framework has been criticized for privileging particular cultural, socio-political, and economic ideologies that potentially have serious implications for the common, collective good (Mochizuki et al., 2025).
7. **Human–machine collaboration and new work paradigms.** Overlapping with the other strategic propositions in our model, this item's focus is on developing AI-enabled technologies to not replace humans but to augment human capabilities. Attention is being given to enhanced conversational systems, collaborative robots (also known as cobots), and virtual assistants or agents that will help human-first systems to boost productivity, creativity, and enable entirely new modes of human–machine symbiosis in the workplace. Again, many small-scale developments are taking place, but access to reliable and scalable systems is still some way off.

AI technology continues to develop and evolve, though its practical applications may not always align with expectations. Public discussions sometimes suggest these advancements are closer than they currently are in reality. So while this list can be seen as already in progress, much of it is yet to scale effectively. The combination of AI and quantum computing offers significant potential for specialized tasks such as cryptography, optimization, and complex modelling. However, practical business solutions are likely still five to ten years away (Gent, 2023).

Other longer-term ambitions are advances in AI hardware and sustainability. The explosion in AI model size and complexity has driven innovation in custom silicon chips, such as application-specific integrated circuits (ASICs), neuromorphic chips, and hardware optimized for low-energy, high-efficiency inference. Data centers are often claimed to be increasingly powered by renewables as sustainability becomes a competitive differentiator. However, based on current projections the environmental impact is still considered to be dire.

Another longer-term ambition is in the much-anticipated AI-powered healthcare and scientific discovery, given the importance of solving current critical global problems. AI can potentially transform healthcare through faster, more accurate diagnosis, personalized medicine, and wearable devices for real-time health monitoring. Many developments and breakthroughs have and will continue to take place, for example, DeepMind's AlphaProteo and AlphaGenome have generated and validated new protein and gene sequences (Varadi et al., 2024). However, innovations have been at a pace that has been slower than anticipated; the example we used in the previous chapter on medical diagnostics is a case in point.

The next generation of AI technologies is focusing on autonomous, contextually aware systems that are deeply embedded in our lives and work, governed ethically, powered efficiently, and customized for every imaginable industry. These trends suggest a future where AI not only transforms creative, professional, and scientific domains but also raises critical questions about trust, governance, and the evolving relationship between humans and machines. An analysis of the literature suggests that these drives for AI-driven innovations are again siloed by specific technologies or specific application domains. This suggests that the overall impact of AI technologies will continue to be uneven.

Given these challenges, the following success factors for next-generation AI technologies have been identified:

- **Observe** the continuing developments in AI technologies – all AI technologies, not just Generative AI.
- **Continual diagnostics** of the impact of technology on your organizational values.
- Technology development and evolution should be on your organizational **risk register**.

How to reimagine next-generation AI technologies:

- Be aware of new technological developments but remember that they will require considerable time to scale and earn a return on invstment - if at all.
- Run regular **strategic foresight** sessions that encourage your stakeholders to **radically reimagine** your organization in light of emergent or fantastical technological capabilities.
- Remember: Business as usual is being challenged.

Strategic Imperative 4: Technology Reimagining. AI advancements are outpacing organizational capability to keep up with developments, let alone invest in the most appropriate infrastructures and software. Understanding how to navigate technological advancements that are realistic and hype-free is a core capability that needs to be developed with all stakeholders.

Question for leaders: How might we develop renewed technology architectures adapted to the unique challenges and opportunities of augmented intelligence?

Overarching questions for leaders: Given the discussion of the four propositions of strategic sassiness, human fearlessness, organizational rewilding, and technology reimagined, what is your reaction to the following questions:

- Do you feel comfortable?
- Is it hard to know where to start?
- Do you know who or what to trust?

If your answers make you feel uncomfortable, then you are in the right place. I'd be worried if you were comfortable – because no one has mastered this yet.

HUMAN–MACHINE COLLABORATION FRAMEWORK

As we have seen, there has been extensive research undertaken into identifying the key enablers of humans-AI collaboration on organizational value creation, and this research has grown exponentially compared to when I started over four years ago. As identified in Figure 2.1, there are a multitude of factors relevant for organizational leaders condensed into **four propositions**, each with a set of **key success factors** categories that will improve your learnings and success rate with your experiments, pilots, and full installations. However, as we have made clear from the outset, AI technology is rapidly changing, return on investment is a grey area, there are challenges in navigating the hype, and each application is dependent on situational factors.

The story in the data presented in this chapter is that leaders need to be sassy and fearless, be able to rewild their organization, and reimagine how they use technology. The socio-economic-political situation and consequences of this pose an enormous challenge. As we will explore later in more detail in Chapters 5 and 6, organizations are doing the opposite and holding back (and sometimes with good reason).

The research literature emphasized building technologies that synergize with human motivation, engagement, and interaction, and on embedding those technologies within renewed organization systems and processes. However, this is a very difficult task to execute, particularly as this research is often naïve to the practical realities of industrial power dynamics at the strategic level and the weight of legacy systems at the operational level.

While the considerable potential of AI technologies is clear, a realignment of the treatment of technology is required to enable human–machine collaboration to reach its full potential. This requires an ongoing investigation of new generation technologies while simultaneously improving the current limitations and potential performance of machine learning. Leaders need to manage both scrupulously; otherwise, rather than add value, AI can destroy value.

AI technology research literature appears to be somewhat fragmented, which reflects the fact that it is siloed by specific technologies in specific application domains. This raises the importance of *strategic alignment and a multidisciplinary approach* that focuses on how organizations can reconfigure their socio-technical systems to enhance human–AI system development and implementation. To partly provide guidance to this challenge, we derived a conceptual framework that overlays the importance of microfoundations as a cohesive approach to embedding AI technologies in legacy systems, illustrated in Figure 2.6.

The Dynamic Capabilities Theory (Teece and Pisano, 2003) is a long-standing framework used in strategic management, and the related framework of microfoundations (Teece, 2007; Palmié et al., 2023) emphasizes the need for organizations to constantly adapt, integrate, and re-configure organizational skills, resources, and functional competencies, particularly in rapidly changing technological environments.

A key finding in the research behind this book is that the value creation from augmented intelligence may depend on the inherent and unique dynamic capabilities and microfoundations of each organization to translate opportunities into tangible outcomes.

While clear enablers of value creation from augmented systems have been identified in our review, to realize value from AI organizations may need to leverage complementary resources and microfoundations (Mikalef and Gupta, 2021) or practice greater alignment of control points along their digital ecosystems (Pagani, 2013). Amplifying the requisite microfoundations is key to enabling your AI strategy in your organization. These are derived in three key areas:

- *Analytical systems, processes, and human capacities* enable strategic sassiness and human fearlessness.
- *Enterprise structures, procedures, designs, and incentives* enable organizational rewilding.
- *Continuous alignment and realignment of tangible and intangible assets* enable technology reimagined.

Using a microfoundations approach deepens our approach to how organizations can realize value from augmented intelligence and opens opportunities for further research and practice. Over Chapters 5 to 8, we will discuss how organizations have been attempting to do this in practice.

CONCLUSIONS

Research into the next generation of augmented human and artificial intelligence is in the early stages of development, particularly in the specialized area of human–machine collaboration in complex environments. The field is challenged by research fragmentation, a lack of generalizability of results across research and application domains, systemic challenges with algorithmic models and limitations in machine learning training data, a lack of critical research on AI capability for value creation, and pressing ethical challenges that have been inadequately addressed.

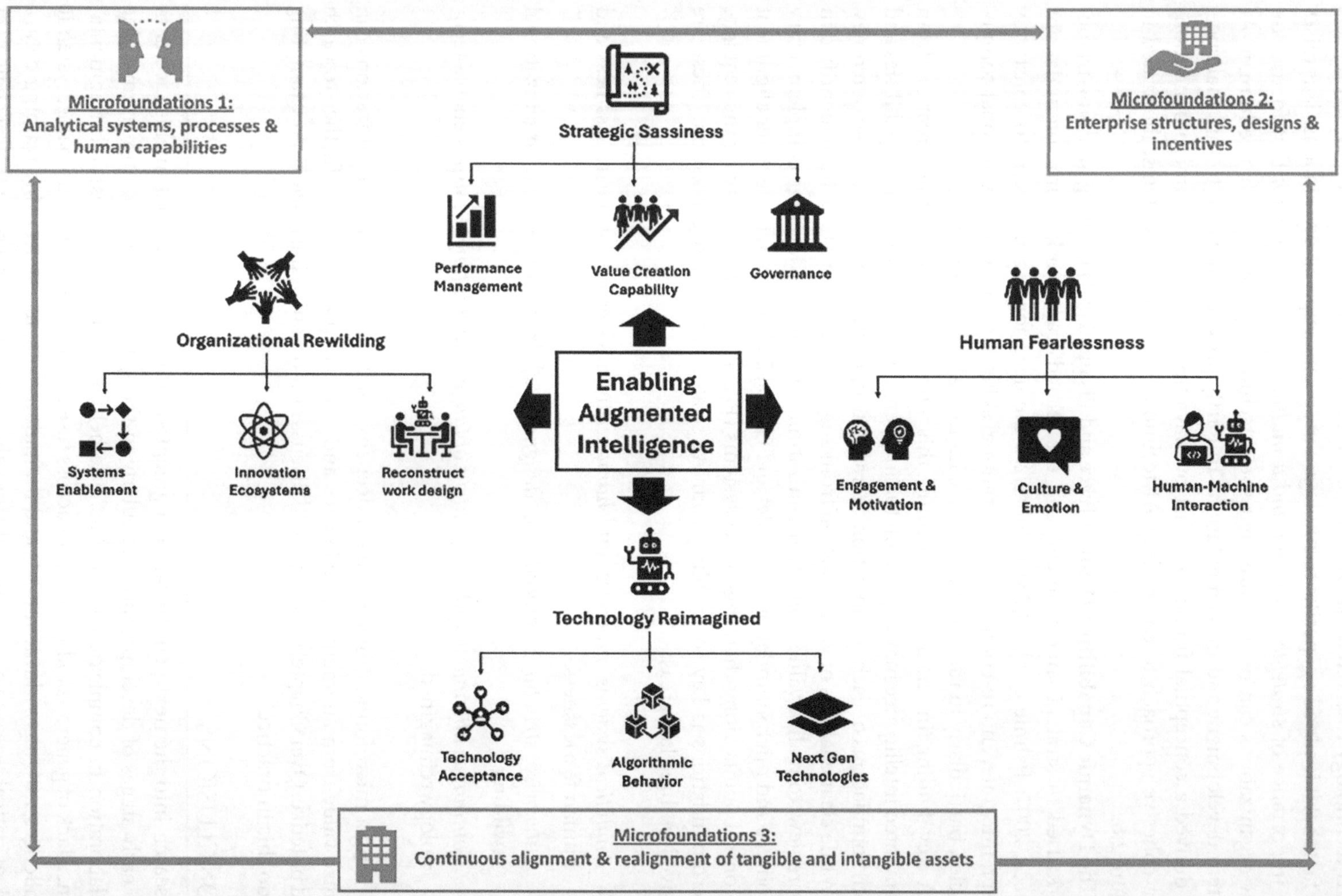

FIGURE 2.6 Conceptual framework of enabling human–AI collaboration.

Furthermore, we are challenged by a range of different world views and ideologies that are muddying the waters when it comes to access to objective, fact-based research for leaders to utilize in their organization. When we peel away the hype, all these challenges are contributing to the unsatisfactory return on investment and slow corporate take-up rates of AI technologies that are being reported.

The potential benefits of AI technologies are undeniable; however, they are still largely underdeveloped and require the maturity that more multidisciplinary approaches may provide. Research points to the reality that value-creation may be in the human, organizational, and strategic ecosystems that support and utilize AI technology rather than in the technology itself.

In the next chapter, we will take a step back into a deep investigation of the nature of human-technology entanglement from anthropological and sociological perspectives to gain a better understanding of the nature of the challenges we face in not only using AI technologies in business applications, but more importantly, the integration and effects of the technologies on human life and society as a whole.

ACKNOWLEDGMENTS

This project has received funding from the European Union's Horizon 2020 research and innovation program under the Marie Sklodowska-Curie Grant Agreement No. 101023024 for the project Augmented Humans. Part of this chapter was first published at the European Conference of Information Systems (ECIS), Kristiansand, Norway, 2023.

REFERENCES

Abdul, A., Vermeulen, J., Wang, D., Lim, B. Y., and Kankanhalli, M. (2018). Trends and trajectories for explainable, accountable and intelligible systems: An HCI research agenda. *Conference on Human Factors in Computing Systems – Proceedings*, April 2018. https://doi.org/10.1145/3173574.3174156

Adadi, A., and Berada, M. (2018). Peeking inside the Black-Box – A survey on explainable artificial intelligence. *IEEE Access*,*6*, 52138–52160.

Adam, M. T. P., Teubner, T., and Gimpel, H. (2018). No rage against the machine: how computer agents mitigate human emotional processes in electronic negotiations. *Group Decision and Negotiation*, *27*(4), 543–571. https://doi.org/10.1007/s10726-018-9579-5

Aguiar, J., Portela, F., Santos, M. F., Machado, J., Abelha, A., Silva, Á., Rua, F., and Pinto, F. (2013). Pervasive information systems to intensive care medicine: Technology acceptance model. ICEIS 2013 – Proceedings of the 15th International Conference on Enterprise Information Systems, 1, 177–184.

Ajenaghughrure, I. B., Sousa, S. C. D. C., and Lamas, D. (2021). Psychophysiological modeling of trust in technology: influence of feature selection methods. Proceedings of the ACM on Human-Computer Interaction, 5 (EICS). https://doi.org/10.1145/3459745

Akata, Z., Balliet, D., de Rijke, M., Dignum, F., Dignum, V., Eiben, G., Fokkens, A., Grossi, D., Hindriks, K., Hoos, H., Hung, H., Jonker, C., Monz, C., Neerincx, M., Oliehoek, F., Prakken, H., Schlobach, S., van der Gaag, L., van Harmelen, F., … Welling, M. (2020). A research agenda for hybrid intelligence: augmenting human intellect with collaborative, adaptive, responsible, and explainable artificial intelligence. *Computer, 53*(8), 18–28. https://doi.org/10.1109/MC.2020.2996587

Aydin, C. E., Rosen, P. N., and Felitti, V. J. (1994). Transforming information use in preventive medicine: learning to balance technology with the art of caring. Proceedings / the ... Annual Symposium on Computer Application [Sic] in Medical Care. *Symposium on Computer Applications in Medical Care*, 563–567. PMID: 7949991; PMCID: PMC2247893.

Baker, C., Saxe, R., and Baker, C. L. (2011). *Bayesian Theory of Mind: Modeling Joint Belief-Desire Attribution*. www.researchgate.net/publication/228727729

Bayern, S. (2025). False agency in artificial intelligence. In *Research Handbook on the Law of Artificial Intelligence* (pp. 232–249). Edward Elgar Publishing.

Bender, E. M., Gebru, T., McMillan-Major, A., and Mitchell, S. (2021, March). On the dangers of stochastic parrots: Can language models be too big? In Proceedings of the 2021 ACM Conference on Fairness, Accountability, and Transparency (pp. 610–623).

Bengio, Y., Hinton, G., Yao, A., Song, D., Abbeel, P., Darrell, T., ... and Mindermann, S. (2024). Managing extreme AI risks amid rapid progress. *Science, 384*(6698), 842–845.

Berente, N., Gu, B., Recker, J., and Santhanam, R. (2021). Managing Artificial Intelligence. *MIS Quarterly, 45*(3), 1433–1450. https://doi.org/10.25300/MISQ/2021/16274

Birhane, A. (2021). Algorithmic injustice: A relational ethics approach. In *Patterns* (Vol. 2, Issue 2). Cell Press. https://doi.org/10.1016/j.patter.2021.100205

Birhane, A., Kalluri, P., Card, D., Agnew, W., Dotan, R., and Bao, M. (2021a). *The Values Encoded in Machine Learning Research*. http://arxiv.org/abs/2106.15590

Birhane, A., Prabhu, V. U., and Kahembwe, E. (2021b). *Multimodal Datasets: Misogyny, Pornography, and Malignant Stereotypes*. http://arxiv.org/abs/2110.01963

Borges, A. F. S., Laurindo, F. J. B., Spínola, M. M., Gonçalves, R. F., and Mattos, C. A. (2021). The strategic use of artificial intelligence in the digital era: Systematic literature review and future research directions. *International Journal of Information Management, 57*, 102225. https://doi.org/10.1016/J.IJINFOMGT.2020.102225

Boschert, S., Coughlin, T., Ferraris, M., Flammini, F., Gonzalez Florido, J., Cadenas Gonzalez, A., Henz, P., de Kerckhove, D., Rosen, R., Saracco, R., Singh, A., Vitillo, A., and Yousif Edited by Theresa Cavrak, M. (2019). Symbiotic autonomous systems. White Paper. *IEEE Digital Reality*. IEEE.

Bruno, M. A., Grimm, L., Pang, L. J., Bezold, A., Fields, B. K., Baird, G. L., ... and Lexa, F. J. (2025). Artificial Intelligence and Its Impact on Radiology. *Journal of the American College of Radiology, 22*(11), 1417–1422.

Brynjolfsson, E., Li, D., and Raymond, L. (2025). Generative AI at work. *The Quarterly Journal of Economics, 140*(2), 889–942.

Cabrera-Sánchez, J. P., Villarejo-Ramos, Á. F., Lié-Cabanillas, F., and Shaikh, A. A. (2021). Identifying relevant segments of AI applications adopters – Expanding the UTAUT2's variables. *Telematics and Informatics, 58*, 101529. https://doi.org/10.1016/j.tele.2020.101529

Callaghan, W., Goh, J., Mohareb, M., Lim, A., and Law, E. (2018). MechanicalHeart: A human-machine framework for the classification of phonocardiograms. Proceedings of the ACM on Human-Computer Interaction, 2(CSCW). https://doi.org/10.1145/3274297

Calvaresi, D., Mualla, Y., Najjar, A., Galland, S., and Schumacher, M. (2019). Explainable multi-agent systems through blockchain technology. In Lecture Notes in Computer Science (including subseries Lecture Notes in Artificial Intelligence and Lecture Notes in Bioinformatics): Vol. 11763 LNAI. https://doi.org/10.1007/978-3-030-30391-4_3

Capgemini Research Institute. (2020). The AI-powered enterprise: Unlocking the potential of AI at scale. / www.capgemini.com/insights/research-library/the-ai-powered-enterprise/ Accessed 13 November 2025.

Carroll, M., Shah, R., Ho, M. K., Griffiths, T. L., Seshia, S. A., Abbeel, P., and Dragan, A. (2019). On the Utility of Learning about Humans for Human-AI Coordination. http://arxiv.org/abs/1910.05789

Castelfranchi, C., and Tummolini, L. (2003). Positive and negative expectations and the deontic nature of social conventions. *Proceedings of the International Conference on Artificial Intelligence and Law*, 119–125. https://doi.org/10.1145/1047788.1047819

Chakraborti, T., Kambhampati, S., Scheutz, M., and Zhang, Y. (2017). AI challenges in human-robot cognitive teaming. arXiv preprint arXiv:1707.04775.

Chan, S. (2001). Complex adaptive systems. In *ESD. 83 Research Seminar in Engineering Systems* (Vol. 31, pp. 1–9). MIT.

Chen, M., Herrera, F., and Hwang, K. (2018). Cognitive computing: architecture, technologies and intelligent applications. *IEEE Access, 6*, 19774–19783. https://doi.org/10.1109/ACCESS.2018.2791469

Chen, S. C., and Liu, Y. C. (2025). Impact of road event recognition reliability in autonomous vehicles on driver trust and takeover performance. *Human Interaction & Emerging Technologies*, 197, 399–406.

Clark, A. (2001, July). Natural-born cyborgs? In *International Conference on Cognitive Technology* (pp. 17–24). Springer.

Collins, C., Dennehy, D., Conboy, K., and Mikalef, P. (2021). Artificial intelligence in information systems research: A systematic literature review and research agenda. *International Journal of Information Management, 60*. https://doi.org/10.1016/j.ijinfomgt.2021.102383

Cooke, N. J., Gorman, J. C., Myers, C. W., and Duran, J. L. (2013). Interactive team cognition. *Cognitive Science, 37*(2), 255–285.

Coombs, C., Hislop, D., Taneva, S. K., and Barnard, S. (2020). The strategic impacts of Intelligent Automation for knowledge and service work: An interdisciplinary review. *Journal of Strategic Information Systems, 29*(4). 101600.

Cooper, S., Khatib, F., Treuille, A., Barbero, J., Lee, J., Beenen, M., ... and Players, F. (2010). Predicting protein structures with a multiplayer online game. *Nature, 466*(7307), 756–760.

Crandall, J. W., Oudah, M., Tennom, Ishowo-Oloko, F., Abdallah, S., Bonnefon, J. F., Cebrian, M., Shariff, A., Goodrich, M. A., and Rahwan, I. (2018). Cooperating with machines. *Nature Communications, 9*(1). https://doi.org/10.1038/s41467-017-02597-8

Crary, A. (2023). The toxic ideology of longtermism. *Radical Philosophy, 214*, 49–57.

Crouser, R. J., and Chang, R. (2012). *An Affordance-Based Framework for Human Computation and Human-Computer Collaboration*. https://scholarworks.smith.edu/csc_facpubs

Cubric, M. (2020). Drivers, barriers and social considerations for AI adoption in business and management: A tertiary study. *Technology in Society, 62*. https://doi.org/10.1016/j.techsoc.2020.101257

D'Amour, A., Heller, K., Moldovan, D., Adlam, B., Alipanahi, B., Beutel, A., ... & Sculley, D. (2022). Underspecification presents challenges for credibility in modern machine learning. *Journal of Machine Learning Research, 23*(226), 1–61.

Davenport, T. H. (2018). From analytics to artificial intelligence. *Journal of Business Analytics, 1*(2), 73–80.

De Cosmo, L. (2022). Google engineer claims AI chatbot is sentient: Why that matters. *Scientific American, 12.* www.scientificamerican.com/article/google-engineer-claims-ai-chatbot-is-sentient-why-that-matters/ Accessed 13 November 2025.

de Cremer, D., Kasparov, G., Wojcicki, A., and Images, G. (2021). Business and Society AI Should Augment Human Intelligence, Not Replace It Summary. https://hbr.org/2021/03/ai-should-augment-human-intelligence-not-replace-it

Dellermann, D., Calma, A., Lipusch, N., Weber, T., Weigel, S., and Ebel, P. (2019). The future of human-AI collaboration: A taxonomy of design knowledge for hybrid intelligence systems. https://hdl.handle.net/10125/59468

Dellermann, D., Lipusch, N., Ebel, P., and Leimeister, J. M. (2019). Design principles for a hybrid intelligence decision support system for business model validation. *Electronic Markets, 29*(3), 423–441. https://doi.org/10.1007/s12525-018-0309-2

Deloitte. (2019). *Artificial Intelligence Augmenting Human Intelligence*. Deloitte Insights.

Demartini, G., Difallah, D. E., Gadiraju, U., and Catasta, M. (2016). An introduction to hybrid human–machine information systems. *Foundations and Trends in Web Science, 7*(1), 1–87. https://doi.org/10.1561/1800000025

Dietvorst, B. J., Simmons, J. P., and Massey, C. (2015). Algorithm aversion: People erroneously avoid algorithms after seeing them err. *Journal of Experimental Psychology: General,* 144(1), 114.

Dorst, K. (2004). On the problem of design problems-problem solving and design expertise. *Journal of Design Research, 4*(2), 185–196.

Dorst, K. (2006). Design problems and design paradoxes. *Design Issues, 22*(3), 4–17.

Dragomir, L. C. (2023). Cyborg: Transhumanism, between mythology and necessity. *Social Sciences and Education Research Review, 10*(1), 103–110.

Duan, Y., Edwards, J. S., and Dwivedi, Y. K. (2019). Artificial intelligence for decision making in the era of Big Data - evolution, challenges and research agenda. *International Journal of Information Management, 48*, 63–71. https://doi.org/10.1016/j.ijinfomgt.2019.01.021

Dwivedi, Y. K., Hughes, L., Ismagilova, E., Aarts, G., Coombs, C., Crick, T., Duan, Y., Dwivedi, R., Edwards, J., Eirug, A., Galanos, V., Ilavarasan, P. V., Janssen, M., Jones, P., Kar, A. K., Kizgin, H., Kronemann, B., Lal, B., Lucini, B., … Williams, M. D. (2021). Artificial Intelligence (AI): Multidisciplinary perspectives on emerging challenges, opportunities, and agenda for research, practice and policy. *International Journal of Information Management, 57*, 101994.

Engelbart, D. C. (1962). *Augmenting Human Intellect: A Conceptual Framework*. Stanford Research Institute.

Enholm, I. M., Papagiannidis, E., Mikalef, P., and Krogstie, J. (2021). Artificial intelligence and business value: A literature review. *Information Systems Frontiers*. https://doi.org/10.1007/s10796-021-10186-w

Esteva, A., Chou, K., Yeung, S., Naik, N., Madani, A., Mottaghi, A., ... and Socher, R. (2021). Deep learning-enabled medical computer vision. *NPJ Digital Medicine,* 4(1), 5.

Fan, W., Liu, J., Zhu, S., and Pardalos, P. M. (2020). Investigating the impacting factors for the healthcare professionals to adopt artificial intelligence-based medical diagnosis support system (AIMDSS). *Annals of Operations Research, 294*(1–2), 567–592. https://doi.org/10.1007/s10479-018-2818-y

Figalist, I., Elsner, C., Bosch, J., and Olsson, H. H. (2022). Breaking the vicious circle: A case study on why AI for software analytics and business intelligence does not take off in practice. *Journal of Systems and Software, 184*, 111135.

Finlayson, S. G., Bowers, J. D., Ito, J., Zittrain, J. L., Beam, A. L., and Kohane, I. S. (2019). Adversarial attacks on medical machine learning. *Science*, 363(6433), 1287–1289.

Fitts, P. M. (1951). *Human Engineering for an Effective Air-Navigation and Traffic-Control System.* National Research Council, USA.

Floridi, L., Cowls, J., Beltrametti, M., Chatila, R., Chazerand, P., Dignum, V., Luetge, C., Madelin, R., Pagallo, U., Rossi, F., Schafer, B., Valcke, P., and Vayena, E. (2018). AI4 people: An ethical framework for a good AI society: Opportunities, risks, principles, and recommendations. *Minds and Machines, 28*(4), 689–707. https://doi.org/10.1007/s11023-018-9482-5

Frauenberger, C. (2019). Entanglement HCI the next wave? *ACM Transactions on Computer-Human Interaction, 27*(1). https://doi.org/10.1145/3364998

Fügener, A., Grahl, J., Gupta, A., and Ketter, W. (2021). Will humans-in-the-loop become borgs? Merits and pitfalls of working with AI. *MIS Quarterly: Management Information Systems, 45*(3), 1527–1556. https://doi.org/10.25300/MISQ/2021/16553

Gallup, (2025). *State of the Global Workplace 2025: Understanding Employees, Informing Leaders.* Gallup.

Gebru, T., and Torres, É. P. (2024). The TESCREAL bundle: Eugenics and the promise of utopia through artificial general intelligence. *First Monday, 29*(4). https://doi.org/10.5210/fm.v29i4.13636

Gent, E. (2023). Quantum Computing's Hard, Cold Reality Check: Hype is everywhere, skeptics say, and practical applications are still far away. *IEEE Spectrum, 22.* https://spectrum.ieee.org/quantum-computing-skeptics Accessed 5 November, 2025.

Giuliano, R. (2020). Echoes of myth and magic in the language of Artificial Intelligence. *AI and Society, 35*(4), 1009–1024. https://doi.org/10.1007/s00146-020-00966-4

Goetze, T. S. (2022). Mind the gap: Autonomous systems, the responsibility gap, and moral entanglement. In *Proceedings of the 2022 ACM Conference on Fairness, Accountability, and Transparency* (pp. 390–400).

Gorman, J. C. (2014). Team coordination and dynamics: Two central issues. *Current Directions in Psychological Science, 23*(5), 355–360.

Grønsund, T., and Aanestad, M. (2020). Augmenting the algorithm: Emerging human-in-the-loop work configurations. *Journal of Strategic Information Systems, 29*(2), 101614.

Gulati, S., Sousa, S., and Lamas, D. (2017). Modelling trust: An empirical assessment. In *Lecture Notes in Computer Science (including subseries Lecture Notes in Artificial Intelligence and Lecture Notes in Bioinformatics).* Vol. 10516 LNCS. https://doi.org/10.1007/978-3-319-68059-0_3

Guo, H., Xing, X., Zhou, Y., Jiang, W., Chen, X., Wang, T., ... and Xu, J. (2025). *A Survey of Large Language Model for Drug Research and Development.* IEEE Access.

Gursoy, D., Chi, O. H., Lu, L., and Nunkoo, R. (2019). Consumers acceptance of artificially intelligent (AI) device use in service delivery. *International Journal of Information Management, 49*, 157–169. https://doi.org/10.1016/j.ijinfomgt.2019.03.008

Hagendorff, T. (2020). The ethics of AI ethics: An evaluation of guidelines. *Minds and Machines, 30*(1), 99–120. https://doi.org/10.1007/s11023-020-09517-8

Hanelt, A., Bohnsack, R., Marz, D., and Marante, C. A. (2021). A systematic review of the literature on digital transformation: Insights and implications for strategy and organizational change. *Journal of Management Studies, 58*(5), 1159–1197.

Heikkilä, M., and Heaven, W. D. (2022). Yann LeCun has a bold new vision for the future of AI. *MIT Technology Review*. www.technologyreview.com/2022/06/24/1054817/yann-lecun-bold-new-vision-future-ai-deep-learning-meta/ Accessed 5 November 2025.

Hemmer, P., Schemmer, M., Vössing, M., and Kühl, N. (2021). Human-AI complementarity in hybrid intelligence systems: A structured literature review. In *PACIS 2021 Proceedings*, Dubai (p. 118). PACIS.

Hinsen, S., Hofmann, P., Jöhnk, J., and Urbach, N. (2022). How can organizations design purposeful human-AI interactions: A practical perspective from existing use cases and interviews. In *HICSS 2022, Conference Proceedings* (pp. 196–205). Association of Information Systems.

Hollnagel, E. (2017). The diminishing relevance of human–machine interaction. *The Handbook of Human–machine Interaction* (pp. 417–429). CRC Press.

Holmström, J. (2022). From AI to digital transformation: The AI readiness framework. *Business Horizons, 65*(3), 329–339.

Hudson, A. D., Finn, E., and Wylie, R. (2023). What can science fiction tell us about the future of artificial intelligence policy? *AI and Society, 38*(1), 197–211.

Humlum, A., and Vestergaard, E. (2025). The unequal adoption of ChatGPT exacerbates existing inequalities among workers. *Proceedings of the National Academy of Sciences, 122*(1), e2414972121.

Huxley, J. (1957) "Transhumanism," in *New Bottles for New Wine* (pp. 13–18). Chatto & Windus.

Huy, Q. N., Corley, K. G., and Kraatz, M. S. (2014). From support to mutiny: Shifting legitimacy judgments and emotional reactions impacting the implementation of radical change. *Academy of Management Journal, 57*(6), 1650–1680. https://doi.org/10.5465/amj.2012.0074

Hyland-Wood, D., Harrison, A., and Kolera, B. (2019). Righting writing's wrongs: Toward effective writing partnerships between humans and AI. *Universal Journal of Educational Research, 7*(5), 1306–1318. https://doi.org/10.13189/ujer.2019.070516

Ilyenkov, E. V. (1968). *On Idols and Ideals*. Politizdat.

Ishowo-Oloko, F., Bonnefon, J.-F., Soroye, Z., Crandall, J., Rahwan, I., and Rahwan, T. (2019). Behavioural evidence for a transparency–efficiency tradeoff in human–machine cooperation. *Nature Machine Intelligence, 1*(11), 517–521. https://doi.org/10.1038/s42256-019-0113-5

Jarrahi, M. H. (2018). Artificial intelligence and the future of work: Human-AI symbiosis in organizational decision making. *Business Horizons, 61*(4), 577–586. https://doi.org/10.1016/j.bushor.2018.03.007

Jick T. D., and Sturtevant K. D. M. (2017). Taking stock of 30 years of change management: Is it time for a reboot? In Shani, A. B., Noumair, D. A. (eds.), *Research in Organizational Change and Development* (Vol. 25, pp. 33–79). Emerald Publishing Limited. https://doi.org/10.1108/S0897-301620170000025002

John, M. M., Olsson, H. H., and Bosch, J. (2022). Towards an AI-driven business development framework: A multi-case study. *Journal of Software: Evolution and Process*, e2432.

Kaber, D. B., and Endsley, M. R. (2004). The effects of level of automation and adaptive automation on human performance, situation awareness and workload in a dynamic control task. *Theoretical Issues in Ergonomics Science, 5*(2), 113–153. https://doi.org/10.1080/1463922021000054335

Katz, Y. (2022). Intelligence under racial capitalism. *Monthly Review*, 74(4), 32–52.

Kaynak, O., He, W., Flammini, F., and Liu, Z. (2021). Towards symbiotic autonomous systems. *Philosophical Transactions of the Royal Society A: Mathematical, Physical and Engineering Sciences, 379*(2207). https://doi.org/10.1098/rsta.2020.0359

Keding, C., and Meissner, P. (2021). Managerial overreliance on AI-augmented decision-making processes: How the use of AI-based advisory systems shapes choice behavior in RandD investment decisions. *Technological Forecasting and Social Change,* 171. https://doi.org/10.1016/j.techfore.2021.120970

Kiesler, S., Sproull, L., and Waters, K. (1996). A prisoner's dilemma experiment on cooperation with people and human-like computers. *Journal of Personality and Social Psychology, 70*(1), 47–65. https://doi.org/10.1037/0022-3514.70.1.47

KPMG. (2019). *Easing the Pressure Points: The State of Intelligent Automation.*

Kurzweil, R. (2005). The singularity is near. In *Ethics and Emerging Technologies* (pp. 393–406). Palgrave Macmillan UK.

Langer, M., and Landers, R. N. (2021). The future of artificial intelligence at work: A review on effects of decision automation and augmentation on workers targeted by algorithms and third-party observers. *Computers in Human Behavior, 123.* https://doi.org/10.1016/j.chb.2021.106878

Lee, K. Y., Sheehan, L., Lee, K., and Chang, Y. (2021). The continuation and recommendation intention of artificial intelligence-based voice assistant systems (AIVAS): the influence of personal traits. *Internet Research.* https://doi.org/10.1108/INTR-06-2020-0327

Lemasters, R. (2024). Religious transhumanism as a new religious movement: Sketching a model of the development of religious transhumanism. *Religions*, 15(8), 885.

Leone, D., Schiavone, F., Appio, F. P., and Chiao, B. (2021). How does artificial intelligence enable and enhance value co-creation in industrial markets? An exploratory case study in the healthcare ecosystem. *Journal of Business Research, 129*, 849–859.

Lewis, S., Passmore, J., and Cantore, S. (2016). *Appreciative Inquiry for Change Management: Using AI to Facilitate Organizational Development.* Kogan Page Publishers.

Leyer, M., and Schneider, S. (2021). Decision augmentation and automation with artificial intelligence: Threat or opportunity for managers? *Business Horizons.* https://doi.org/10.1016/j.bushor.2021.02.026

Licklider, J. C. (2008). Man-computer symbiosis. *IRE Transactions on Human Factors in Electronics, 1*, 4–11.

Liu, H., Lai, V., and Tan, C. (2021). Understanding the effect of out-of-distribution examples and interactive explanations on human-AI decision making. *Proceedings of the ACM on Human-Computer Interaction, 5*(CSCW2). https://doi.org/10.1145/3479552

Liu, Q., Zhao, X., and Sun, B. (2018). Value co-creation mechanisms of enterprises and users under crowdsource-based open innovation. *International Journal of Crowd Science, 2*(1), 2–17. https://doi.org/10.1108/ijcs-01-2018-0001

Loh, E. (2018). Medicine and the rise of the robots: A qualitative review of recent advances of artificial intelligence in health. *BMJ Leader, 2*(2), 59–63. https://doi.org/10.1136/leader-2018-000071

Longo, F., Padovano, A., and Umbrello, S. (2020). Value-oriented and ethical technology engineering in industry 5.0: A human-centric perspective for the design of the factory of the future. *Applied Sciences, 10*(12), 4182.

Lu, L., Cai, R., and Gursoy, D. (2019). Developing and validating a service robot integration willingness scale. *International Journal of Hospitality Management*, 80, 36–51.

Lundberg, J., Arvola, M., and Palmerius, K. L. (2021). Human autonomy in future drone traffic: Joint human–AI control in temporal cognitive work. *Frontiers in Artificial Intelligence, 4*. https://doi.org/10.3389/frai.2021.704082

Luscombe, R. (2022). Google engineer put on leave after saying AI chatbot has become sentient. *The Guardian, 12*(06.2022).

Maadi, M., Khorshidi, H. A., and Aickelin, U. (2021). A review on human–AI interaction in machine learning and insights for medical applications. *International Journal of Environmental Research and Public Health, 18*(4), 1–21. MDPI AG. https://doi.org/10.3390/ijerph18042121

Marabelli, M., Newell, S., and Handunge, V. (2021). The lifecycle of algorithmic decision-making systems: Organisational choices and ethical challenges. https://ssrn.com/abstract=3908190

Marcus, G. (2022). Artificial general intelligence is not as imminent as you might think. *Scientific American, 327*(4), 42–45.

McCarthy, J., Minsky, M. L., Rochester, N., and Shannon, C. E. (2006). A proposal for the Dartmouth Summer Research Project on artificial intelligence. August 31, 1955. *AI Magazine*, 27(4), 12–12.

McKinsey. (2021). *The State of AI in 2021*. McKinsey Analytics.

Metcalf, L., Askay, D. A., and Rosenberg, L. B. (2019). Keeping humans in the loop: Pooling knowledge through artificial swarm intelligence to improve business decision making. *California Management Review, 61*(4), 84–109. https://doi.org/10.1177/0008125619862256

Methnani, L., Aler Tubella, A., Dignum, V., and Theodorou, A. (2021). Let me take over: variable autonomy for meaningful human control. *Frontiers in Artificial Intelligence, 4*. https://doi.org/10.3389/frai.2021.737072

Mikalef, P., and Gupta, M. (2021). Artificial intelligence capability: Conceptualization, measurement calibration, and empirical study on its impact on organizational creativity and firm performance. *Information and Management, 58*(3), 103434.

Mochizuki, Y., Bruillard, E., and Bryan, A. (2025). The ethics of AI or techno-solutionism? UNESCO's policy guidance on AI in education. *British Journal of Sociology of Education*, 1–22. https://doi.org/10.1080/01425692.2025.2502808

Morley, J., Elhalal, A., Garcia, F., Kinsey, L., Mökander, J., and Floridi, L. (2021). Ethics as a service: A pragmatic operationalisation of AI ethics. *Minds and Machines, 31*(2), 239–256. https://doi.org/10.1007/s11023-021-09563-w

Morley, J., Morton, C., Karpathakis, K., Taddeo, M., and Floridi, L. (2021). Towards a framework for evaluating the safety, acceptability and efficacy of AI systems for health: an initial synthesis. *arXiv preprint arXiv:2104.06910*.

Morozov, E. (2023). The True Threat of Artificial Intelligence. International New York Times.

Mueller, M. (2024). *The Myth of AGI*. Internet Governance Project.

Naughton, J. (2022). Long termism: how good intentions and the rich created a dangerous creed. *The Guardian*. www.theguardian.com/technology/commentisfree/2022/dec/04/longtermism-rich-effective-altruism-tech-dangerous Accessed 5 November 2025.

Newlands, G. (2021). Lifting the curtain: Strategic visibility of human labour in AI-as-a-Service. *Big Data and Society, 8*(1). https://doi.org/10.1177/20539517211016026

Newman, S., Birhane, A., Zajko, M., Birhane, A., Osoba, O. A., Prunkl, C., Lima, G., Bowen, J., Sutton, R., and Adams, C. (2019). *AI and Agency*. https://escholarship.org/uc/item/8q15786s

Niehaus, F., and Wiesche, M. (2021). A socio-technical perspective on organizational interaction with AI. *A Literature Review*. https://aisel.aisnet.org/ecis2021_rp/156

Oh, C., Lee, T., Kim, Y., Park, S. H., Kwon, S., and Suh, B. (2017). Us vs. them: Understanding artificial intelligence technophobia over the Google DeepMind Challenge Match. *Conference on Human Factors in Computing Systems – Proceedings*, 2017-May, 2523–2534. https://doi.org/10.1145/3025453.3025539

ÓhÉigeartaigh, S. (2025). *The Most Dangerous Fiction: The Rhetoric and Reality of the AI Race.* Available at SSRN: https://ssrn.com/abstract=5278644 or http://dx.doi.org/10.2139/ssrn.5278644

Pagani, M. (2013). Digital business strategy and value creation: Framing the dynamic cycle of control points. *Mis Quarterly*, *37*(2), 617–632.

Palmié, M., Rüegger, S., and Parida, V. (2023). Microfoundations in the strategic management of technology and innovation: Definitions, systematic literature review, integrative framework, and research agenda. *Journal of Business Research*, *154*, 113351.

Parasuraman, R., and Wickens, C. D. (2008). Humans: Still vital after all these years of automation. *Human Factors*, *50*(3), 511–520. https://doi.org/10.1518/001872008X312198

Parent-Rocheleau, X., and Parker, S. K. (2022). Algorithms as work designers: How algorithmic management influences the design of jobs. *Human Resource Management Review*, *32*(3), 100838.

PwC. (2017a). *Human in the Loop*. PwC Research.

PwC. (2017b). *Sizing the Prize. What's the Real Value of AI for Your Business and How Can You Capitalise*? PwC Research.

Rabinowitz, N. C., Perbet, F., Song, H. F., Zhang, C., and Botvinick, M. (2018). Machine theory of mind. In *International Conference on Machine Learning* (pp. 4218–4227). PMLR.

Rafner, J., Gajdacz, M., Kragh, G., Hjorth, A., Gander, A., Pal, B., Berditchevskaia, A., Grey, F., Gal, K., Segal, A., Walmsley, M., Miller, J. A., Dellerman, D., Haklay, M., Michelucci, P., Sherson, J., and Vencortex, H. (2021). Revisiting citizen science through the lens of hybrid intelligence. *arXiv preprint arXiv:2104.14961*.

Raisch, S., and Krakowski, S. (2021). Artificial Intelligence and Management: The Automation-Augmentation Paradox. *Academy of Management Review*, *46*(1), 192–210.

Ramesh, N., and Delen, D. (2021). Digital transformation: How to beat the 90% failure rate? *IEEE Engineering Management Review*, *49*(3), 22–25.

Redfern, N. (2023). *Runaway Science: True Stories of Raging Robots and Hi-Tech Horrors*. Visible Ink Press.

Ritala, P., and Almpanopoulou, A. (2017). In defense of "eco" in innovation ecosystem. *Technovation*, *60*, 39–42. https://doi.org/10.1016/j.technovation.2017.01.004. Accessed 12 Oct 2020. https://doi.org/10.1109/JPROC.2018.2889678

Rzepka, C., and Berger, B. (2018). User interaction with AI-enabled systems. A systematic review of IS research. In *39th International Conference on Information Systems*, San Francisco. https://aisel.aisnet.org/icis2018/general/Presentations/7/

Scheuerman, M. K., Hanna, A., and Denton, E. (2021). Do datasets have politics? Disciplinary values in computer vision dataset development. *Proceedings of the ACM on Human-Computer Interaction*, *5*(CSCW2), 1–37.

Seeber, I., Bittner, E., Briggs, R. O., de Vreede, T., de Vreede, G. J., Elkins, A., Maier, R., Merz, A. B., Oeste-Reiß, S., Randrup, N., Schwabe, G., and Söllner, M. (2020). Machines as teammates: A research agenda on AI in team collaboration. *Information and Management*, *57*(2). https://doi.org/10.1016/j.im.2019.103174

Sharma, R., and Rana, G. (2020). *Revitalizing Talent Management Practices through Technology Integration in Industry 4.0*. Internet of Things and Businesses in a Disruptive Economy.

Shea, V. J., Dow, K. E., Chong, A. Y. L., and Ngai, E. W. T. (2019). An examination of the long-term business value of investments in information technology. *Information Systems Frontiers, 21*(1), 213–227. https://doi.org/10.1007/S10796-017-9735-5

Shin, D. (2021). The effects of explainability and causability on perception, trust, and acceptance: Implications for explainable AI. *International Journal of Human Computer Studies, 146*, 102551. https://doi.org/10.1016/j.ijhcs.2020.102551

Sima, V., Gheorghe, I. G., Subić, J., and Nancu, D. (2020). Influences of the industry 4.0 revolution on the human capital development and consumer behavior: A systematic review. *Sustainability (Switzerland), 12*(10). https://doi.org/10.3390/SU12104035

Singer, T., and Tusche, A. (2013). Understanding Others: Brain Mechanisms of Theory of Mind and Empathy. *Neuroeconomics: Decision Making and the Brain*. Second Edition. https://doi.org/10.1016/B978-0-12-416008-8.00027-9

Smorodinskaya, N., Russell, M. G., Katukov, D., and Still, K. (2017). *Innovation Ecosystems vs. Innovation Systems in Terms of Collaboration and Co-creation of Value*. http://hdl.handle.net/10125/41798

Sohn, K., and Kwon, O. (2020). Technology acceptance theories and factors influencing artificial intelligence-based intelligent products. *Telematics and Informatics, 47*. https://doi.org/10.1016/j.tele.2019.10132

Stahl, B. C. (2021). *Artificial Intelligence for a Better Future: An Ecosystem Perspective on the Ethics of AI and Emerging Digital Technologies* (p. 124). Springer Nature.

Stowers, K., Brady, L. L., MacLellan, C., Wohleber, R., and Salas, E. (2021). Improving teamwork competencies in human–machine teams: perspectives from team science. *Frontiers in Psychology, 12*. https://doi.org/10.3389/fpsyg.2021.590290

Taddeo, M., and Floridi, L. (2018). How AI can be a force for good. *Science, 361*(6404), 751–752. https://doi.org/10.1126/science.aat5991

Teece, D. J. (2007). Explicating dynamic capabilities: The nature and microfoundations of (sustainable) enterprise performance. *Strategic Management Journal, 28*(13), 1319–1350.

Teece, D. J., and Pisano, G. (2003). The dynamic capabilities of firms. In *Handbook on Knowledge Management* (pp. 195–213). Springer.

Tirosh-Samuelson, H. (2012). Transhumanism as a secularist faith. *Zygon®, 47*(4), 710–734.

UNESCO. (2025). *Ethics of Artificial Intelligence: The Recommendation*. www.unesco.org/en/artificial-intelligence/recommendation-ethics# Accessed August 2, 2025

Van den Hoven, J. (2007, November). ICT and value sensitive design. In *The Information Society: Innovation, Legitimacy, Ethics and Democracy: Proceedings of the Conference "Information Society: Governance, Ethics and Social Consequences," University of Namur, Belgium 22–23 May 2006* (pp. 67–72). Springer US.

Varadi, M., Bertoni, D., Magana, P., Paramval, U., Pidruchna, I., Radhakrishnan, M., ... and Velankar, S. (2024). AlphaFold Protein Structure Database in 2024: providing structure coverage for over 214 million protein sequences. *Nucleic Acids Research, 52*(D1), D368–D375.

Wang, C., Fang, R., Park, K., Feng, Y., Lu, Z., and Cui, Y. (2012). Perceived usefulness, perceived security and adoption of mobile government: An empirical research. *Advances in Information Sciences and Service Sciences, 4*(6), 234–244. https://doi.org/10.4156/AISS.vol4.issue6.27

Wang, Y., Kinsner, W., Kwong, S., Leung, H., Lu, J., Smith, M. H., Trajkovic, L., Tunstel, E., Plataniotis, K. N., and Yen, G. G. (2020). Brain-inspired systems: a transdisciplinary exploration on cognitive cybernetics, humanity, and systems science toward autonomous artificial intelligence. *IEEE Systems, Man, and Cybernetics Magazine, 6*(1), 6–13. https://doi.org/10.1109/msmc.2018.2889502

Wang, Y.-Y., and Wang, Y.-S. (2019). Interactive learning environments development and validation of an artificial intelligence anxiety scale: An initial application in predicting motivated learning behavior development and validation of an artificial intelligence anxiety scale: an initial application in predicting motivated learning behavior. https://doi.org/10.1080/10494820.2019.1674887

Wilkins, J. (2025). Company Regrets Replacing All Those Pesky Human Workers with AI, Just Wants Its Humans Back. https://futurism.com/klarna-openai-humans-ai-back Accessed 29 July, 2025.

Wills, J. (2017). *Library of Congress Film Essay: The Terminator*. Library of Congress.

Xu, L., and Yu, F. (2020). Factors that influence robot acceptance. *Kexue Tongbao/Chinese Science Bulletin, 65*(6), 496–510. https://doi.org/10.1360/TB-2019-0136

Xu, W. (2019). Toward human-centered AI: A perspective from human-computer interactions. *Interactions, 26*(4), 42–46.

Xu, Y., Liu, X., Cao, X., Huang, C., Liu, E., Qian, S., ... and Zhang, J. (2021). Artificial intelligence: A powerful paradigm for scientific research. *The Innovation, 2*(4), 100179

Yang, Q. (2021). SIGCHI Outstanding Dissertation Award: Profiling Artificial Intelligence as a Material for User Experience Design. *Conference on Human Factors in Computing Systems Proceedings*. https://doi.org/10.1145/3411763.3457783

Zhang, Z., Genc, Y., Wang, D., Ahsen, M. E., and Fan, X. (2021). Effect of AI explanations on human perceptions of patient-facing AI-powered healthcare systems. *Journal of Medical Systems, 45*(6). https://doi.org/10.1007/s10916-021-01743-6

Zhuge, H. (2020). Cyber-physical-social intelligence. In *Cyber-Physical-Social Intelligence*. Springer Singapore. https://doi.org/10.1007/978-981-13-7311-4

II

Entanglement

CHAPTER 3

Human–Technology Entanglement

We're forever teetering on the brink of the unknowable and trying to understand what can't be understood.

—ISAAC ASIMOV

INTRODUCTION

To understand human–technology entanglement, we need to take a journey through anthropology, history, psychology, and philosophy.Without these perspectives, we are limited in being able to understand the AI phenomenon, how it came to be, and where it's potentially headed. This deep dive into the long history of human–technology entanglement can be summarized by the words of Eugene O'Neill (2006), "There is no present or future – only the past, happening over and over again – now." In other words, we have been here before.

At its core, technology is an evolution of tools that boost human capability. From a philosophical standpoint, the things we invent serve as mirrors that reveal insights about who we are and deepening our understanding of ourselves and the societies we have created. Lewis Mumford (1935), a technology historian, sociologist, and philosopher – maintained that the machines we have created reflect our fascination with ourselves; put simply, we have created machines in our own image. Looking at some of our most iconic technologies – whose evolved forms remain important fixtures in western cultures to this very day – the telephone, the phonograph (an early form of the gramophone), and motion pictures can all be seen as growing out of our innate interest to understand and extend ourselves: the human voice, the human eye, somatic movement, and human relationships.

DOI: 10.1201/9781003616566-5

These mechanical technologies have evolved out of our own intimate knowledge of the human physiology and anatomy that inspired their development – technologies that imitate and superpower our biological abilities.

The trajectory of technology development can be clearly seen today with AI. For example, in AI's 70-year history, the biggest single push and success has been in the development of generative AI – particularly in accessible image, text, music, and video generation – which has captured the public's imagination. These tools have given every citizen the tools to recreate the human form and extend ourselves. As Mumford would put it, *the machines we have created are a reflection of our fascination with ourselves.*

So, what fascinates us with AI, especially the technologies that have evolved from generative AI? It seems to have become an obsession to replicate our humanness and our intelligence, or even to supercharge it onto larger or more-than-human fantastical forms. This obsessiveness has led us to anthropomorphize robots in a planet already overpopulated with able-bodied humans. It has led to replicating human artwork, music, and knowledge and imitating our images and voices – which was never a problem to solve in the first place. We have created virtual worlds and metaverses that emulate the natural world that sustains us, while simultaneously doing nothing to protect the real thing from human destruction. We are obsessed with the creation of cyborgs, trans-humans, and a singularity with machines but are unable to address a technology-induced alienation, addictions, and psychoses in humans.

At a deep, psychological level, Mumford would maintain that humans have created these intelligent machines to enable us to understand ourselves and our relationships to each other and the world. And perhaps, this need for understanding and connection has become even more elusive than ever as the size and scale of the technology has become a monstrous form of what was innately human. There are even elements of weaponizing our intelligence and creativity in ways that demean what it means to be human by developing uber intelligence to the extent that many high-profile scientists, AI technology companies, and politicians are now claiming that AI technologies may soon become an existential threat that may lead to our annihilation as we inevitably lose control over them (Brown, 2023; Federspiel et al., 2023).

Subconsciously, what might this be saying about humanity's relationship with ourselves at this point in history? Understanding the machine has almost become a proxy for attaining a deeper understanding of ourselves, and it can be argued that we are reaching a critical point of discomfort with what we see. But there is hope. Mumford maintains that we have choices in how we create and integrate technology. These choices are many, but they are exercised by a few. The choices are deliberate, unconscious, logical, or irrational – *but they are still choices* – and they must be made transparent, understood, and agreed upon by all of us collectively. We can exercise our choices by reflecting on the technology we have created and assimilating only that which serves humanity's purpose.

In terms of moving deeper into the era of AI, we need to remember that we still have choices; the trajectory that is being presented to us in the media is not inevitable. The machine does not make demands; the human spirit does. Going back to first principles, remember that the **development of technology is not isolated and self-contained – it is a product of the environment which nurtures it**. In other words, technology does not occur in isolation; it is not an independent system; it's an integral component of the socio-economic-political ecosystems that have created it. It reacts to the wider ecosystem but influences it as well – an important concept we explore in the next section.

The person who understands this inextricable link between technology and humanity is Hayao Miyazaki, the founder of Studio Ghibli. The studio creates art, stories, and animated films that tell emotional stories about humanity and our connection with the natural world. Miyazaki and his studio continue to produce hand-crafted artwork for their films, to tell their stories. When he found out that his artwork was appropriated as learning data and then replicated by ChatGPT, he claimed that "*AI was an insult to life itself*" (Khattak et al., 2025). Miyazaki's concern was not primarily over the theft of their art, but that the AI reproductions had failed to reflect the beauty of the human and natural world, something that was fundamental in the studio's creations. Perhaps Mumford's take on this would be that we have reached an inflection point with our technologies – that they are no longer a reflective expression of our humanity, but rather an aberration of it.

This chapter is focused on a *meta view* of AI in our contemporary society. To do this, we explore the concept of *technogenesis*, which is the view that humans and technology have co-evolved since the beginning of time and are inextricably linked (Hodder, 1990; 2012; 2014; Latour, 1993; 2017). We then explore the nature of the entangled relationships between humans and technology or "things" as Hodder (2012; 2014) refers to them from an anthropological perspective. We then explore the impacts and *consequences of these entangled systems* in terms of dependence and dependency, and the *perplexity* they create for citizens and organizations striving to cope with and lead through technology-induced change and transformation. This builds the case for the *critical post-human* perspective taken in the remainder of this book. But first, let's look at an *ecosystem view* of the current AI landscape as an anchor for the deeper work that follows.

Given the fundamental challenges we're facing with AI technologies, we need to anchor ourselves in a meta question similar to what was asked by Samuel Beckett in "Waiting for Godot": *What are we doing here, that is the question*? (Beckett, 1954).

Key message in** Chapter 3**: History is important.

I promise you; this chapter is important. The tools we have created for you in the latter part of this book will be more meaningful, and your wisdom in how to use them will be more astute after you explore the concepts in this chapter. Come walk with me...

THE ENTANGLED AI ECOSYSTEM

> *Invention, it must be humbly admitted, does not consist in creating out of void, but out of chaos; the materials must, in the first place, be afforded:* it can give form to dark, shapeless substances, but cannot bring into being the substance itself.
>
> —MARY WOLLSTONECRAFT SHELLEY, FRANKENSTEIN.

Looking at how our AI ecosystems work is the starting point in understanding where the leverage points are in attempting to influence AI systems design in organizations. Socio-technical perspectives have always formed the foundation of information systems (IS) research, and this has to a large extent been the key enabler of its success in forming practical and useful theoretical foundations with the business systems and computer science communities. A key tenet of the socio-technical systems perspective is that technology innovation is considered inseparable from the social processes of organizational development and change (Avgerou, 2001). Socio-technical systems *co-evolve* with their users, and this provides for a more nuanced and dynamic approach to understanding AI and how it can be better designed, developed, and enabled in organizations.

As introduced in the previous chapter, the increasing complexity of our business, investment, cultural, and political environments necessitates taking socio-technical approaches a step further, by considering *ecosystems* as a more appropriate approach to understanding AI system functions and emergent behaviours. This is considered essential for a technological environment that is dominated by rapid development and change (Crouser and Chang, 2012; Grønsund and Aanestad, 2020; Lundberg et al., 2024; Methnani et al., 2021; Yang, 2021).

Ecosystems are fundamentally *complex adaptive systems* that emerge during collaboration among networked actors in the system (not only human and machine but also systems and materials) to co-create value (Chan, 2001; Newlands, 2021; Smorodinskaya et al., 2017). A socio-technical system in the IS tradition is different from an ecosystem. A critical point made by Smorordinskaya et al. is that "*Ecosystems are tailored to interactive co-creation of values, while systems are not*" (2017), implying that traditional systems have been designed to produce a predetermined outcome. **This distinction is important.** In the current corporate and management consultant mindset of "strategic planning," socio-technical systems have been designed to produce preferred or planned results. However, the fundamental workings of increasingly complex systems often produce less than expected outcomes, as these design decisions are often based on weak or uninformed assumptions about how the world operates.

In a complex adaptive environment, straight line assumptions between cause and effect do not apply, as cause and effect are much more distant in time and space. At best, they are naïve, and at worst they lead to spurious correlation that leaves organizations with empty promises of productivity and ROI based on atypical use cases. Our research shows that the current nascent stage AI research has focused predominantly on the emergent technologies and the value creation opportunities they represent, and less so on the human, organizational, and social aspects that support them. This has led to calls from researchers for a more holistic approach for the development and implementation of AI-enabled systems (Enholm et al., 2022; Niehaus and Wiesche, 2021; Rzepka and Berger, 2018). Therefore, an AI strategy focused only on the technology and not on the ecosystem is set to fail.

Complex adaptive systems tend to be agile, self-organizing, and self-governing and create synergy effects; they are also dynamic, constantly adapting and evolving. It could also be argued from a systems perspective that the value is within the entirety of the ecosystem rather than being attributable to any single actor or event. This is where different mental models of how different systems work come in; those who view our systems as organic (such as technology anthropologists) and those who view them as mechanistic (such as many computer scientists) have different opinions and solutions on AI development, enablement, and success.

Within complex adaptive systems, human behavior is indeterminable as they are embedded in social systems that are inherently uncertain, ambiguous, and fluid, which renders current approaches to AI development and deployment as fraught with difficulties as artificial systems need to operate within boundaries of accuracy, reliability, and predictability if they are to be utilized as business systems. This is because they're based on assumptions about human nature and systems that are limited, incomplete, and indeterminable (Smorodinskaya et al., 2017; Birhane, 2021; Chan, 2001). Machine-imposed determinability on human–AI systems is believed to not only be based on inaccurate assumptions but has consequences for people at the margins in society – a situation which is further exacerbated in an environment where issues of ethics and safety remain at the periphery of business interests (Birhane, 2021; Newlands, 2021; Bender et al., 2021). As discussed in Chapters 1 and 2, the potential benefits of AI technologies are undeniable; however, the value may be in the complex human, organizational, and social ecosystems that support and utilize the technology rather than in the technology itself.

Researchers believe that the current computer science bias of AI development is embedded in traditional mental models predicated on prediction, stability, order, uniformity, and equilibrium: these are considered as Cartesian and Newtonian inheritances (philosophies prefaced on determinism and predictability) and not adequately applicable to complex, dynamic, and ambiguous environments (Birhane, 2021). Our socio-economic-political systems surpassed the comfort of predictability long ago; we are firmly embedded in an era of complex and ambiguous environments where all the networked actors are not transparent in their existence, influence, or motivations. An example of the complexity of the current AI ecosystem entanglement at the base level is outlined in Figure 3.1. Please note that this system's complexity has been reduced for a high-level focus on LLMs to illustrate this point.

In this example, the AI ecosystem comprises seven primary nodes or actors, along with eight additional entities that play essential supporting roles in maintaining system operations. Each actor serves as an entity engaging within the ecosystem to drive actions and generate outputs, which continuously circulate to either reinforce or modify the ecosystem's dynamics. Every line in the diagram is a connection that is a negotiated position in the ecosystem, a position made up of different motivations, agreements, trade-offs, capabilities, and return on investment – these positions are dynamic, shifting to changes in the overall environment. A discovery or shift in one area reverberates through the rest of the system. The seven critical actors and their interactions with other components in the system are outlined below:

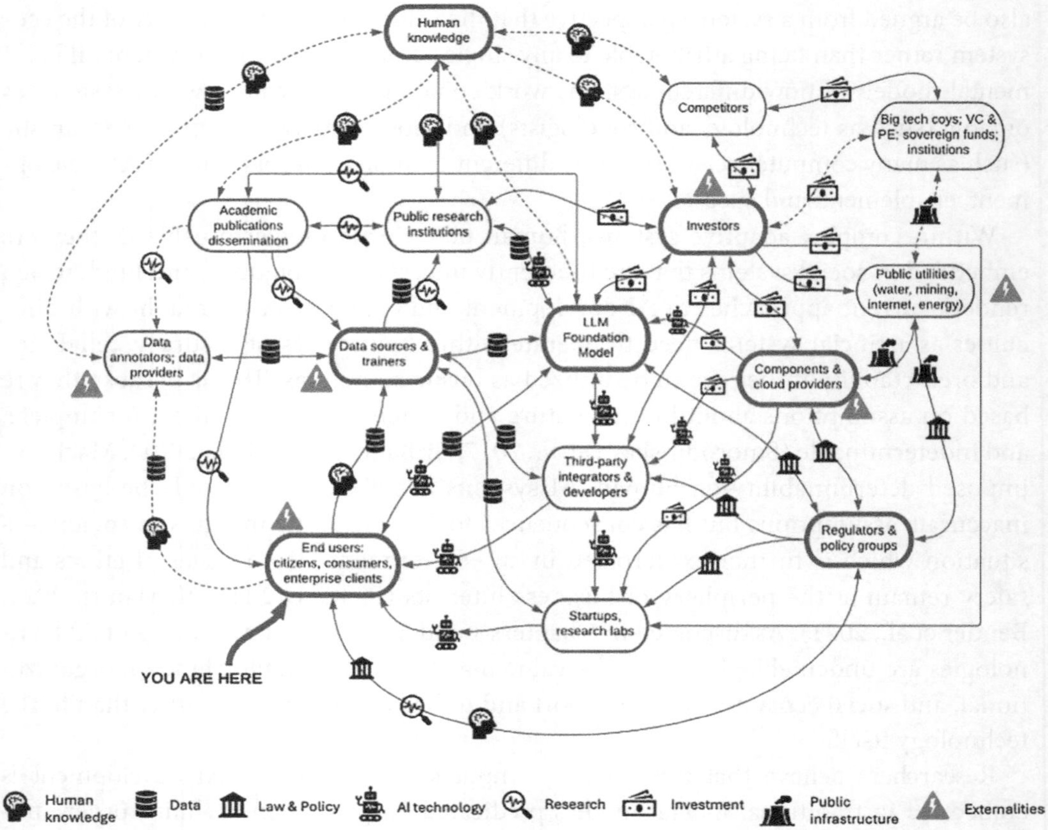

FIGURE 3.1 AI ecosystem entanglement (LLMs).

- **Human knowledge base.** This is the corpus of human-generated content that forms the foundation of all training data that has been sourced to train foundational models. This is usually unstructured data, such as text, images, videos, and audio, that's been scraped from various sources such as databases, books, videos, and websites (or derived from proprietary datasets). To train an AI model, AI algorithms are given training data, which they use iteratively to tune their intended function (see the "data sources" item below in this list). Beyond the human knowledge base, *synthetic data* is also being used by developers, as humans can't create new data fast enough to keep up with the enormous demands of AI models. These are data generated by algorithms and for algorithms (Jacobsen, 2023). This is artificially generated data that mimics real-world data through statistical abstraction and simulation and is forecast to form 70% of all data used by 2030 (Kiran and Kumar, 2024). The challenges of synthetic data is discussed in Part III of this book.
- **Developers of LLM foundation models and model management platforms.** In this example, developers of foundation models and model management platforms are currently dominated by five organizations, such as OpenAI, Microsoft, Google, AWS, and Anthropic, that control over 86% of the market between them[1]. An

extension of this group of actors is a larger group of *Third-Party Integrators and Developers* who provide GenAI services. This group has a very long tail, with the largest actors being Accenture with 7% of the market, Deloitte with 3%, and 2% each for IBM, McKinsey, CapGemini, and BCG. Over 76% of the market comprises many smaller players with little influence, each with less than 1% of the market. Many of these smaller players are bought out by the larger players as companies move into land-grab mode.

- **Investors.** Many top-tier venture capital (VC) investors have been building up their Generative AI portfolios. Notably, Andreessen Horowitz and Sequoia have made nearly 50% more Generative AI investments than anyone else so far.[2] The top five VCs are Andreessen Horowitz, Sequoia Capital, Lightspeed Venture Partners, Khosla Ventures, and Accel. Since 2019 (to May 2024), the US has been the top country globally for Generative AI funding with a large lead (US$54), followed by China and the UK at US$3 each, while Israel, Canada, France, and Germany have also raised over US$1B.
- **Data sources.** These companies specialize in data collection, annotation, and curation to meet the specific needs of AI development. Data for AI requires high-quality, human-annotated datasets across various modalities, including text, image, audio, and video, for training generative AI models. This includes sourcing and curating datasets from numerous countries. Leading data vendors in this domain include Appen, Shaip, Twine AI, Nexdata, DataOcean AI, and Pixta AI.
- **Components, cloud providers, data centers.** Behind the scenes of your AI interface is a network of major companies producing high-performance GPUs and custom-designed AI chips, as well as cloud infrastructure and data centers, and other data-generating components such as sensors and cameras. For example, the largest players are Nvidia, AMD, Intel, and AWS for chips. In an interesting turn of developments, the term **AI Factories** entered the AI lexicon in 2024 but became popularized during the 2025 Nvidia GTC conference. AI factories are large-scale data centers or computational infrastructures designed to train, deploy, and run AI models – especially large-scale models like OpenAI's GPT, Google DeepMind's Gemini, or Meta's LLaMA. These "factories" aren't traditional manufacturing plants, but rather massive clusters of GPUs and other AI-optimized hardware that enable the production and operation of artificial intelligence systems.

  "AI factories" consist of high-performance compute infrastructure (e.g., Nvidia H100 GPU clusters), advanced cooling systems to manage heat from hardware, data pipelines for ingesting and processing vast volumes of training data, AI model development stacks (frameworks, algorithms, and toolchains), and software orchestration for training, fine-tuning, and inference deployment. Organizations building them are the AI giants such as NVIDIA, Microsoft-OpenAI, Google DeepMind, and Amazon AWS. The most interesting development was that prior to the popularization of the term AI Factories, this area was known as the AI ecosystem to describe the interconnected network of actors, tools, infrastructure, and practices involved in AI development. However, the emergence of a more industrial term signaled the emergence of mass production of "intelligence," closed-loop systems of AI technology development, and enclosures of open ecosystems into corporate conglomerates. In Chapter 4, we revisit this pattern as the emergent behavior of empires.

- **Regulators and policy makers.** While global AI regulation is still evolving, there is a growing consensus on the need for guardrails on AI development and deployment. Key areas of regulation are focused on risk management, transparency and explainability, accountability, bias and fairness, data governance, and human oversight. However, there is a wide range of implementation and enforcement approaches that are still being negotiated. The Organisation for Economic Co-operation and Development (OECD) has developed a set of principles for promoting trustworthy AI, which have been adopted by many countries, and the G20. Several international commitments have been established at bilateral, regional, and multilateral levels to collaborate and cooperate on AI. The European Union, in particular, is taking a leading role in AI regulation with the Artificial Intelligence Act. The Act prohibits certain AI systems that are deemed to violate fundamental rights or democratic values, and establishes requirements for high-risk AI systems, including registration, technical documentation, and transparency obligations. At the time of this book's publication, the EU was reported as looking to scale back these regulations.
- **You as citizens** or "users" of LLMs only see the interface on your devices and the utility you get from LLM-based products. It may be your AI agent dealing with some of your workflows to free your time, it could be a program that helps you research a project or rewrite your reports, or you could even be using it to write your code or marketing copy or your PhD. This utility is what you're after, and the ecosystems deliver it to you seamlessly. The downsides are just the **cost of doing business** with this new tool, such as environmental externalities, data theft, potential community job losses – or is it?

The stocks and flows in this ecosystem can be seen in the legend in Figure 3.1 and are illustrated as elements that are produced, exchanged, or leveraged between all the networked actors. These elements are human knowledge, data, law and policy, AI technologies, AI research, investment, public infrastructures, and externalities that are produced.

But what happens if you do care beyond "**the cost of doing business**"? What if you care about where the training data comes from, or about the externalities that are produced? Is it possible to "disentangle" these complex ecosystems to produce different outcomes? The current ecosystem exists because we use these tools, so surely we can have more say. Are the AI facts and trajectories presented by those with vested interests in the current system represent the whole story, or is there more to the story of how we got here and where we're going?

In the next section, we delve deeper into human–technology entanglement. However, we complicate things in Chapter 4 to make an argument that the technology entanglement, since Classical Greece to the Middle Ages, supported the growth and development of the military industrial-complex and the rise of empires, and we are inadvertently complicit in its continuation to this day with the digital-AI revolution. The good news is that we all have a choice about where we go from here. First, let's explore the concept of technogenesis and the origin story of how humans become entangled with the technologies we create.

TECHNOGENESIS: HUMANS MAKE TOOLS, TOOLS SHAPE HUMANS

Humans have been making and using tools since the beginning of time. The earliest known stone implements are associated with the Oldowan culture in Africa from over 2.5 million years (Toth, 1985; Leakey, 1976). They were simple flakes chipped from rocks and used to cut, scrape, or crack materials for eating or building. This point in time marks the beginning of toolmaking, which forced a profound shift in the evolution of early humans in being conscious of our ability to transform raw material into a purposeful tool or technology. Anthropologists believe that this represented more than momentary human ingenuity, but it created a significant *cognitive leap* for our species. The development and use of tools and retaining them for later use was a deliberate and instinctual interaction with the world that involved mediated agency, knowledge retention, and planning (Leakey, 1976).

This point in time is the beginning of human–technology entanglement.

Bernard Stiegler's concept of technogenesis (1998) highlights that technology and human evolution are deeply intertwined, with tools being essential to our humanity rather than just external objects. Stiegler views this as a reciprocal relationship, where tools shape human cognition, societal structures, and cultural dynamics. Technology is a foundational lens for understanding human civilization. For instance, the emergence of early tools, such as those in the Oldowan culture around 2.6 to 1.7 million years ago, marked a revolutionary shift where we started to practice knowledge retention, problem-solving, and knowledge transfer about our tools into the fabric of our human development (Toth, 1985; Leakey, 1976).

This trajectory of human-tool entanglement will continue to evolve, twist, and turn. Homo sapiens from 300,000 BCE started to create more specialized tools that were fit for purpose, such as spears for fishing, blades for cutting, and shovels for digging. The central thesis of technogenesis is that tool creation and use changed our evolution; the development of the opposable thumb on our hands, the expansion of the neocortex of our brains, and the shift in the social dynamics of early hominin groups were shaped over time by our interaction with our environment and the tools we created (Steigler, 1998; Hayles, 1999).

The symbiosis between humans and our tools and technologies is a recursive loop explained succinctly by the phenomenon *We shape our tools, and thereafter our tools shape us* (Hurme and Jouhki, 2017). This loop also appears in media studies led by McLuhan (1967), who viewed media as extensions of our physical and mental capabilities, and Vilém Flusser, whose concept of the *Apparatus-Operator complex* describes the dynamic relationship between technical devices (apparatuses) and the individuals (operators) who use them (Pandilovski, 2016). This symbiosis is also consistent with the cybernetics perspective that emphasizes the role of the observer in understanding and interacting with systems; observers are always part of the system they are observing, and their observations and actions influence the system they are studying (Axelsson, 2025; Heylighen and Joslyn, 2001).

These symbioses and recursive loops are at the heart of human–technology entanglement.

Our tools were the first external memory systems for humans. Philosopher Andy Clark, in *Natural-Born Cyborgs?* (2001), maintains that humans are *cognitively extended* through tools, symbols, and technologies. Our neural pathways were developed through the act of problem contemplation (how to crack open a nut) and tool creation (forge a stone tool that fits in the human hand) as part of developing a solution for an anticipated outcome (eat the soft seed). Technology and human development became inseparable.

However, human cognition is also embodied (Hutchins, 2014; Hayles, 1999), as our learning experiences were internalized through how we used our hands, the tools we created that solved problems, the social systems that we developed, and the forests and savannahs we observed for our survival. Human cognition extends outside of our brains and into our connection with environment and our interactions with materials, other humans, and other species. For example, Clark (2001) says that western civilization's thinking is prejudiced only to respect the biology of the brain or cognition or "inside the ancient fortress of skin and skull," as he calls it. Our true power, he believes, lies in our ability to physically integrate our extended environment in a continual loop between brain, body, external environment, and technology; a capability that makes humans "natural born cyborgs" (Clark, 2001).

Similarly, Hayles (1999; 2014) rejects the traditional reductionist view of human cognitive development that just looks at how the brain works in isolation from the complex physiological and neurological systems that sustain it. Hayles emphasizes that the *embodied nature* of human cognition includes the contribution of the endocrine system, hormone regulation, and the sensory system in making up true human intelligence. This has been an integral part of our technogenesis since early humans and is hard-wired within us. This becomes an important issue in our later discussions on the reductionist bias of how we derive "artificial" intelligence and how AI attempts to emulate the disembodied human brain.

These anthropological and sociological perspectives of human–technology entanglement maintain that the confluence of humans and technology development has become ingrained over time and over countless waves of technological advancements and entanglements.

TOOLS AS BOUNDARY OBJECTS, SYSTEMS OF ABSTRACTION, AND SYMBOLIC SYSTEMS

In sociotechnical studies, the tools that humans have developed that have a significant impact on our societies are often referred to as *boundary objects*. In organizations or communities, a boundary object enhances our knowledge transfer, shared understanding of events, and co-ordinates activities (Doolin and McLeod, 2012). It is the artefact of our ingenuity that serves as a shared point of reference for different actors in our communities. The flint of stone deliberately chipped by the Oldowans mentioned earlier in this chapter is a boundary object for that technological epoch. A recent example is the introduction of the first smartphone, the iPhone, in 2007 during the Information Revolution. In Figure 3.2, we illustrate how a tool or technology emerges from a given epoch as a boundary object and then continues to embed itself into deeper layers of our systems.

For example, following Figure 3.2, the boundary object integrates itself into human life by the creation of *symbolic systems* (a set of symbols and rules that allow for the representation, manipulation, and communication of information) and *systems of abstraction* (ways of thinking about and understanding phenomena). The next layer is that of sociomateriality, or the development of sociotechnical systems that integrate the tools (or boundary objects) into our everyday lives.

When a tool becomes part of human life, it often becomes difficult to imagine functioning without it; an example would be a smartphone. The embedding of a boundary object is what Bruno Latour (1993) and others call *delegation*: we assign tasks to objects, and in doing so, we surrender certain forms of agency. The tool or technology may free humans to do more precise work, but it also commits humans to patterns of tool-based action and transmission. For example, the smartphone's utility has become highly enmeshed in our banking system, so that we need it for payments, authentications to get into our online accounts for various services, and connecting to our digital social networks. The removal of smartphones from use will entail dismantling all the secondary systems (which, for most of us, will be virtually impossible).

The key point here is that a tool or technology is more than its existence; it's the sum of the systems that have been set up to understand it and to integrate it within our society.

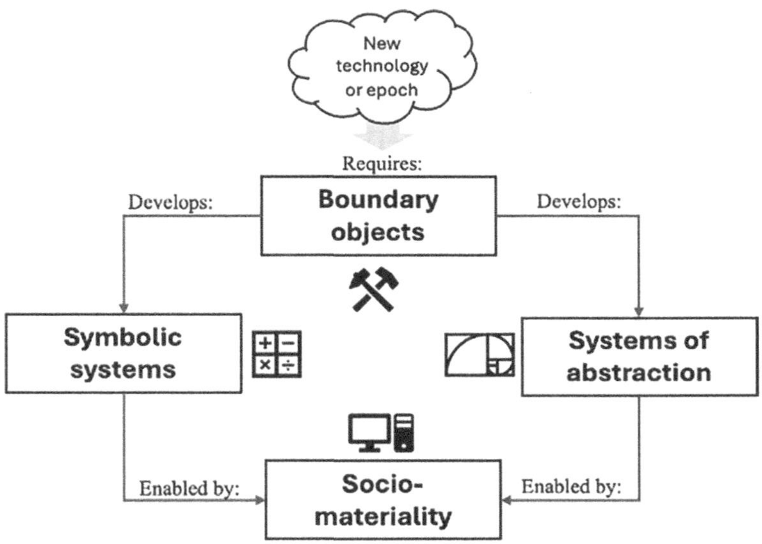

FIGURE 3.2 Technogenesis and entanglement.

Removing or replacing the tool entails the dismantling of the systems that have been set up to support it.

Now let's look at the more intimate entanglement between humans and technology, and its consequences.

THE ENTANGLEMENT OF HUMANS AND THINGS

Ian Hodder's theory on human entanglement offers an important lens through which we can explore the intricate relationships between humans and technology. From an anthropological perspective, Hodder maintains that entanglement represents the interplay of dependency and constraint, where humans and what he calls "things" are mutually bound in dynamic, evolving interactions (Hodder, 2012; 2014). This entanglement creates human material *dependency* on objects, as well as *constraints* that then shape our societal behaviors and cultural norms. Hodder breaks down entanglement as the sum of four types of relationships between *humans and things,* which I've outlined below and have illustrated in Figure 3.3:

- Humans depend on things (HT),
- Things depend on other things (TT),
- Things depend on humans (TH),
- Humans depend on humans (HH),
- Thus entanglement = (HT) + (TT) + (TH) + (HH).

Entanglement at the functional level is explained by four types of relationships: HT + TT + TH + HH. The entanglement of humans and things is relationally produced and becomes a perpetual loop.

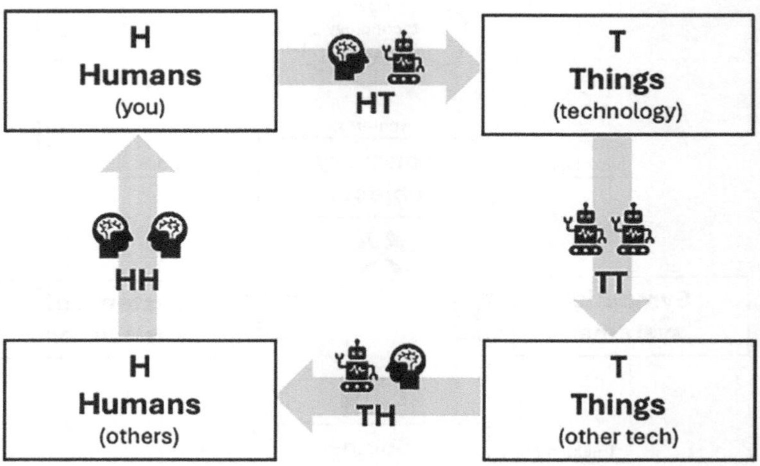

FIGURE 3.3 Entanglement: Four types of relationships.

Source: Adapted from Hodder (2012; 2014).

Ian Hodder (2014) gives the example of the **Neolithic Revolution** at the end of the last Ice Age and the start of the Holocene epoch (11,000 years ago), which is characterized as the period that instigated a step change in human–technology entanglement. In this era, a significant agricultural revolution took place where humans began to domesticate cereal crops; these required greater co-ordination of labor and attention in dealing with the seed development, farming, cropping, storage, and use of grain cereals. Humans also began to domesticate cattle and sheep, which required herding, protection, milking, and shearing. This not only required the development and transfer of skills and knowledge, but tooling of the technologies required to support these new agricultural activities.

In evolutionary terms, these Neolithic changes resulted in human *dependence* on the food, textiles, and other materials that new agricultural systems and technologies produced. This introduced our first step-change in intimate entanglement of humans with the technologies of agriculture – not only as a means of survival, but of living what we saw as a good life and eventually, what we perceived to be wealth and power creation. As agriculture developed, humans continued to evolve – technologically, biologically, and socially – and eventually formed villages, cities, and empires. We required systems to support the physical production of food, textiles, and tools, and consequently developed rudimentary trade and accounting systems to manage surpluses.

The developments that began with the Neolithic Revolution continue today, with cereals, livestock, and key technologies providing essential food and materials to support the current population. **We are entangled** with the technologies needed to keep the agriculture machinery churning out produce, **we are entrapped** as agricultural production is essential to feed and clothe millions on Earth living in cities. These consequences are illustrated in Figure 3.4.

Hodder explains (2012, p.32): "There is a long-term trend towards greater human-thing entanglement that is a product of the fact that humans *depend on things*, and because things depend on other things that depend on humans." Hodder maintains that "things

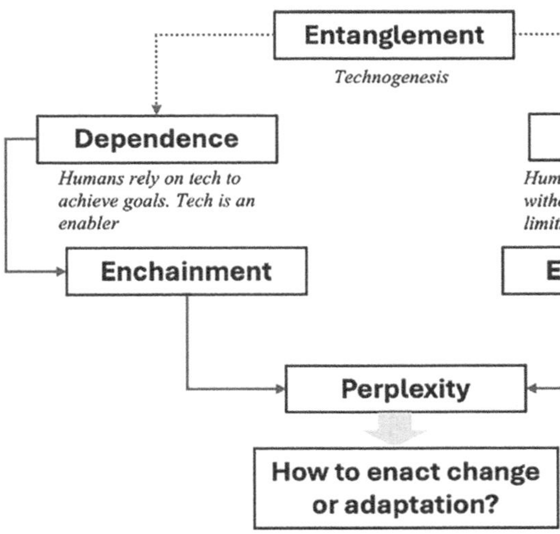

FIGURE 3.4 Consequences of entanglement.

are unstable and finite, so that change within entanglements is continually produced." As discussed in our section on complex adaptive systems, as our tools or technology constantly change, it sets off consequential changes like pulses throughout the ecosystem.

In entanglements, humans and objects *are relationally produced.* This means that humans create objects, and objects then help shape humans, resulting in an entanglement between the two. However, there is also a *dialectical struggle* in this entanglement, as there are both positive and negative outcomes of this entanglement. As shown in Figure 3.4, there is a positive form of *dependence* and a more difficult relationship, which is a *dependency* that impacts human actions. Dependence and dependencies create complex entanglements that are challenging to extricate ourselves from. The concept of "entanglement" therefore means a mutual ensnaring of humans and objects, the dialectic of dependence, and dependency between humans and objects.

Hodder warns that it is very difficult for humans to become less entangled because of the costs that have been invested in existing technologies and in the material and social worlds that have incorporated them. Unravelling one part of an entanglement often involves disentangling too many other parts to make it humanly or practically possible.

The directionality of entanglement is a by-product of (a) the instability and finite nature of things, (b) the dependence of things on other things and on humans, and (c) the difficulty of going back and disentangling. Those of us who have worked on "change management" or "digital transformation" initiatives know well that

> *iFixing or improving one part of the machine often leads to the need to improve or fix other parts; soon the fixes themselves need fixing, thus proliferating change.*
>
> (HODDER, *2012, p.32)*

The increasing rates of entrapment and entanglements create a gradual reduction in the independence of the external environment until all aspects of the environment have become human artifacts, and there is less and less in our environment that can "take care of itself." Our whole environment has now become an artifact in itself that needs constant care, fixing, and manipulation.

Ever since the first tool was created, we have taken the path of being dependent on things, and we have been caught up in the intimate entanglement of the things we have created. It's been an evolutionary pathway that can be seen as "one long movement, initially slow, but speeding up exponentially as the strands of human-thing entanglement lengthened and intensified" (Hodder, 2020).

A tool, once invented, brings with it a host of material demands, knowledge requirements, and unintended consequences. It is also a double-edged sword: The first blade did not just allow cutting; it enabled new forms of violence. It also created social distinctions where those who had better tools had more power. Conversely, we also need to consider what shapes technology in the first place, such as the social shaping of technology (MacKenzie and Wajcman,1999). For example, the time standardization was a process of establishing a shared, uniform time framework, like Greenwich Mean Time or time zones, which differed from the subjective experiences of time experienced by early humans.

This standardization of time was crucial for facilitating communication and coordination in modern societies, particularly with the advent of technologies like railways and telegraphs (Zerubavel,1982), a process deeply intertwined with bureaucracy, control, and coordination. Time as a technological artefact peaked with the *time and motion studies* that became the foundation of modern management,[3] where employees need to clock in and out, meet quotas, and match their productive rhythm to that of machines (such as avoiding toilet breaks when packing boxes on an Amazon production line).

Hodder argues that the long-term perspectives offered by archaeology and human evolution suggest that we need to look deep inside ourselves and into what it means to be human. He challenges us with a significant moral choice: to change what it is to be human and to become something other than ourselves. Certain theorists maintain that we are naturally born cyborgs, that transhumanism is destiny, and that we will reap massive benefits because of this. Others will question this position and ask, *is there a tipping point*, as there is in nature, when a system collapses in on itself? Ecosystems often have a critical threshold beyond which even a small change can trigger a disproportionately large and often irreversible shift in the system's state. After all, collapse and renewal is a important and natural part of every ecosystem.

In the realm of AI, entanglement is especially relevant, as intelligent technologies increasingly dictate not just practical functions of work and leisure but also our emotional and cognitive landscapes more than any other time in our long history of technology entanglements. Hodder would call this the long-term evolutionary paradox, arising from entanglement, that includes both creation and destruction. In the next section, we discuss the concept **of perplexity** and how this may provide a tool for greater understanding of an entangled environment, and perhaps in navigating some levels of disentanglement.

ENTANGLEMENT BEGETS PERPLEXITY (AND THE CATALYST FOR CHANGE)

The most interesting part of entanglement is not just the architecture of the interwoven human–technology elements, but the perplexity that entanglement creates in the minds of citizens when we try to disentangle or understand the various moving, interconnected parts. Especially then cause and effect is indiscernible.

Perplexity is an epistemic emotion and often provides a catalyst for deep questioning about our current state (in organizations or communities, or even in our personal lives) and sets the wheels in motion for transformation (de Cruz, 2021). Perplexity is a state of puzzlement when we've reached an impasse in a problem we're facing and feel at a loss in finding a solution. It's an **affective state that draws our attention to gaps in our knowledge** and highlights discrepancies between our mental states and the world as we experience it (Morton, 2010). These discrepancies create a state of maladjustment between the self and the environment, where they have trouble finding meaning in the world as they once could (Humpston and Broome, 2016).

The deepening human–machine entanglement we are experiencing in society at this point in time is **creating a profound sense of perplexity among citizens**. For example, this can be seen in the lack of clarity on the impact of AI on job losses or erosion of human autonomy in the workplace, a lack of understanding of the capabilities of AI as its decisions are "black-boxed." It is being witnessed through the disagreements among computer scientists on the trajectory of the AGI development and the impact this will have on the fabric of society in the context of potential dystopian futures. It can also be seen in the limited community trust in the small group of AI tech companies in making decisions that have significant planetary outcomes.

Despite these downsides, we are *still pulled toward* AI, fascinated by its human mimicry, its ability to make us better writers, artists, and musicians, or its potential to save on business costs and raise productivity and profit. Others are pulled toward the God-like potential of AI or beliefs that the merging of man and machine is a natural and desirable endgame. These are confusing, emotive, and testing times for citizens, leaving us in a state of perplexity and a sense of powerlessness in trying to decipher what we feel, what we want, and what we want to avoid. It is therefore important to understand this emotional state as it provides a baseline for the behaviors it generates. While this is endemic within our communities in general, it is also present in the workplaces we need to manage and the customers and patients we need to reach.

Let us unpack the effect of perplexity across five stages of manifestation and resolution, and how organizations can facilitate a shift from destructive technology-driven complexities or entanglements toward more sympathetic sociotechnical systems. While anthropologies like Hodder, as discussed in the previous section, argue that change in entanglement is difficult (and in some situations, impossible), several sociologists and technologists maintain that change is still possible through collective deliberation, consensus, and action. As depicted in Figure 3.5, we illustrate the flow from entanglement to perplexity to potential resolution.

We begin with any human–technology entangled situation, as discussed in the previous section, which creates either enchainment or entrapment. The example we discussed was with the smartphone's entanglement with our banking and authentication systems.

Entangled situation begets emotions of perplexity. To people, this feels like discomfort at an innate loss of autonomy, which tends to manifest in three types of emotional effects on citizens: puzzlement, alienation, and cognitive dissonance. These feelings of perplexity and discomfort are the beginnings of questioning the current situation driven by an inner will to better adapt or change the human–technology relationship. For example, Sergeeva et al. (2020) present a post-phenomenological study of the views and feelings of theater nurses when working with doctors using the high-tech da Vinci robot – an endoscopic system for minimal invasive surgery. Prior to the use of the robot in surgical operations, the nurses had an important role to play during surgery; however, the new technology disempowered them and left them feeling empty and alienated as they felt: "We were only allowed to make the instrument tables ready and (at the end) clean up the whole mess…we didn't really have a role" (Sergeeva et al., 2020, p.1256).

These are the emotions at the crux of perplexity in terms of disillusionment feelings about what to do next and how AI affects our jobs and careers. This works at a personal level as well. For example, while ChatGPT may give a citizen functional assistance in

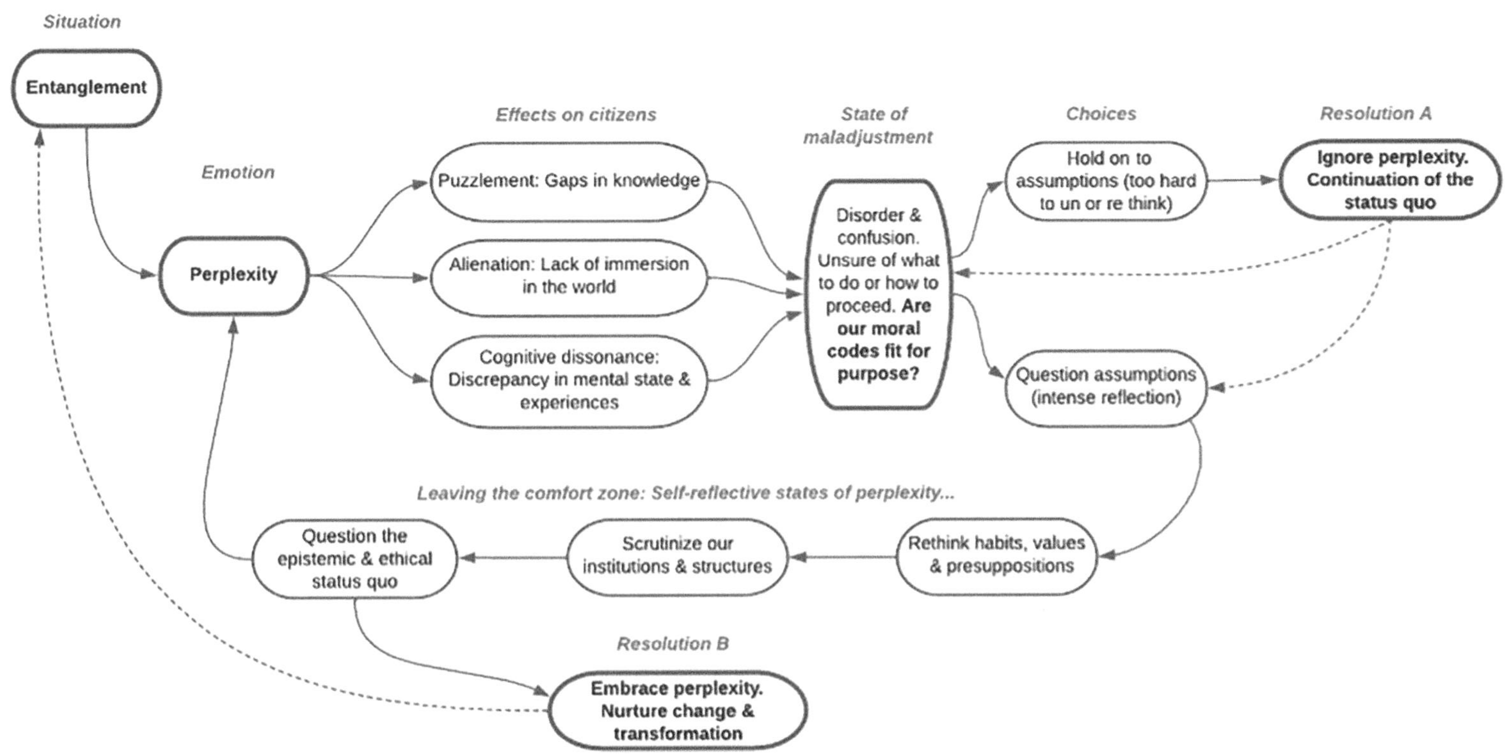

FIGURE 3.5 Entanglement begets perplexity begets change.

Source: Adapted from de Cruz (2021).

writing essays, articles, or emails, there are adverse effects such as losing our cognitive abilities and confidence as independent, free-thinking writers (Kosmyna et al., 2025).

This then flows into a state of maladjustment and leaves citizens with a choice: to hold onto tightly held assumptions about the world or allow themselves to question the situation through intense self-reflection.

This leads to two potential resolutions. The first is to ignore perplexity and continue with the status quo – the head-in-the-sand strategy. The other resolution requires a longer journey that involves leaving the comfort zone. In the Sergeeva et al. (2020) example, the changes instigated by the da Vinci robot were complex as they involved embodied perspectives of how the human practitioners moved around the operating theater, co-ordinated with one another, and conducted the surgery. Reports suggest that there is still some continuing resistance to da Vinci robot due to surgeons preferring the direct control of traditional methods and the limitations in tactile feedback in using the robot (McCartney, 2023).

Despite the benefits of AI technologies, citizen resistance is often based on the negative effects that are suspended in the lags between the introduction of the technology and the setup of supporting systems needed for legacy system integration and adjustment. Sergeeva et al. found that over time, the required reconfiguration of roles took place in this particular hospital to support the da Vinci robot, which included the adaptation of secondary systems such as expanded occupational knowledge, emergence of new specializations, body co-ordination in the theatre, and shifts in status and boundaries between the different practitioners.

In essence, perplexity that arises out of entanglement is part of the feedback loop; provides the impetus to deeply investigate and interrogate all the implications of a shift in a new entangled technology to better integrate it and set it up for operational success. The message here is to lean into the discomfort rather than ignore it or belittle the critics.

SOCIOMATERIALITY AS A HOLISTIC PERSPECTIVE

While ideological foundations and values are embedded in our organizational and socio-economic-political systems at a high level, they are sustained through everyday sociotechnical practices by humans in their jobs and daily life. This occurs in localized sites such as offices, checkpoints, server rooms, software development labs, and surveillance control centers. **Sociomateriality** emphasizes the *inseparability of the social and the material* in everyday practices, highlighting how technologies and humans mutually shape one another in situated contexts.

Wanda Orlikowski (2007) argues that technologies and humans should be analyzed not as separate entities but as *sociomaterial assemblages* rather than dichotomies such as subject/object, tool/user, designer/user, or social/technical. For Orlikowski, practices are always sociomaterial because the material (machines, software, architecture) and the social (norms, discourses, roles) mutually constitute one another in practice. Similarly, Lucy Suchman (2007) in her work in human–machine interaction maintains that technologies do not act alone or in isolation from human interpretation; agency arises through relational configurations such as the "information traffic going back and forth between them."

Figure 3.6 illustrates how our systemic structures, such as worldview and ideological foundations, are performed through sociomaterial practices (infrastructures,

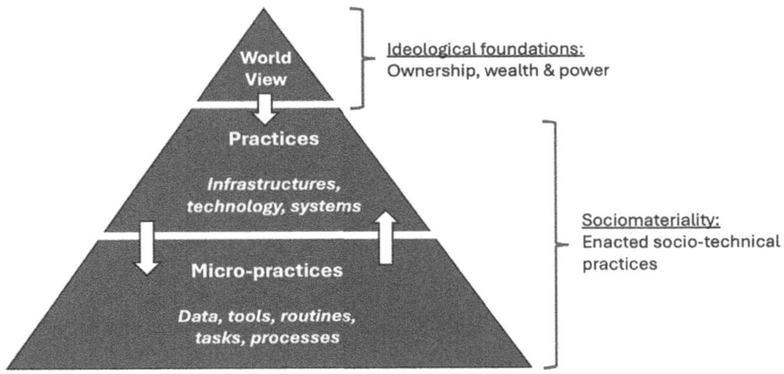

FIGURE 3.6 Sociomaterial practices shaped by the prevailing worldview.

technologies, and systems) and micro-practices (the routines, tools, data, and bodies come together to perform the tasks) that have preassigned socially constructed meanings and values associated with them. Sociomateriality can be used in two ways: as a theoretical lens for understanding how our systems work and how they may need to be modified, and secondly, to identify how physical and digital tools influence employee behavior, communication, and overall work practices.

The introduction of AI in a system or organization prompts your stakeholders to practically engage with the technology through sensemaking (Sandberg and Tsoukas 2011; 2015).

Through the principles of sociomateriality, leaders can gain a more nuanced understanding of the complex interplay between technology, social dynamics, and organizational practices that can lead to more effective strategies for technology implementation, workplace design, and change management (Orlikowski, 2007). The key tenets of sociomaterial principles are as follows:

Technology implementation and adoption. All elements of the sociomaterial are important, not just the technology. What kind of new organization realities are being signaled?

Everyday practices. Everyday practices are affected by the introduction of AI. How do we redefine the boundaries of the workday? What are the new (spoken and unspoken) expectations and obligations? Are we trying to separate the technical from the sociomaterial aspects rather than treat them as a whole?

Workplace design and management. The cohesiveness of the environment in which we do our work is important in giving us a sense of place, and this includes spatial layout, communication channels, experiential stimulation and socialization amenities.

Organizational and change stability. New practices may be needed in navigating disruptions, enabling workplace sensemaking and adaptation, and facilitating a positive change environment and support structures.

Thinking deeply. Organizations often take it for granted that change will happen as it is everyone's job to adapt. We tend to treat relationships with stakeholders as transactional rather than partnerships or collaborations. What are we assuming to be inevitable or too abstract to think about?

Opening an engaging space for change in your organization is a key step toward understanding the nature of your entanglements and to begin conversations around negotiating for a choice architecture of your sociotechnical systems (Battenberg and Verve, 2012a, b). Most organizations by now have an AI strategy of some description, but the majority are focused on the technology rather than on the sociomaterial assemblages that they constitute.

CONCLUSIONS

Entanglement mangles human and technology issues; therefore, your systems need to be treated as sociomaterial entanglements. Entanglement generally cannot be disentangled, but in situations where elements are interwoven rather than entangled, a kind of meshwork can be found twith openings for potential leverage points for interventions. Holistic sociomaterial approaches are premised on the fact that technologies do not act alone or in isolation from human or social elements; agency arises through relational configurations between them.

However, we need to be mindful that there are limitations in sociomaterial approaches due to the widening *deep asymmetries between humans and machines.* For example, certain AI technologies that are being developed to expand situational awareness (such as autonomous weapons systems) are in reality reducing awareness and are maintaining the strucutres of closed-loop worlds (Gross and Suchman, 2021). Suchman maintains that:

> *You will never get from those models of situational awareness the kind of openness, contingency and indeterminacy that characterizes and forms the basis of human interaction…It becomes increasingly clear that in order to make AI systems operate in the openness and contingency of human worlds it is necessary to reengineer these worlds as closed worlds.*
>
> (GROSS AND SUCHMAN, *2021, 182)*

Therefore, while assemblages are the norm, we need to be cognizant of where these asymmetries may exist in our systems so that we may accommodate them with openness and transparency. Furthermore, when we are modelling a facsimile of the world for our AI systems to understand, we need to be mindful that these models are closed-loop simulations rather than the real thing.

NOTES

1 Data from https://iot-analytics.com
2 Data from https://dealroom.co/guides/generative-ai
3 See the works by Frederick Winslow Taylor, Frank, and Lillian Gilbreth.

REFERENCES

Avgerou, C. (2001). The significance of context in information systems and organizational change. *Information systems journal*, 11(1), 43–63.

Axelsson, J. (2025). Implications of second-order cybernetics and autopoiesis on systems-of-systems engineering. *Systems*, *13*(2), 119.

Beckett, S. (1954). *Waiting for Godot: Tragicomedy in 2 Acts*. Grove Press.

Bender, E. M., Gebru, T., McMillan-Major, A., and Mitchell, S. (2021). On the Dangers of Stochastic Parrots: Can Language Models Be Too Big? In *Proceedings of the 2021 ACM Conference on Fairness, Accountability, and Transparency* (pp. 610–623). ACM.

Birhane, A. (2021). Algorithmic injustice: A relational ethics approach. *Patterns*, 2(2), 100205.

Bratteteig, T., and Verne, G. B. (2012a). Creating a space for change within sociomaterial entanglements. *Scandinavian Journal of Information Systems*, *24*(2), 7.

Bratteteig, T., and Verne, G. B. (2012b). Conditions for autonomy in the information society: Disentangling as a public service. *Scandinavian Journal of Information Systems*, *24*(2), 3.

Brown, S. (2023). Why neural net pioneer Geoffrey Hinton is sounding the alarm on AI| MIT Sloan. *Mitsloan. mit. edu*.

Chan, S. (2001). Complex adaptive systems. In *ESD. 83 research seminar in engineering systems* (Vol. 31, pp. 1–9). MIT.

Clark, A. (2001). Natural-born cyborgs? In *International Conference on Cognitive Technology* (pp. 17–24). Springer Berlin Heidelberg.

Crouser, R. J., and Chang, R. (2012). An affordance-based framework for human computation and human-computer collaboration. *IEEE Transactions on Visualization and Computer Graphics*, 18(12), 2859–2868.

De Cruz, H. (2021). Perplexity and philosophical progress. *Midwest Studies in Philosophy*, 45, 209–221.

Doolin, B., and McLeod, L. (2012). Sociomateriality and boundary objects in information systems development. *European Journal of Information Systems*, *21*(5), 570–586.

Enholm, I. M., Papagiannidis, E., Mikalef, P., and Krogstie, J. (2022). Artificial intelligence and business value: A literature review. *Information systems frontiers*, *24*(5), 1709–1734.

Federspiel, F., Mitchell, R., Asokan, A., Umana, C., and McCoy, D. (2023). Threats by artificial intelligence to human health and human existence. *BMJ Global Health*, *8*(5). doi: 10.1136/bmjgh-2022-010435

Grønsund, T., and Aanestad, M. (2020). Augmenting the algorithm: Emerging human-in-the-loop work configurations. *Journal of Strategic Information Systems*, *29*(2), 101614.

Gross, A., and Suchman, L. (2021). Lucy Suchman in conversation with Ana Gross. *Sociologica*, *15*(2), 179–185.

Hayles, N. K. (1999). *How We Became Posthuman: Virtual Bodies in Cybernetics, Literature, and Informatics*. University of Chicago Press.

Hayles, N. K. (2014). Cognition everywhere: The rise of the cognitive nonconscious and the costs of consciousness. *New Literary History*, 45(2), 199–220.

Heylighen F. and Joslyn C. (2001): "Cybernetics and Second Order Cybernetics," in R. A. Meyers (ed.), *Encyclopedia of Physical Science & Technology*, Vol. 4 (3rd ed.) (pp. 155–170). Academic Press.

Hodder, I. (1990). *The Domestication of Europe: Structure and Contingency in Neolithic Societies*. Basil Blackwell.

Hodder, I. (2012). *Entangled: An Archaeology of the Relationships between Humans and Things*. Wiley Blackwell.

Hodder, I. (2014). The entanglements of humans and things: A long-term view. *New Literary History*, *45*(1), 19–36.

Hodder, I. (2020). The paradox of the long term: Human evolution and entanglement. *Journal of the Royal Anthropological Institute*, 26(2), 389–411.

Humpston, C. S., and Broome, M. R. (2016). The spectra of soundless voices and audible thoughts: Towards an integrative model of auditory verbal hallucinations and thought insertion. *Review of Philosophy and Psychology*, 7(3), 611–629.

Hurme, P., and Jouhki, J. (2017). We shape our tools, and thereafter our tools shape us. *Human Technology*, *13*(2), 145–148. http://dx.doi.org/10.17011/ht/urn.201711104209

Hutchins, E. (2014). The cultural ecosystem of human cognition. *Philosophical Psychology*, 27(1), 34–49.

Jacobsen, B. N. (2023). Machine learning and the politics of synthetic data. *Big Data & Society*, *10*(1), 20539517221145372.

Khattak, M., Cohen, S. E., and Taylor, K. (2025). Who holds the camera? Filmmaking justice in the era of generative AI. *GRACE: Global Review of AI Community Ethics*, *3*(1). https://doi.org/10.60690/7qv2j005

Kiran, A., and Kumar, S. S. (2024). A methodology and an empirical analysis to determine the most suitable synthetic data generator. *IEEE Access*, *12*, 12209–12228.

Kosmyna, N., Hauptmann, E., Yuan, Y. T., Situ, J., Liao, X. H., Beresnitzky, A. V., ... Maes, P. (2025). Your brain on ChatGPT: Accumulation of cognitive debt when using an AI assistant for essay writing task. *arXiv preprint arXiv:2506.08872*.

Latour, B. (1993). *We Have Never Been Modern* (C. Porter, Trans.). Harvard University Press. (Original work published 1991).

Latour, B. (2017). *Facing Gaia: Eight Lectures on the New Climatic Regime* (C. Porter, Trans.). Polity Press.

Leakey, M. (1976). A summary and discussion of the archaeological evidence from bed I and bed II, Olduvai Gorge, Tanzania. In G. L. Isaac and E. McCown (eds.), *Human Origins: Louis Leakey and the East African Evidence* (pp. 431–59). Staples Press.

Lundberg, J., Stirna, J., and Andersson, K. (2024). Designing military command and control systems as system of systems–an analysis of stakeholder needs and challenges. In *International Conference on Advanced Information Systems Engineering* (pp. 336–351). Springer Nature Switzerland.

MacKenzie, D., and Wajcman, J. (1999). *The Social Shaping of Technology*. Open University.

McCartney, J. (2023). Robotic surgery is here to stay—and so are surgeons. *Bulletin of the American College of Surgeons*. www.facs.org/for-medical-professionals/news-publications/news-and-articles/bulletin/2023/may-2023-volume-108-issue-5/robotic-surgery-is-here-to-stay-and-so-are-surgeons/ Accessed 13 November 2025

McLuhan, M. (1967). *The Medium Is the Massage: An Inventory of Effects*, Penguin Books.

Methnani, L., Aler Tubella, A., Dignum, V., and Theodorou, A. (2021). Let me take over: Variable autonomy for meaningful human control. *Frontiers in Artificial Intelligence, 4*, 737072.

Morton, T. (2010). *The Ecological Thought*. Harvard University Press.

Newlands, G. (2021). Algorithmic surveillance in the gig economy: The organization of work through Lefebvrian conceived space. *Organization Studies, 42*(5), 719–737.

Niehaus, F., and Wiesche, M. (2021). A Socio-Technical Perspective on Organizational Interaction with AI: A Literature Review. ECIS 2021 Research Papers.

Orlikowski, W. J. (2007). Sociomaterial practices: Exploring technology at work. *Organization Studies*, *28*(9), 1435–1448.

Pandilovski, M. (2016). What lies behind modern technology? The approaches of Marshall McLuhan and Vilém Flusser. *Glimpse, 17*, 77–85.

Rzepka, C., and Berger, B. (2018). User interaction with AI-enabled systems: A systematic review of IS research. *Thirty Ninth International Conference on Information Systems*, San Francisco.

Sandberg, J., and Tsoukas, H. (2011). Grasping the logic of practice: Theorizing through practical rationality. *Academy of Management Review, 36*(2), 338–360. https://doi.org/10.5465/amr.2009.0183

Sandberg, J., and Tsoukas, H. (2015). Making sense of the sensemaking perspective: Its constituents, limitations, and opportunities for further development. *Journal of Organizational Behavior, 36*(S1), 6–32. https://doi.org/10.1002/job.1937

Sergeeva, A. V., Faraj, S., and Huysman, M. (2020). Losing touch: An embodiment perspective on coordination in robotic surgery. *Organization Science*, 31(5), 1248–1271.

Smorodinskaya, N., Russell, M., Katukov, D., and Still, K. (2017). Innovation ecosystems vs. innovation systems in terms of collaboration and co-creation of value. In *Proceedings of the 50th Hawaii International Conference on System Sciences* (pp. 5245–5254). Association of Information System.

Stiegler, B. (1998). *Technics and Time, 1: The Fault of Epimetheus* (Vol. 1). Stanford University Press.

Suchman, L. A. (2007). *Human-Machine Reconfigurations: Plans and Situated Actions*. Cambridge University Press.

Toth, N. (1985). The Oldowan reassessed: A close look at early stone artifacts. *Journal of Archaeological Science, 2*, 101–120.

Yang, S. J., Ogata, H., Matsui, T., and Chen, N. S. (2021). Human-centered artificial intelligence in education: Seeing the invisible through the visible. *Computers and Education: Artificial Intelligence*, 2, 100008.

Zerubavel, E. (1982). The standardization of time: A sociohistorical perspective. *American Journal of Sociology, 88*(1), 1–23.

CHAPTER 4

Entanglement and Empire

There are no happy endings in history, only crisis points that pass.

—ISAAC ASIMOV

INTRODUCTION

Human–technology entanglement from the anthropological and sociological perspectives discussed in the previous chapter focuses on the social and relational level of the development of civilization as we co-evolved with technology. This baseline of understanding is important as it forms the foundation of how humans have utilized, embodied, and co-evolved with different technologies over time. However, there are other forces at play. It can be argued that the main driver of human–technology entanglement is also shaped by a higher order driven by the needs of empires for continuous economic and political power acquisition.

The thesis from the viewpoint of **empire studies** is that the co-evolution and entanglement of humans and technology have also been deeply shaped and accelerated by the entanglement of empire and technology. There are key points in our history to evidence this: ancient and classical Greece, the Roman Empire, and the European Middle Ages had set the pace for empire formation, and this was consolidated during the Scientific Revolution, the Enlightenment, and the Industrial Revolution. Our modern history of the Information Revolution from World War 2 (WW2) until today has further consolidated and entrenched the historic drive of empires to dominate technological development for economic and political gain.

It can be argued that Western technological development and entanglement have a near-uninterrupted lineage since these epochs.[1] This chapter intends to provide a

DOI: 10.1201/9781003616566-6

background on how AI has emerged in the here and now from this lineage. For this book, this chapter takes a meta view of a *Western perspective* on the key influences that have shaped the trajectory of AI empires throughout history to give us a perspective on the *origins of the technology empires* that are dominating our global civilization today. Please note that dates in this chapter are approximate as they differ between different historical accounts in the different literature used in this research.

Again, I ask you to bear with me as this history is important for leaders to gain a better perspective on the here and now. History is vitally important.

ENTANGLEMENT'S BEGINNINGS IN THE ANCIENT WORLD

For an overview of the beginnings of the empire-technology entanglement, we can arbitrarily start in the **early Hellenic Period** of 3200–2000 BCE with the proliferation of "city states" operating different and independent forms of government. Socio-political development in this period was essentially decentralized, and elitist power structures and militarization formed the basis of power and control in each city-state. The economic systems in these states were based on maritime development and exploration, trade, agriculture, and craft production. However, it wasn't until the last phase of the Bronze period, when the **Mycenean civilization** grew to power between 1600 and 1100 BCE and overlapped with the **Minoan civilization** between 2000 and 1450 BCE, that the shift occurred from disparate Greek city-states to larger empire models of power and governance.

It is often claimed that these two civilizations made a significant contribution to the early development of Western European civilization in terms of systems of governing complex social structures, trade, language, culture, and the arts. This is also where empire-technology entanglement took a quantum leap forward compared to Neolithic civilizations toward the models we use today. Figure 4.1 illustrates the evolution of Western empires from the early Hellenic period to the Roman Republic.

The socio-political models that evolved during the period of the Myceneans and the Minoans became one of centralized control through hierarchical societies. Strong elite classes formed and were protected by fortified palaces and a military elite embedded into the ruling class. Sophisticated centralized administration in these civilizations made it possible to keep track of agricultural and craft production and trade, and to enable the accumulation of surpluses for the elite classes. It is important to note that slavery was extensive during this period, and this had set the practice of bonded or exploited labor to enable the growth of empires. This is what Fynn-Paul (2009) calls the greater Mediterranean slavery that had featured in western empires from antiquity to the end of the early modern era.

While the Myceneans didn't engage in large-scale colonization (apart from islands in the Aegean and Mediterranean) in the way the Greeks and Romans would later do, they did expand their influence and control over areas beyond their homeland. This wasn't a direct colonization of other lands per se, but rather it was a form of domination and cultural exchange, often through military power and economic control (Tartaron, 2013).

The economic models during this period were based on mercantilism, which established extensive trade routes throughout the Mediterranean and Aegean, stretching

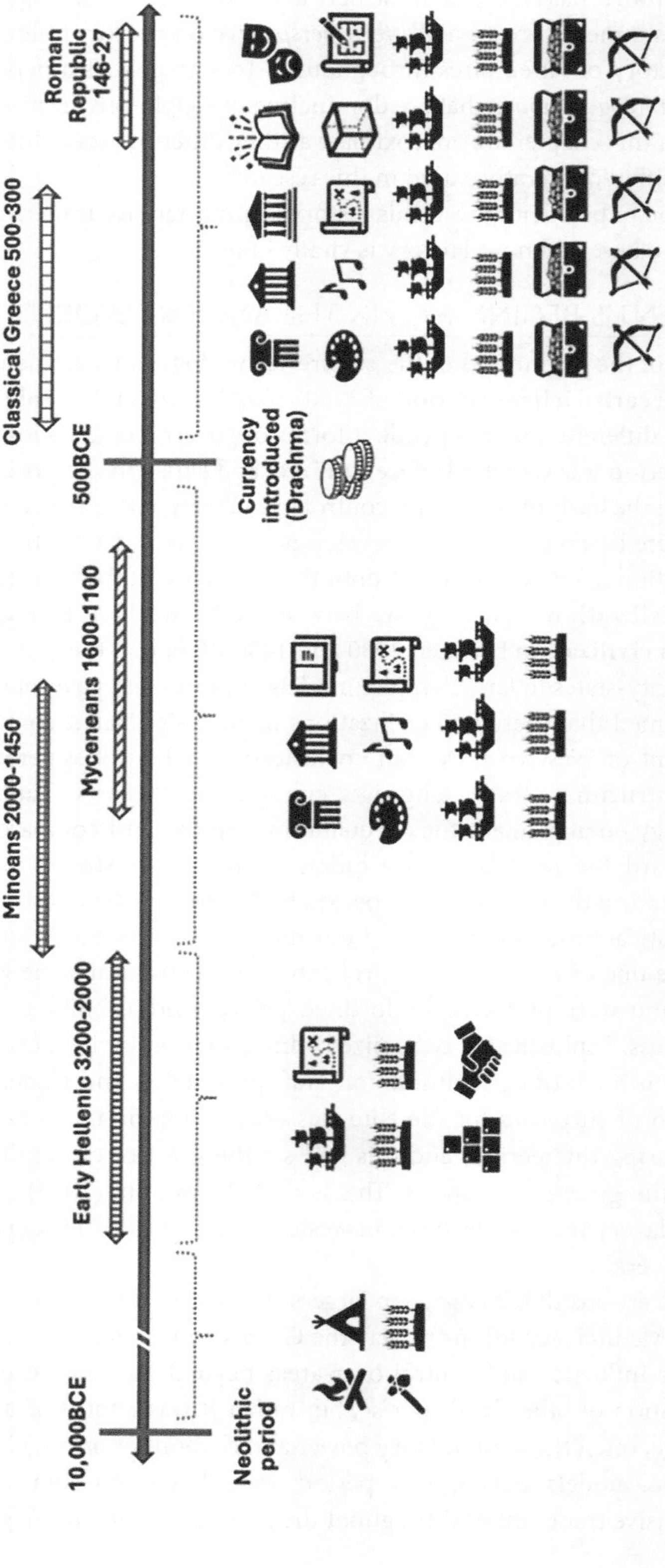

FIGURE 4.1 Growth of technology empires in the ancient world timeline.

from (what is now) Spain, Italy, Egypt, Turkey, and North Africa. The most important outcome of this extensive trade was also the spread and exchange of ideas, information, and networks. This period was known for building wealth, power, and influence through groundbreaking innovations in engineering, architecture, the arts, and military systems. The backbone of the economic growth in the era was the extensive maritime trade and the growth of agriculture (Gates, 2003).

These civilizations eventually declined for a variety of different reasons. While there are many unknowns, historians maintain that the Mycenean and Minoan civilizations were thought to have ended due to a multitude of dramatic events such as invasions, political unrest, overpopulation, as well as natural disasters, resource depletion, and climate change (Maran and Wright, 2019; Chew, 2002). It's surmised that these successful and affluent civilizations had hit their limits to growth during the testing economic, political, agricultural, and climatic environments in this era. This led to their eventual demise and the beginning of the Dark Ages of the ancient world, much of it thought it be climate change-induced droughts, famines, and mass migrations of peoples, and the military conflicts that ensued (Finné et al., 2017; Kaniewski et al., 2015). Many of these events are already starting to sound familiar.

The next most significant event in the growth of empire entanglement was the rebirth and resurgence in the region that occurred during the **Golden Age of Ancient Greece** from 500 to 300 BCE. This era drove a period of significant cultural, artistic, and intellectual flourishing, which saw the rise of democracy, advancements in philosophy, art, architecture, and literature. This period brought about the flourishing of Athenian influence throughout Greece, but most importantly, this Golden Age developed innovations that formed the foundations of Western civilization in terms of values, governance, and economic development. Economically, Greece already had extensive trade routes and colonies throughout the Mediterranean, Asia Minor, and North Africa, but this reach became more extensive with the military campaigns of **Alexander the Great,** 336–323 BCE.

Until this point, all trade in the region was based on barter systems. Coins made of gold and silver were first minted as a currency in Greek, Sicilian, and Lydian communities. This formed the beginnings of monetary currency with the **Greek Drachma** taking hold by the 6th century BCE. It should be noted that prior to these coins being minted, traders in Mesopotamia, Egypt, and Palestine were using ingots and pieces of metal as a unit of measure in bartered value exchanges in the 3rd century BCE.

The Golden Age of Greece fell like most empires – wars, conquests, political and social instability, and a failing economy because of war and instability. The Roman Republic eventually conquered Greece around 146 BCE. The technological and cultural legacy of the Golden Age of Greece continued into the rise of the **Roman Republic** and eventually the Roman Empire. Greek culture and philosophy significantly influenced Roman culture, and the Romans adopted many aspects of Greek art, literature, and philosophy. This becomes a pattern where the innovations of one empire are passed on to the next for continued application and improvements.

The rise in the **Roman Empire,** 27 BCE to 478 CE, consolidated the ingenuity, ideas, artefacts, and technologies inherited from the Empires before it and launched a massive wave of renewed innovations and socio-economic and political developments. The Roman Empire had, over the following two centuries, conquered (modern-day) Italy, Greece, Spain, the North African coast, much of the Middle East, France, and even as far as Britain. With this conquering of territories came an explosion of wealth not only through trade but through the appropriation of wealth, the use of slavery and the plundering of colonized lands. Their technological superiority was correlated with their ability to accumulate wealth on the backs of colonization and slavery.

A fundamental dynamic of empires is the inequality of exchange of wealth and value between the ruling classes and the colonized lands (Goff, 2020). For example, the policy of *wealth for the Romans* focused on the standard of living, rights, and freedoms of the Romans but not for their periphery states. To ensure this wealth was maintained at the center of the empire, this had to be largely acquired with military expansions abroad. This inequality of exchange that was dominant in this era was the foundation of the growth as a zero-sum game in the development of Western milieux: that the growth of wealth in my land came at the expense of yours.

The development and innovations of these ancient worlds were the beginnings of the empire-technology entanglements, shaped by the same factors that we see to this day. The entanglements that took shape, as we discussed earlier in Chapter 3, are discursive; humanity shaped the technology, then the technology shaped us.

ENTANGLEMENT FROM THE MIDDLE AGES

From the Middle Ages onward, European civilizations experienced accelerated political formations and territorial ambitions of empires that were critical to the foundations of the Western economic and political logic. The Middle Ages from a European perspective span from the fall of the Roman Empire in 500AD to 1500AD, which led into the beginning of the Renaissance period. Again, I'm taking a European perspective as the philosophies developed in this period survive in the foundations of the socio-economic-political landscape that dominates technology development to this day.

Here's a closer look at how and why of this phenomenon:

A Brief History of the Rapid-Fire Developments during the Middle Ages

The one thousand years in this period were an engine of technological innovation that fueled the rise of empires – or vice versa. This era is known for its development of feudalism, improvements in warfare, and the rise of Christianity and Islam as the dominant religions. Warfare was motivated by religious crusades and geopolitical aspirations. The Christian church replaced the Roman Empire as a key powerful force in Europe from 590CE, and European monarchies not only grew their own expansionist agendas, but they also drew their authority and power from their relationships with the church for populist appeal.

The Middle Ages represented the rise of **imperial Christianity**, the growth of monasticism, and the beginnings of early Western values based on Christian world views. There were considerable territorial and economic expansions fueled by technological progress, but these were also tumultuous socio-economic periods of significant wars, famines, diseases, and plagues. The ambitions of empires and religion were aligned.

This period also saw the **emergence of Islam** in the 7th century with Muhammad's initial revelations and migration to Medina in 622 CE and the subsequent unification of the Arabian Peninsula under Islamic rule through a series of extensive conquests in the region (Hoyland, 1997). This marked yet again a transformative era in history, fostering advancements in mathematics, science, and technology. Under the Islamic Caliphates, scholars preserved and expanded upon ancient knowledge from Greece, Rome, and India, leading to significant breakthroughs such as the development of algebra by Al-Khwarizmi and advancements in astronomy, medicine, and engineering. The House of Wisdom in Baghdad became a hub for intellectual exchange, translating key texts and pioneering innovations that would influence global progress for centuries (Gutas, 2002). Figure 4.2 highlights the proliferation of significant empires between the Roman Empire and 1900 and the acceleration of technological revolutions.

As can be seen in Figure 4.2, there were many significant, interconnecting events taking place during this period, including technological development and dissemination that altered the shape of society from predominantly agrarian to industrial. The **boom in agriculture** between 900 and 1300 CE occurred in Europe due to climatic shifts and advances in farming technologies. This agricultural boom had a profound economic impact on European societies and economies, such as increased food production, population growth, urbanization, and expansions in trade. This agricultural revolution was further enabled by advancements in farming techniques and technologies, which not only boost agricultural output but also free up labor for other sectors due to their productivity and efficiencies.

There was significant activity taking place within each empire and their interactions with others that facilitated knowledge sharing and trade, as well as war and conquest. The Vikings were active from the late 8th to early 11th centuries (800–1050 CE) and were seafaring warriors and traders originating from Scandinavia. Their influence extended across Europe and even as far as North America, where they established settlements like Vinland around 1000 CE. Renowned for their advanced shipbuilding techniques and navigation skills, the Vikings opened up significant trade routes and facilitated cultural exchanges between distant regions. They played a pivotal role in shaping medieval economies and political landscapes, often integrating into local societies while also contributing to the spread of technological knowledge. Their legacy is evident in the socio-political structures and maritime traditions of many European territories (Sawyer, 2001).

The religious wars of **the Crusades** during 1096–1291 CE were initiated by the Christians to reclaim what they saw as the Holy Land from Muslim rule. However, the Crusades also targeted other regions like the Iberian Peninsula and the Baltic, largely driven by religious fervor and political ambitions, which had a lasting impact on the empires and their rule in both Europe and the Middle East.

The **Mongol Empire** was established in the 13th century (1206–1368 CE) and became one of the largest contiguous empires in history, spanning from Eastern Europe to Asia.

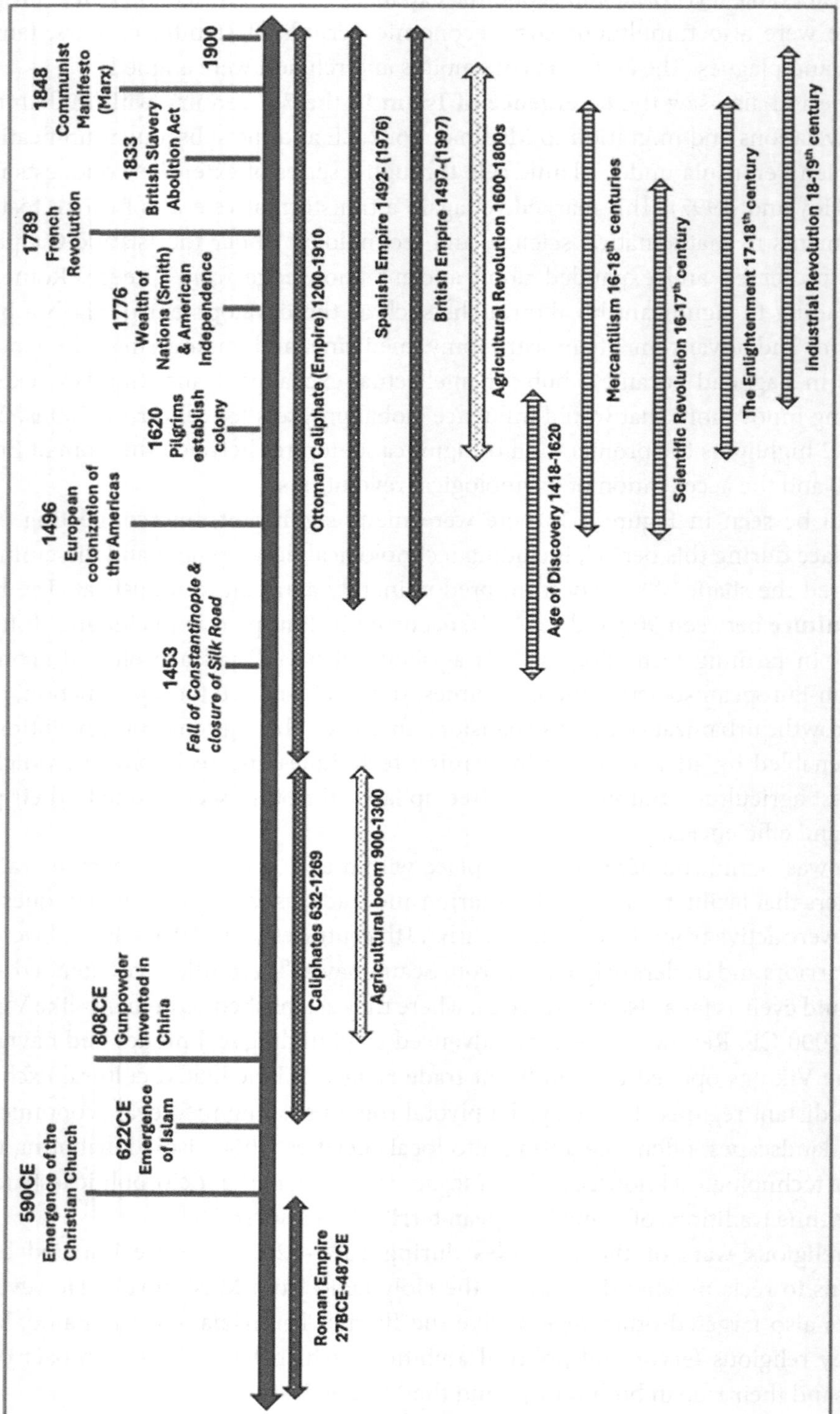

FIGURE 4.2 Growth of technology and empires from Middle Ages to 1900.

The Mongol Empire had a transformative impact on global trade, cultural exchange, and the spread of technology. The Mongols established a period of peace that facilitated trade along the Silk Road, connecting diverse civilizations and fostering economic integration. Their innovations in governance and military strategies influenced subsequent empires, while their tolerance for various religions and cultures allowed for vast cultural interactions. According to Weatherford (2005), the Mongols were instrumental in creating "the first global economy" by linking distant regions through trade and communication networks.

The invention of gunpowder in **China during the Tang dynasty** in the 9th century spread along the Silk Road nations reaching the Middle East by 1240 CE. The invention of gunpowder marked a turning point in global history, revolutionizing warfare and shaping political power dynamics. Initially used for fireworks and rudimentary weapons, gunpowder's military applications quickly expanded, transforming siege tactics and battlefield strategies. Its spread along the Silk Road facilitated cultural and technological exchanges, with the substance reaching the Middle East by 1240 CE, where it was incorporated into advanced weaponry and military innovations. The dissemination of gunpowder not only altered the course of regional conflicts but also laid the groundwork for the rise of empires that relied on gunpowder warfare. Gunpowder technology is believed to be one of the key engines driving the early modern world (Andrade, 2016). The **Fall of Constantinople** to the Ottoman Turks marked the end of the Byzantine Empire in 1453 CE. By this time, the Ottomans, armed with gunpowder-fueled munitions, were able to close off the Silk Trade routes that had been operating for 1500 years since 130BCE.

The **Mughal Empire** (1526–1857) significantly influenced economic and technological development in South Asia. Renowned for its administrative efficiency, the Mughal Empire implemented a centralized system of revenue collection and land management that boosted agricultural productivity and trade. Mughal rulers supported advancements in architecture, urban design, and engineering, exemplified by constructions like the Taj Mahal and sophisticated irrigation systems. These achievements facilitated the growth of commerce, particularly through the integration of regional markets into a broader economic framework. Furthermore, Mughal artisans and craftsmen contributed to technological innovation in textiles, metallurgy, and weaponry, which were essential for both domestic prosperity and military dominance (Richards, 1995).

Approaching the end of the Middle Ages was a massive shift and consolidation of power.

The **Spanish Empire,** which commenced in the 15th century, was a heavy contributor to the Age of Discovery as Columbus discovered the "New World" and the colonization of the Americas through Spanish Imperialism, leading to the conquest of the Aztecs between 1492 and 1521. The British Empire began near the end of the Middle Ages with smaller settlements in the 16th century, but they grew to its peak influence later in the 19th and 20th centuries, fueled by further Agricultural Revolution, the Scientific Revolution, the Enlightenment, and the Industrial Revolution. The growth of the **British Empire** was made possible through a spike in wealth derived from the colonization of North America, the West Indies, India, and eventually parts of Asia and Latin America.

Mercantilism was the dominant nationalist economic policy in Europe from the 16th to 19th centuries, which aimed to maximize a nation's wealth and power by promoting exports and restricting imports. Its fundamental belief and motivation is that a country's strength is directly linked to its accumulation of gold and silver, which were seen as the true measure of wealth. This system however was supported through various government interventions like tariffs and subsidies, designed to encourage domestic production and trade while discouraging foreign competition.

Mercantilism was aligned to both colonization and slavery, and to the laissez-faire economists. Mercantilism viewed colonies as sources of raw materials and markets for finished goods, fueling the expansion of European empires and the transatlantic slave trade (Klein, 2010). The transatlantic slave trade operated between the 16th and 19th centuries, forcibly transporting 10 million Africans to the Americas (which devastated African societies and economies) and embedded racist hierarchies and ideologies into Western thought (Klein, 2010; Smith, 2016).

POST MIDDLE AGES BOOM – THE DISCOVERY OF NEW WORLDS

The rate of economic and political expansion of empires accelerated after the Middle Ages through the recurring pattern of technology-fueled growth through resource exploitation, geographic expansion, and trade.

The European discovery of **North America** fundamentally altered global economics and trade by integrating the Americas into existing European trade networks. This event facilitated the Columbian Exchange, which introduced new goods such as tobacco, maize, and potatoes to Europe while exporting European technologies, livestock, and crops to the Americas. It also spurred the development of transatlantic trade, which included the exploitation of natural resources, land colonization, and the establishment of plantation economies reliant on enslaved labor. The influx of wealth from the Americas, particularly gold and silver, significantly contributed to the rise of mercantilist policies and the economic dominance of European empires. (Cipolla, 1965; Fernández-Armesto, 2006)

The Pilgrims arrived in North America in 1620, which began the spread of British and European influence on the Americas. The American Revolutionary Wars took place between 1775 and 1783, and American independence from Britain was profound, as it marked the end of colonial economic constraints imposed by British mercantilism. Freed from restrictive trade policies and taxation without representation, the newly established United States began to develop its own economic systems, fostering domestic industries and opening trade with other nations. This autonomy laid the groundwork for the rise of American capitalism and its eventual transformation into a global economic power.

However, history continued to repeat the same patterns established since ancient Greece.

The growth of America since its independence in 1776 was significantly shaped by slavery, exploitation, and colonization. The forced labor of enslaved individuals underpinned the economic foundation of agricultural industries, particularly in the South, enabling the production of cash crops such as cotton while fueling trade networks. The subsequent territorial expansion, including the annexation of Mexican lands and the displacement of Indigenous peoples, further solidified America's economic and geographic dominance. These practices of exploitation and colonization not only expanded resource access but also entrenched social hierarchies that continued to influence the nation's socioeconomic trajectory (Fernández-Armesto, 2006; Cipolla, 1965).

Adam Smith published the *Wealth of Nations* in 1776, a foundational text for modern capitalism. He advocated minimal government intervention and believed individuals pursuing their own interests would ultimately meet society's material needs through "the invisible hand." He also had concerns about the limitations of this system, which is infinitely observable in our modern economies today. However, Smith's critical assumptions were that the wealthy were ambitious but the poor hated work and were prone to resentment, and his views were tilted toward protecting the status quo:

> *But avarice and ambition in the rich, in the poor the hatred of labour and the love of present ease and enjoyment, are the passions which prompt to invade property, passions much more steady in their operation, and much more universal in their influence. Wherever there is great property, there is great inequality. For one very rich man, there must be at least five hundred poor, and the affluence of the few supposes the indigence of the many. The affluence of the rich excites the indignation of the poor, who are often both driven by want, and prompted by envy, to invade his possessions. It is only under the shelter of the civil magistrate that the owner of that valuable property, which is acquired by the labour of many years, or perhaps of many successive generations, can sleep a single night in security.*
>
> (SMITH, *1998* V.II.*2)*

We can see this mental model is still present in our modern societies and organizations today, either in whole or part, or stated or implied, perhaps being unaware of the history of how it evolved to where we are today.

Seventy years after Adam Smith wrote *The Wealth of Nations*, **Karl Marx** and Friedrich Engels published the *Communist Manifesto* in 1848. Marx presented a critique of Adam Smith's theories, especially regarding capitalism, suggesting that Smith's emphasis on individual self-interest and free markets did not fully address aspects such as class relations and labor. Marx recognized Smith's contributions to understanding the division of labor and economic development but argued that Smith did not sufficiently consider issues like class dynamics and the potential for worker alienation under capitalist systems (Felluga, 2011; Dupré, 1980).

It was during this period of **rapid industrialization** that communities began to witness catastrophic impacts on wealth disparities, colonization, environmental degradation, poverty, and disease as industrial cities began to rapidly expand. This marks the beginning of more intense questioning of the behaviors of empires and ideation that there could be alternative ways of thinking and governing, and economy, and the society it serves. However, this questioning of the dominant narratives started well before industrialization.

Immediately preceding this era, the **English Revolution of 1640** established foundational ideas about individual rights and parliamentary sovereignty, which influenced later movements advocating social and economic justice, including the rise of constitutional governance. However, the impact of these early ideas took some time to take effect. For example, it was only with the Slavery Abolition Act of 1833 that slavery was ended throughout most of the British Empire.

The **French Revolution of 1789** directly addressed systemic inequalities by overthrowing monarchical oppression and instituting reforms aimed at achieving universal equality and fraternity, serving as a powerful model for subsequent radical ideologies. Historians argue that these revolutions reshaped political discourse globally, promoting the ideals of justice and equity (Karmel, 1972; Soboul, 1980).

However, the ideals behind social and economic justice go back to the beginnings of the empire in ancient Greece, documented in **Plato's *Republic*** written in 375 BCE. According to Fronterotta (2010), there are two cities depicted in the *Republic*, one is a modest city and is considered healthy, and the other is a luxurious city but is sick with a fever due to its desire for more wealth and expansion. The difference between the two cities is that the citizens of the latter "have surrendered themselves to the endless acquisition of money and have overstepped the limit of their necessities" (Fronterotta, 2010). However, the luxuriousness of this city requires the seizure of neighboring lands and consequently a standing army to defend those lands and the city's wealth. Plato was commenting on what he had seen during the Golden Age of ancient Greece with the expansions in trade, warfare, and wealth acquisition. According to Plato, war originates in communities living beyond the natural limits of necessity.

In short, the healthy or true city is sustainable, limiting its consumption to actual needs, while the luxurious city seems not to be sustainable, living beyond its needs in a perpetual warring quest for more. In the *Republic*, Plato attempted to reveal the political organization and virtues of a city to be just, healthy, and thereby sustainable. These were highlighted in his four virtues of wisdom, courage, moderation, and justice (Rowe, 2017). The two cities in Plato's philosophy and political theory raise important questions about social and economic justice, consumption, and sustainability, issues that we have yet to resolve over 2000 years later.

In summary, the empires that formed and grew during the Middle Ages needed higher-order technologies to support domestic production, exploration, trade, and industrialization. The technologies developed during this period were tools of conquest and imperial management, and empires became entangled with these technologies to develop, maintain, and expand their power. The technologies that evolved during this period have continued to be developed for centuries to come. To provoke a deeper reflection on entanglement, below we reframe these technologies as tools of conquest and imperial management.

TECHNOLOGICAL SYSTEMS AS TOOLS OF CONQUEST

Empires that rose and fell over the one-thousand-year period of the Middle Ages and then consolidated their powers during the Enlightenment and Industrial Revolution were pivotal in shaping the development and application of technologies – as well as the Western Empire mindset that facilitated their development.

Technology development over this period was not for the purpose of human flourishing, but to expand control, extract resources, and maintain dominance of the ruling classes. Understandably, that sentence may be provocative to many. However, it is by no means made from an ideological position, but one anchored in history. Let's now consider three key technologies developed in this period that had a significant impact on wealth accumulation in Europe: maritime technologies, military technologies, the printing press, and tools of imperial management.

Navigation and Maritime Technologies. The rise of European empires during the Middle Ages (such as the Portuguese, Spanish, and later, the British) was built on the back of navigation, shipbuilding, and cartography. These technologies were developed and refined to enable exploration, colonization, and exploitation of distant lands. The compass, the astrolabe, improved hull designs, and later steam power all expanded imperial reach compared to classical and ancient times. For example, before the Middle Ages, maritime technologies enabled the growth of the Greek, Phoenician, Roman, and Egyptian empires during the Classical period (1200–900 BCE). Seafaring as a whole dates back to 6000 BCE, where ancient civilizations used boats for transport and trade. However, it was the specific navigation and maritime technologies developed during the Middle Ages that provided a significant leap in the growth of European empires (Cipolla, 1965; Fernández-Armesto, 2006).

Gunpowder and Military Technologies. Empires rapidly adopted and innovated in military technologies. Gunpowder was invented during the Tang Dynasty in China in the 9th century, and this technology spread westward through Asia, reaching the Middle East by 1240 (Cipolla, 1965). The so-called "gunpowder empires" in Islamic empires such as the Ottoman, Safavid, and Mughal empires are examples of how the control of firearms, cannons, and fortification engineering reshaped how wars were fought between warring empires and how territory was controlled once conquered. For example, Chase (2003) highlights how empires like the Ottomans and Mughals used gunpowder tech to consolidate power. As discussed earlier, by the end of the 14th century, gunpowder had completely changed the face of warfare in Europe and was then used by the Spanish Empire to invade and colonize the Americas.

Printing Press. The legend of the impact of this well-known technology is often compared to the introduction of the internet given its revolutionary impact on knowledge sharing and distribution. However, the printing press was primarily intended as a key imperial tool for administrative control, religious standardization (especially in colonial missions), and to produce imperial ideologies that were spread to Western communities and their colonies.

Technological Systems as Tools of Imperial Management. As empires expanded, they needed more sophisticated systems to govern diverse populations and territories. These include communication technologies, extraction technologies, and census and surveillance (Crawford, 2021; Headrick, 2010). In terms of bureaucratic and communication technologies, the telegraph, railways, and later radio were not just advances in human communication in the social sense; they were primarily infrastructures for imperial management. For example, the British Empire's global telegraph network allowed London to manage distant colonies in real time.

Extraction technologies such as mining, plantation agriculture, and later oil drilling were all enabled by mechanical innovations. But these technologies were embedded in the imperial logic of extracting and exploiting resources to advance our growing economies. In terms of census and surveillance, empires increasingly relied on statistical technologies to make colonized populations visible, accountable, and measurable, or as Scott (2020) describes it as rendering complex societies into categories they can control. For example, fingerprinting, ID systems, and mapping were not neutral tools; they were technologies of domination (Scott, 2020).

Historians have shown that even **scientific discovery** was entangled with imperial botany and control colonial bioprospecting in the Atlantic region (Schiebinger, 2004) and traces modern **surveillance technologies** back to slavery, colonial control, and biometric classification (Browne, 2015). However, more troubling is where Darwin's theory of evolution by natural selection influenced the development of **Social Darwinism**, which was then used to justify laissez-faire capitalism and other social hierarchies. Thomas (2009) explains that Darwin's biological concepts of competition and "survival of the fittest" were applied to human societies, arguing that economic and social inequalities were natural and inevitable outcomes of this competition. These perspectives, while faced with scientific disagreement, were still used by conservative economists and politicians to argue against government intervention in the economy and social welfare programs, as it was seen as interfering with natural selection. This can be understood as a biological justification of laissez-faire and had links with eugenics and imperialism (Thomas, 2009). The most extreme ideological expression of Social Darwinism is nationalism and imperialism. In populist thought, the concepts of biological evolution justified the exploitation by the "superior races" of "lesser breeds" and that saying that "strong nations" are those that were successful at expanding industry and empire; they would survive while the "weaker nations" would not (Chase et al., 2013).

One cannot help but see elements of Social Darwinism persisting to this day in some form. This is not a position of despair, however. History gives us information on where we have come from. On where we are headed – here have a choice.

THE ENLIGHTENMENT

The Enlightenment provided renewed critical intellectual and fostered a belief in human progress and the perfectibility of society through reason and knowledge. This intellectual climate encouraged the use of scientific methods and rational inquiry to understand and control nature, which directly contributed to technological innovation, which had become the core driver of the Industrial Revolution (Mokyr, 2009).

Enlightenment philosophy also influenced more just and fairer economic and political systems. It contributed to the decline of mercantilism and the rise of more open, competitive economic systems. Enlightenment thinkers advocated for free markets, property rights, and the reduction of rent-seeking, which created an environment more conducive to industrial and commercial expansion. The liberalization of business, government, and religion during the Enlightenment helped foster a society where innovation and entrepreneurship were valued and rewarded, further accelerating industrial growth (Grayling, 2016).

There is a strong correlation between regions most influenced by the Enlightenment in the eighteenth century and those that led the way in industrialization by the 19th century. Countries that experienced Enlightenment thought, such as Britain, France, and parts of Germany, were among the first to industrialize, suggesting that the Enlightenment's influence was a key factor in enabling the Industrial Revolution (Mokyr, 2011).

Enlightenment Ideals Still Dominate Today

The ideologies and approaches developed during the Enlightenment have persisted to today, particularly in influencing the development of artificial intelligence and its prioritization among political agendas, technology advocacy, and economic policy.

The Western model of the importance of AI can be seen as rooted in Enlightenment ideals of personal autonomy and human dignity, viewing AI as a tool to expand opportunities and improve lives rather than a means of control. This aligns with thinkers like Voltaire, who championed individual reasoning, and Diderot, who advocated openness to disruptive innovation. Global leadership voices today are even openly drawing these parallels themselves, with recent politicization of this at the *Boston Global Forum* (Kennedy, 2025) and at the World Economic Forum (Livesey, 2025), as well as leaders of AI tech companies advocating that AI will be a liberating rather than controlling technology.

The Enlightenment established a strict divide between humans (intelligent, creative) and machines (mechanical, deterministic), a concept we questioned in the previous chapter. AI disrupts this framework, creating systems that exhibit intelligence *and* mechanistic traits, forcing a re-evaluation of concepts like agency, creativity, and morality. Enlightenment optimism about human progress now confronts AI's paradox of solving global challenges (e.g., climate change or diseases) while threatening jobs and social stability.

Society's AI obsession reflects a mix of Enlightenment-informed optimism and grounded skepticism. While experts often echo Enlightenment faith in progress (56% of AI researchers predict positive impacts), public anxiety about job displacement and existential risks mirrors historical "technology panics" experienced in the past (Huang et al., 2024), which is something we will explore in detail in Chapters 5 and 6.

Enlightenment ideas persist as both guideposts and contested frameworks in the AI era. The movement's emphasis on reason, progress, and human dignity underpins efforts to harness AI for empowerment, while its legacy of critical scrutiny informs debates over ethics and control. Society's hyperfocus on AI reflects a quintessentially Enlightenment struggle: balancing optimism about human ingenuity with vigilance against its unintended consequences.

Limitations to Enlightenment Principles

Contemporary critics raise several significant challenges to Enlightenment philosophies when addressing current and future human challenges. These criitiques can be grouped in six areas of debate:

Environmental and Climate Crisis. Critics argue that Enlightenment rationality created a mechanistic worldview that treats nature as a mere resource to be exploited. The "disenchantment of nature" and "technological domination of nature" rooted in Western scientific thought are seen as fundamental causes of environmental destruction. The resentment of dependence leads to the exploitation of the natural world, suggesting that the Enlightenment emphasis on human autonomy and mastery over nature directly contributes to the ecological crisis.

Postcolonial and Cultural Critiques. Postcolonial theorists argue that Enlightenment universalism masked European cultural imperialism, imposing Western values while suppressing indigenous knowledge systems. This critique is particularly relevant to climate solutions, where traditional ecological knowledge is increasingly recognized as valuable but was historically dismissed by Enlightenment-influenced science.

Feminist and Intersectional Challenges. Post-modern feminists argue that "the essentialism and universalism associated with Enlightenment ideals are both false and intrinsically hostile to the aspirations to self-realization of women and of other traditionally oppressed groups. Critics contend that Enlightenment reason privileged masculine, white, European perspectives while marginalizing other ways of knowing.

Technological Determinism and Scientism. Critics argue that Enlightenment faith in reason has devolved into uncritical "scientism," which treats scientific methods as the only valid form of knowledge. This narrow rationality is seen as inadequate for addressing complex social and environmental challenges that require emotional intelligence, spiritual wisdom, and holistic thinking.

Crisis of Meaning and Community. Some critics argue that Enlightenment individualism and secularization have contributed to modern alienation, mental health crises, and the breakdown of traditional communities that provided meaning and social cohesion.

Inadequacy for Global Challenges. Contemporary global challenges like climate change, pandemics, and economic and political inequality may require forms of cooperation, long-term thinking, and value systems that transcend the Enlightenment framework of individual rational actors pursuing self-interest.

However, defenders argue that many current solutions to these challenges, including environmental science, human rights frameworks, and democratic institutions, still depend fundamentally on Enlightenment principles of reason, evidence, and universal human dignity.

Human–Technology Entanglement: A Springboard to Modernity

Entanglement can be seen as a feedback loop between empire, technology, and humanity. What we see is a set of recursive entangled relationships:

- Empire needs technology to expand, govern, and extract.
- Technology reshapes societies, altering how people live, work, and think.
- These shifts feed back into the empire by reinforcing hierarchies and ideologies (e.g., racial science, industrial capitalism, etc.).
- Humans use the technology and thus reinforce the dominant logic and mental models.

This feedback loop plays an evolutionary role to continuously restructure local technologies. For example, colonial science often dismisses indigenous knowledge systems as inferior and replaces them with "modern" or imperial science, which itself was shaped by the needs of expansion and control. This has a lasting effect on local community and culture and reshapes history. Even after formal empires end, the imperial logic persists in global technological infrastructures since this logic remains invisible to us. For example, global supply chains for rare earth minerals in today's economy reflect older colonial extraction patterns.

Even if previously colonized nations are granted political independence, the patterns of resource acquisition by global companies, negotiated by their governments, are still not seeing the trickling down of the benefits to the populace (Schiebinger, 2004). An example of this is the extraction of critical minerals from developing nations where toxic spills, environmental destruction, declining community welfare, and increased corruption are endemic. Reports from experiences in Asia, Africa, and South America show the correlation of increased mining activity with increased militarization to protect foreign mining companies at the expense of local communities.[2]

The behavior of Big Tech platforms appears to parallel that of neo-imperial actors, organizing vast territories of digital labor, developing and undertaking community surveillance, and undertaking mass data extraction without impunity, all dressed up as being for the greater good. Profits are privatized, yet externalities are pushed into the public domain (Crawford, 2021; Birhane, 2021). AI and automation mirror the same centralizing, extractive logic – though now detached from land and wedded to data (Zuboff, 2019).

When we examine human–technology entanglement through the lens of empire, we see that this relationship has rarely been neutral or egalitarian. It has been historically shaped by the prevailing structures of power, conquest, and governance (Mumford, 1934; Headrick, 2010).

The tools we often think of as "human progress" were in fact **often born from imperial needs** and continue to carry those legacies in their design and deployment to this very day. From the perspective of the message in this book, understanding this history is essential for any meaningful conversation not only about ethics, justice, and design in today's AI and data-driven systems, but also in terms of the distribution of power, ownership, and control in the current and future societies we wish to build for the future.

ENTANGLEMENT: WHAT DOES THIS ALL MEAN FOR YOU?

Entanglement is by its nature complicated. As shown in Chapters 3 and 4, entanglement weaves across time since the beginnings of early fhumans in Africa, across to the early ancient western civilizations in the Mediterranean. From there, empires grew out of the technological expansion during the Middle Ages and set the blueprint for empire-technology entanglement that's relevant to this very day. The actors are different, but the behaviour is the same. However, they are embedded in patterns of behavior and mental models citizens take for granted and without question or examination. History is important as it continually repeats itself. So now we have a choice if this pattern stops with you.

Empire technology entanglements since the conclusion of World War 2 signaled the decline of territorial empires and the emergence of a new regime of power. Technological systems birthed in wartime quickly became infrastructures for postwar expansion, surveillance, governance, and capital accumulation. From Cold War supercomputers to contemporary AI factories, technological revolutions have not merely been tools of modernization; they have been instruments of empire, embedding domination into the very materials and operations of daily life (Edgerton, 2006; Parikka, 2015).

The pattern continues to this very day. I won't detail the specifics here, particularly as it will start getting contentious given the current domination of a handful of nations and tech corporations that control this space technologically and politically. Since WW2, over such a relatively short space of time compared to what we discussed in these last two chapters, eight major technological revolutions, along with numerous mini revolutions, have taken place. These advances have profoundly influenced individuals, organizations, communities, and even the planet, especially through growing human-empire-technology entanglements. Each of these revolutions was contingent on the others and is deeply interconnected and interdependent. These include:

- The Electronics Revolution (1947–1960s)
- The Space-Age Revolution (1957–1970s)
- The Computer Revolution (1970s–1980s)
- The Information Revolution (1990s–2000s)
- The Mobile and Social Media Revolution (2007–2015)
- The Cloud and Big Data Revolution (2010s–Present)
- The Biotech and Genomics Revolution (2000s–Present)
- The Artificial Intelligence Revolution – current wave (2012–Present)

The pattern across all post-WW2 technology revolutions is one of recursive entanglement, where each new technological wave is absorbed into the logic of empire, only to reconfigure its mechanisms and intensify its reach. What began as analogue and tangible manifestations of human–technology entanglements in Chapter 3 has become planetary-scale computation, predictive governance, and biopolitical consequences by the end of this Chapter 4. Technology-mediated empires no longer just conquer territories; they capture human cognition, public infrastructure, planetary resources, and shape our potential future destinies.

However, this story doesn't end here. We have agency and we have choices.

CRITICAL POST-HUMAN APPROACHES IN THE AGE OF AI

Understanding history empowers us to adopt critical strategies for leveraging technology responsibly to benefit citizens, organizations, and stakeholders. Today's socio-economic-political climate reflects post-Enlightenment imperial mindsets, and tech companies increasingly act like empires or oligopolies. While their power may seem impressive, it often harms most businesses and organizations.

Critical posthumanism offers a powerful lens for interrogating the assumptions embedded in contemporary artificial intelligence. Unlike transhumanism, which celebrates AI as a tool for human enhancement without question, critical posthumanism invites a deeper reflection on how technologies like AI challenge the very notion of what it means to be human and explores the consequences of our entanglements. What makes humans different from other species is our capacity to fully incorporate tools and supporting cultural practices into our existence (Clark, 2001) which is being slowly compromised by technology use.

Things to keep in mind as we end this chapter and engage with the remaining chapters are that critical posthumanism is an interdisciplinary philosophical approach that challenges foundational assumptions of humanism and explores the implications of emerging technologies, ecological interdependence, and nonhuman agency. It builds on and critiques both humanism and transhumanism, emphasizing the need to rethink what it means to be human and considering the role of empire in shaping our current approaches to technology and power.

The Key Tenets of Critical Posthumanism

Below, I flesh out eight key tenets of critical posthumanism to provide a baseline for our work to follow in subsequent chapters. Some of these may sound difficult to accept or grasp, but I urge you to try, as this is also an exercise to challenge our mechanistic thinking about the world to help us embrace a future of increasing complexity and ambiguity.

1. **Critique of human exceptionalism.** Critical posthumanism rejects the idea that humans are fundamentally separate from or superior to other forms of life or matter. It challenges anthropocentrism, which privileges human perspectives and interests, arguing that this view has led to ecological devastation, systemic inequality, and epistemological blind spots. Critical posthumanism rejects the idea that humans are uniquely rational, creative, or autonomous (Haraway, 1985; Latour, 1993; 2017). This tenet challenges the tendency to evaluate AI systems only by how closely they mimic human traits; therefore, instead of asking whether AI is "as intelligent as a human," posthumanism asks how intelligence can be rethought as distributed, situated, and nonhuman.

2. **Decentering the "liberal human subject."** Posthumanism critiques the Enlightenment perspective of the autonomous, rational, male, which is a Western construct of what it means to be human. It argues that this construct is often exclusionary, which marginalizes women, non-Western peoples, animals, and machines (Braidotti, 2013; 2019; Latour, 2017). This highlights how AI systems often encode and reproduce biased assumptions about humanity, e.g., facial recognition failing on darker skin, and language models marginalizing non-Western perspectives.
3. **Redefining the nature of reality and existence.** Rather than treating actors as isolated entities, posthumanism emphasizes that humans, technologies, animals, and environments are interdependent and co-constituted. This idea is influenced by thinkers like Donna Haraway's (1985) "companion species" and Karen Barad's (2007) "intra-action" which maintains that we are all distinct actors with entangled agencies that emerge through our interactions. Posthumanism critically examines humanism's emphasis on reason and language, instead highlighting that we experience complex connectedness with the world through infinite entanglements (Wolfe, 2010). The implication is that AI is not an isolated tool but part of this entangled network that is shaped by data, infrastructures, users, and feedback loops. As humans and AI co-evolve, our behaviors, perceptions, and decisions are enmeshed (Bratteleig and Verne, 2012a; 2012b).
4. **Nonhuman agency.** Posthumanism acknowledges the agency of animals, machines, and environments, examining their roles in shaping the world beyond human-centered perspectives. Agential realism (Barad, 2007) challenges the division between subject and object, arguing that reality is created through relational intra-actions rather than independent entities. For example, algorithms shape hiring, policing, and content moderation, as if it has agency. AI systems act within social systems and exert power, often without transparency or accountability, thus requiring a broader view of agency.
5. **Intersections with feminism, postcolonialism, and queer theory.** Critical posthumanism often intersects with feminist, postcolonial, and queer critiques, sharing concerns about power, marginalization, and the construction of identity. It resists totalizing narratives and embraces multiplicity, hybridity, and difference (Wynter, 2003; Mbembe, 2017; Braidotti, 2019). It exposes how AI can reinforce dominant norms (gender, race, coloniality) through biased training data, surveillance practices, or techno-solutionism. It calls for inclusive, decolonial, and nonbinary engagements with technology.
6. **Ethical and political responsibility.** Posthumanism calls for new forms of ethical responsibility that account for technology's human and nonhuman entanglements. This includes ecological responsibility, social justice, and the recognition of difference in race, culture, or gender without the need for domination (Latour, 2017; Haraway, 1985). This includes the ecological footprint of training large models, the social impacts of automation, and the responsibility to both human and nonhuman stakeholders in AI systems.

7. **Technological mediation of the human.** Posthumanism explores how technologies (e.g., AI, biotechnology, digital media) transform what it means to be human and how we think, feel, and relate. Unlike transhumanism, which often celebrates human enhancement and mastery over nature, critical posthumanism remains skeptical of techno-utopianism (Latour, 2017; Hayles, 1999) and emphasizes the risks of replicating existing hierarchies under the name of AI-led "progress." For example, AI hype cycles and visions of "superintelligence," often obscure current issues like bias, exploitation, and control. Critical posthumanism warns against narratives of inevitable progress and promotes the fact that we still have choices and the future is not inevitable but contested.
8. **Epistemological pluralism.** Posthumanism emphasizes that there isn't one single, universally correct way of knowing things and that there are alternative ways of knowing and being, including indigenous knowledge systems, affective modes of understanding, and non-linear temporalities. It suggests that various approaches, methodologies, and perspectives can be equally valid for understanding the world rather than relying on teleological progress narratives of modernity that are prevalent in the media (Wynter, 2003; Mbembe, 2017). Posthumanism values indigenous, embodied, and affective ways of understanding technology and resists the reduction of intelligence or knowledge to quantifiable metrics or Western logic systems.

I've provided a concise summary of the guiding principles of critical posthumanism to apply when rethinking and reconfiguring AI systems design. I will bring up this list again in Chapter 8 when we will play with some tools for hands-on AI system design. For now, this is a summary of the longer discussion provided above:

1. Intelligence is distributed throughout the ecosystem.
2. Arrest archaic assumptions and mindsets.
3. Technology is not a tool but a relational element in an entangled network.
4. Non-human actors have agency (not sentience).
5. Beware of structural inequality and normative thinking.
6. We are all responsible for sustained planetary outcomes.
7. Beware of techno-optimism and techno-solutionism.
8. There are many ways of knowing.

As I mentioned in the first chapter, the meta question we need to keep in mind as humans is "what are we here for, that is the question."

CONCLUSION

Modernity's dominant position toward technology has been one of control: we design systems, deploy tools, solve problems, set targets, and achieve power. But in an entangled world, control is often illusory. Technologies have emergent effects. They shape the conditions under which humans think, act, and relate. The more realistic orientation toward AI technology is co-creation if we want to create positive futures that serve humanity and the planet.

In Chapters 3 and 4, we have discussed that technology is not outsdie of us; we are always co-producing meaning, values, and futures with it. Philosopher Bruno Latour's "actor-network theory" (1993) reminds us that agency is distributed through humans and nonhumans acting together, often unpredictably, as behavior in any complex adaptive system is emergent. The implication is that our task is not to master the machine or resist it but to know how to co-evolve with it. We need to design holistic systems of accountability, learning, and mutual flourishing. This is what we will look at in more detail in Part IV of this book, *Flourishing.*

Much of the public debate about technology focuses on making systems more transparent. However, even with transparency, many AI infrastructures or platform systems are opaque and too complex for humans to fully understand, and in many cases, they are simply *blackboxed* to humans. This calls for technological literacy in an interpretive capacity and the ability to ask critical questions, understand the trade-offs, and identify the consequences.

Entanglement is not a glitch in the human story; it's the origin story. What changes now is our awareness of it. To live in the mesh is to accept that there are no clean separations, only knots, tensions, and patterns that must be traced, felt, and sometimes re-tied. We need to recognize that we are always acting within systems, not outside them. This is not a call to surrender. It is a call to compose: to treat every interaction as a site of possible co-creation. The goal is human participation in our technological futures with integrity.

NOTES

1 It must be noted that China, India and many other nations have had an equally impressive history based on a different trajectory and narrative.

2 Article from www.euractiv.com/section/eet/news/how-developing-countries-are-paying-a-high-price-for-the-global-mineral-boom/

REFERENCES

Andrade, T. (2016). *The Gunpowder Age: China, Military Innovation, and the Rise of the West in World History*. Princeton University Press.

Barad, K. (2007). *Meeting the Universe Halfway: Quantum Physics and the Entanglement of Matter and Meaning*. Duke University Press.

Birhane, A. (2021). Algorithmic injustice: a relational ethics approach. *Patterns, 2*(2). https://doi.org/10.1016/j.patter.2021.100205

Braidotti, R. (2013). *The Posthuman*. Polity Press.

Braidotti, R. (2019). *Posthuman Knowledge*. Polity Press.

Bratteteig, T., and Verne, G. B. (2012a). Creating a space for change within sociomaterial entanglements. *Scandinavian Journal of Information Systems, 24*(2), 7.

Bratteteig, T., and Verne, G. B. (2012b). Conditions for autonomy in the information society: Disentangling as a public service. *Scandinavian Journal of Information Systems, 24*(2), 3.

Browne, S. (2015). *Dark Matters: On the Surveillance of Blackness*. Duke University Press.

Chase, K. (2003). *Firearms: A Global History to 1700*. Cambridge University Press.

Chase, M., Jacob, J., Jacob, M., Perry, M., and Von Laue, T. (2013). *Western Civilization: Ideas, Politics, and Society*. Cengage Learning.

Chew, S. C. (2002). Globalisation, ecological crisis, and dark ages. *Global Society*, *16*(4), 333–356.

Cipolla, C. M. (1965). *Guns, Sails and Empires: Technological Innovation and the Early Phases of European Expansion*. Pantheon Books.

Clark, A. (2001). Natural-born cyborgs? In *International Conference on Cognitive Technology* (pp. 17–24). Springer Berlin Heidelberg.

Crawford, K. (2021). *Atlas of AI: Power, Politics, and the Planetary Costs of Artificial Intelligence*. Yale University Press.

Dupré, L. (1980). Marx's critique of culture and its interpretations. *The Review of Metaphysics*, *34*(1), 91–121.

Edgerton, D. (2006). *The Shock of the Old: Technology and Global History since 1900*. Oxford University Press.

Felluga, D. (2011). *Introductory Guide to Critical Theory – Modules on Marx: On the Stages of Economic Development*. Purdue University.

Fernández-Armesto, F. (2006). *Pathfinders: A Global History of Exploration*. WW Norton & Company.

Finné, M., Holmgren, K., Shen, C. C., Hu, H. M., Boyd, M., and Stocker, S. (2017). Late Bronze Age climate change and the destruction of the Mycenaean Palace of Nestor at Pylos. *PloS one*, *12*(12), e0189447.

Fronterotta, F. (2010). Plato's *Republic* in the recent debate. *Journal of the History of Philosophy* *48*(2), 125–151. https://dx.doi.org/10.1353/hph.0.0203.

Fynn-Paul, J. (2009). Empire, monotheism and slavery in the greater Mediterranean region from antiquity to the early modern era. *Past and Present*, *205*(1), 3–40.

Gates, C. (2003). *Ancient Cities: The Archaeology of Urban Life in the Ancient Near East and Egypt, Greece and Rome. Routledge.*

Goff, S. (2020). Public policy and the military-industrial complex. *The Business of War: Theological and Ethical Reflections on the Military-Industrial Complex*. Wipf and Stock Publishers.

Grayling, A. (2016) *The Age of Genius*, Bloomsbury.

Gutas, D. (2002). The study of Arabic philosophy in the twentieth century an essay on the historiography of Arabic philosophy. *British Journal of Middle Eastern Studies*, 29(1), 5–25.

Haraway, D. J. (1985). A cyborg manifesto: Science, technology, and socialist-feminism in the late twentieth century. In *Simians, Cyborgs, and Women: The Reinvention of Nature* (pp. 149–181). Routledge.

Hayles, N. K. (1999). *How We Became Posthuman: Virtual Bodies in Cybernetics, Literature, and Informatics*. University of Chicago Press.

Headrick, D. R. (2010). *Power over Peoples: Technology, Environments, and Western Imperialism, 1400 to the Present*. Princeton University Press.

Hoyland, R. (1997). *Seeing Islam as Others Saw It: A Survey and Evaluation of Christian, Jewish and Zoroastrian Writings on Early Islam (Studies in Late Antiquity and Early Islam)*. The Dawrwin Press, Inc.

Huang, S., Lai, X., Ke, L., Li, Y., Wang, H., Zhao, X., Dai, X., and Wang, Y. (2024). AI technology panic – is AI dependence bad for mental health? A Cross-Lagged Panel Model and the mediating roles of motivations for AI use among adolescents. *Psychology Research and Behavior Management*. DOI: 10.2147/PRBM.S440889. PMID: 38495087; PMCID: PMC10944174.

Kaniewski, D., Guiot, J., and Van Campo, E. (2015). Drought and societal collapse 3200 years ago in the Eastern Mediterranean: A review. *Wiley Interdisciplinary Reviews: Climate Change*, *6*(4), 369–382.

Karmel, A. (1972). *Guillotine in the Wings: A New Look at the French Revolution and Its Relevance to America Today*. McGraw-Hill.

Kennedy, M. (2025). *Preserving the Ideals of the Enlightenment in the Age of Artificial Intelligence*. Wilson Centre. www.wilsoncenter.org/article/preserving-ideals-enlightenment-age-artificial-intelligence accessed 7 August 2025.

Klein, H. S. (2010). *The Atlantic Slave Trade*. Cambridge University Press.

Latour, B. (1993). *We Have Never Been Modern* (C. Porter, Trans.). Harvard University Press. (Original work published 1991).

Latour, B. (2017). *Facing Gaia: Eight Lectures on the New Climatic Regime* (C. Porter, Trans.). Polity Press.

Livesey, J. (2025), Data in the GenAI era: Reclaiming our digital selves. World Economic Forum. www.weforum.org/stories/2025/01/new-enlightenment-era-of-generative-ai-genai/ Accessed 6 November 2025.

Maran, J., and Wright, J. C. (2019). The rise of the Mycenaean culture, palatial administration and its collapse. *A Companion to the Archaeology of Early Greece and the Mediterranean* (pp. 97–132). John Wiley & Sons. https://doi.org/10.1002/9781118769966.ch5

Mbembe, A. (2017). *Critique of Black Reason* (L. Dubois, Trans.), Duke University Press.

Mokyr, J. (2009). *The Enlightened Economy*, Yale University Press.

Mokyr, J. (2011). The European enlightenment, the industrial revolution, and modern economic growth. In *Law, Economics and Evolutionary Theory*. Edward Elgar Publishing.

Mumford, L. (1934). *Technics and Civilization*. Harcourt, Brace and Company.

Parikka, J. (2015). *A Geology of Media*. University of Minnesota Press.

Richards, J. F. (1995). *The Mughal Empire: The New Cambridge History of India*. Cambridge University Press.

Rowe, C. (2017). The City of Pigs: A key passage in Plato's *Republic. Philosophie Antique. Problèmes, Renaissances, Usages*, *17*, 55–71.

Sawyer, R. K. (2001). Emergence in sociology: Contemporary philosophy of mind and some implications for sociological theory. *American Journal of Sociology*, 107(3), 551–585.

Schiebinger, L. (2004). *Plants and Empire: Colonial Bioprospecting in the Atlantic World*. Harvard University Press.

Scott, J. C. (2020). *Seeing Like a State: How Certain Schemes to Improve the Human Condition Have Failed*. Yale University Press.

Smith, A. (1998). *An Inquiry into the Nature and Causes of the Wealth of Nations: A Selected Edition*. Oxford University Press.

Smith, B. (2016). Slavery as free trade: The 18th-century thinkers behind laissez-faire economics saw slavery as a great example of global free trade. Aeon. https://aeon.co/essays/why-the-original-laissez-faire-economists-loved-slavery

Soboul, A. (1980). *Le Premier Empire (1804-1815)*. Presses Universitaires de France.

Tartaron, T. F. (2013). *Maritime Networks in the Mycenaean World*. Cambridge University Press.

Thomas, L. (2009). Origins of the myth of social Darwinism: The ambiguous legacy of Richard Hofstadter's Social Darwinism in American Thought. *Journal of Economic Behavior and Organization*, *71*, 37–51.

Weatherford, J. (2005). *Genghis Khan and the Making of the Modern World*. Crown.

Wolfe, C. (2010). *What Is Posthumanism*? University of Minnesota Press.

Wynter, S. (2003). Unsettling the coloniality of being/power/truth/freedom: Towards the human, after man, its overrepresentation—An argument. *CR: The New Centennial Review*, *3*(3), 257–337.

Zuboff, S. (2019). *The Age of Surveillance Capitalism: The Fight for a Human Future at the New Frontier of Power*. PublicAffairs.

III

Disentanglement

CHAPTER 5

Deep Dive into Enablement

If knowledge can create problems, it is not through ignorance that we can solve them.

—ISAAC ASIMOV

INTRODUCTION

From our exploration of the anthropological, sociological and historical nature of human-technology entanglement, we now come back to the organisational experience with AI in the here and now. As we have established in previous chapters, we have limited knowledge about the necessary and unique attributes of a successful organizational implementation of artificial intelligence in business applications (Pumplun et al., 2019; Sohn and Kwon, 2020). Recent studies suggest that many organizations are falling short in creating tangible business value through AI (Shollo et al., 2022) and that returns on AI investment are below expectations (Mikalef and Gupta, 2021).

The failure to realize the potential of AI-enabled technologies is largely attributable to the oversimplified, yet pervasive ways that society and organizations treat the relationship between AI and humans in the value creation process (Metcalf et al., 2019). Furthermore, the advancement of AI is evolving well beyond being treated as mere technological tools for human use and is instead becoming capable of operating as interdependent agents (Fügener et al., 2021; Seeber et al., 2020).

This is creating unprecedented challenges to current models of strategic decision-making, technology investment, human–machine collaboration, and business and organizational transformation (Berente et al., 2021; Collins et al., 2021).

Uncertainty and instability created by the speed of AI technology advancement, changes in the regulatory environment with regard to the development and scaling of AI technologies, and uncertainty in current economic conditions have created a challenging

DOI: 10.1201/9781003616566-8

environment that organizations need to navigate to achieve sustainable AI-led digital transformation (Dwivedi et al., 2021).

Given this context, we ran in-depth interviews with 30 international industry experts on the enablers and barriers of adopting and implementing AI. We specifically sought perspectives from AI solution providers, strategic advisors, and consultants who work directly with organizations in investing and implementing AI technologies predominantly in the USA and Europe.

Our findings show that there is a complex heterogeneity of issues surrounding AI adoption, implementation, and subsequent value-creation. These issues are clustered in five groups: macro-environmental factors, technology maturity issues, strategy and leadership, systems enablement, and the shifting nature of work.

We conclude this chapter with a contribution to theory development and a conceptual model on the factors affecting organizational adoption and implementation of AI technology that have practical implications for practice.

As intelligent technologies proliferate throughout organizations, the process of making strategic decisions is becoming more complex and uncertain (Faraj and Leonardi, 2022). Furthermore, the blurred boundaries between AI technology development and use make it necessary to theorize beyond narrow approaches for a more accurate approximation of current and future challenges (Waardenburg and Huysman, 2022; Wagner, 2020). This becomes a pressing issue given the lack of consensus on the mechanisms that can generate business value from AI (Mikalef and Gupta, 2021).

BEGIN WITH A REFLECTION ON MANAGEMENT THEORY FOR CONTEXT

As I have done in other chapters in this book, I will continue to reference theory due to its importance to maintaining perspective. Technology is new, but human behavior, our power relationships, and our organizational constructs remain largely the same. The real clues to technology entanglement and human flourishing are contained in management science theories that have become refined over time. Come walk with me…

We draw on the behavioral theory of the firm (BTF) to understand the complex dynamics surrounding AI adoption and implementation. BTF is influential in the fields of strategic management and organization theory and provides a useful framework that complements information systems research. The key tenets of BTF seek to explain how organizations engage in decision-making for investing in innovative technologies (Gavetti et al., 2012; Cyert and March, 1963; Lewellyn and Bao, 2015) and thereby provide insight for current global challenges in AI adoption.

The BTF is considered a landmark behavioral theory of the firm that was developed by Cyert and March (1963), concerned with the way organizations make economic decisions to create business value. Related works using BTF include the implications for innovation management of AI technologies and machine learning-based AI systems (Haefner et al., 2021), the bounded rational process of managerial decision-making for technology investment (Dong et.al., 2013), and firm international investment decision-making (Surdu et al., 2021).

BTF posits the importance of the role of managers' heuristics and cognitive biases in explaining variation in strategic decisions (Argote and Greve, 2007; Lewellyn and Bao, 2015). This provides insight into situations where organizational behavior is complex, dynamic, and heterogeneous, as is evidenced in the literature and in our research into AI adoption. It is also an important theory to consider in situations where an industry is fast changing and subjected to hype which makes it difficult for leaders to navigate.

Put simply, our findings show that in the current environment organizational leaders are taking pragmatic approaches to AI investment that are "good enough" rather than fully optimized. As we will discuss at the end of the chapter, this is not necessarily a bad thing.

Let us take a closer look at BTF theory. One of its key tenets relevant to this chapter is that **firms need to accommodate multiple stakeholders and goals.** Organizations are often described as a coalition of different stakeholders such as shareholders, managers, and employees, and each has their own business goals and expectations. Furthermore, there isn't a simple relationship between these different and often competing goals and subsequent decision-making (Cyert and March, 1963). Organizations are in a perpetual state of quasi-resolution of conflict and seek to negotiate a more predictable operating environment to stabilize the business.

Another insightful behavior in complex contexts is that **firms do not optimize; they suffice.** In environments with information asymmetries, management decision-making is problem-directed by engaging in *problematic search* prompted by finding a sufficient solution to a specific problem, which may not necessarily be an optimal one (Surdu et al., 2021; Mahoney, 2004).

Decisions to suffice are not always rational, as they are influenced by emotion and bias of the leadership team and organizational culture. Closely tied to sufficing is **uncertainty avoidance,** where organizations avoid the requirement to correctly anticipate future events and trends by using decision rules that emphasize short-run reactions to short-run feedback. This behavior tends to focus on maintaining the status quo over proactive transformation (Surdu et al., 2021). The final tenet of BTF is **continuous organizational learning and adaptation.** Managerial decision-making is an adaptive process of organizational learning from performance feedback. However, they often repeat strategies that have worked in the past and show a bias in favor of solutions that they are familiar with (Mahoney, 2004).

Now let's take a deeper look at what the research found.

METHODOLOGY

Prior to running the expert interviews, we had conducted an extensive systematic literature review to scope the extant literature on enablers and barriers to organization adoption of AI (Raftopoulos and Hamari, 2023). As discussed in Chapters 1 and 2, the key themes in the literature can be summarized into four clusters of implementation challenges: human, organization, strategic, and technology factors. While the literature review provided important insight on the enablers and barriers of AI adoption, there remained a gap in understanding the strategic decision-making and behavior of organizations investing and implementing AI – in other words, *why* did leaders make those specific decisions?

Therefore, we designed a study using expert interviews to investigate this specific gap. Our key objective was to ground-truth the findings of our literature review and seek a deeper understanding of the issues affecting organizational experiences with AI implementations. We identified that this is an effective method to complement and contextualize findings of a literature review (Lutz et al., 2019). More importantly, we wanted to hear directly from decision makers at the coalface of AI investment decision-making, implementation, and enablement.

We adopted the definition of an expert to be an **individual with advanced knowledge** in the investigated field of research (Meuser and Nagel, 2009). Our focus was on the identification and selection of industry experts who had specialized experience in the procurement, development, or implementation of AI technologies in organizations. We identified a range of industry experts through a scan of social media activity on LinkedIn and X (formerly known as Twitter), which included a scan of our own professional social media networks. For example, we curated a Twitter list of 470 accounts that we verified as credible, active, and influential industry experts in AI implementations.

We decided to focus our selection of experts operating as consultants, advisors, and AI technology solution providers to organizations. The experts we selected had extensive experience across multiple AI projects, technologies, use cases, and organizations, and had a comprehensive overview of issues and patterns of organizational decision-making on AI adoption and implementation. This formed our search criteria on their LinkedIn and X accounts, and we verified with the expert when we first contacted them.

A key advantage of selecting this expert group is that these individuals have intimate technical knowledge of AI technology development. We deliberately chose senior or C-level AI practitioners for a more nuanced understanding of hands-on AI-led business transformation. In terms of sample size, we followed the recommendations of Creswell and Creswell (2018), who suggest using between three and ten experts for the type of scientific academic study that we ran. In the first round of interviews in 2024, of 10 global experts, we reached a conceptual saturation point after eight interviews.

This study was extended in 2025 with an additional 20 global experts and found the same level of saturation of key themes. This tells us that **despite the rapid advancement of AI technologies over this period, the same problems with implementation and enablement had persisted.** This makes logical sense as the implementation and enablement problems raised in the interviews are concerned about human and systems integration, which has been a perennial challenge for all technology transformations for decades. The technology changes, but the socio-technical and organizational challenges persist.

Our experts in this study included the following:

- Senior C-suite level executives at global technology companies based in the USA, Europe, Nordics, India, and Singapore.
- Global consultants and former technology executives who provide advisory services to industry and policy makers focusing on AI.

- Technology executives at AI innovation hubs servicing organizations looking to invest and experiment with AI technologies.
- Machine learning specialists at global technology consultancies.

Examples of expert experiences with a range of AI implementations included medical imaging, customer profiling, supply chain optimization, automated detection models, big data analytics, image-to-text recognition systems, and risk management and statistical process models. We conducted semi-structured interviews that each ran for over an hour, consisting of four core questions:

1. What is the current state of business interest and investment in AI technologies?
2. What challenges are you seeing with business adoption and implementation of AI technologies?
3. What would you describe as the key barriers and enablers of AI adoption and its overall performance once implemented?
4. What are the key opportunities for improvement from your experience?

The first round of open coding was informed by the methods of Williams and Moser (2019) and utilized the *Atlas.ti* software. We identified and organized the data into 161 initial codes and collected unique quotes from the experts for each code to capture nuance and meaning. Axial coding was applied in the second level of coding to further refine, align, and categorize the themes identified in the first round of open coding. Keeping in mind that the purpose of this phase is to create distinct thematic categories (Williams and Moser, 2019), we conducted several iterations of continuous clustering and distillation using thematic analysis and grounded theory methods to establish relationships between the themes in the data (Strauss, 1987).

After several iterations, we settled on **18 key code groups derived from the 161 codes** that represented the range and depth of the views of the 30 experts. Using selective coding in the final step of our data analysis (Strauss, 1987), we aimed to integrate and refine the code groups into key categories to form a larger theoretical scheme. After several iterations of thematic analyzes, we settled on **five distinct cluster groups:** macro-external environment factors, technology factors, strategy and leadership issues, enablement of AI implementations, and the nature of work.

A summary of the 5 clusters and 18 categories is provided in Figure 5.1. We found challenges in initially conducting the thematic analysis due to an unexpectedly high concentration of themes under the two clusters of macro-external and enablement. By comparison, the themes under the other three clusters were familiar to us from our prior research, as they presented as commonly occurring themes in extant literature. This suggests that industry experts are more attuned to the dynamics of organizational entanglements with the macro environment and the micro entanglements of technology integration and enablement.

The **conceptualization stage** in our thematic analysis, where Meuser and Nagel (2009) suggest looking *at specific characteristics of the commonly shared knowledge of the experts to condense and formulate categories*, was instrumental in finalizing our results. It was

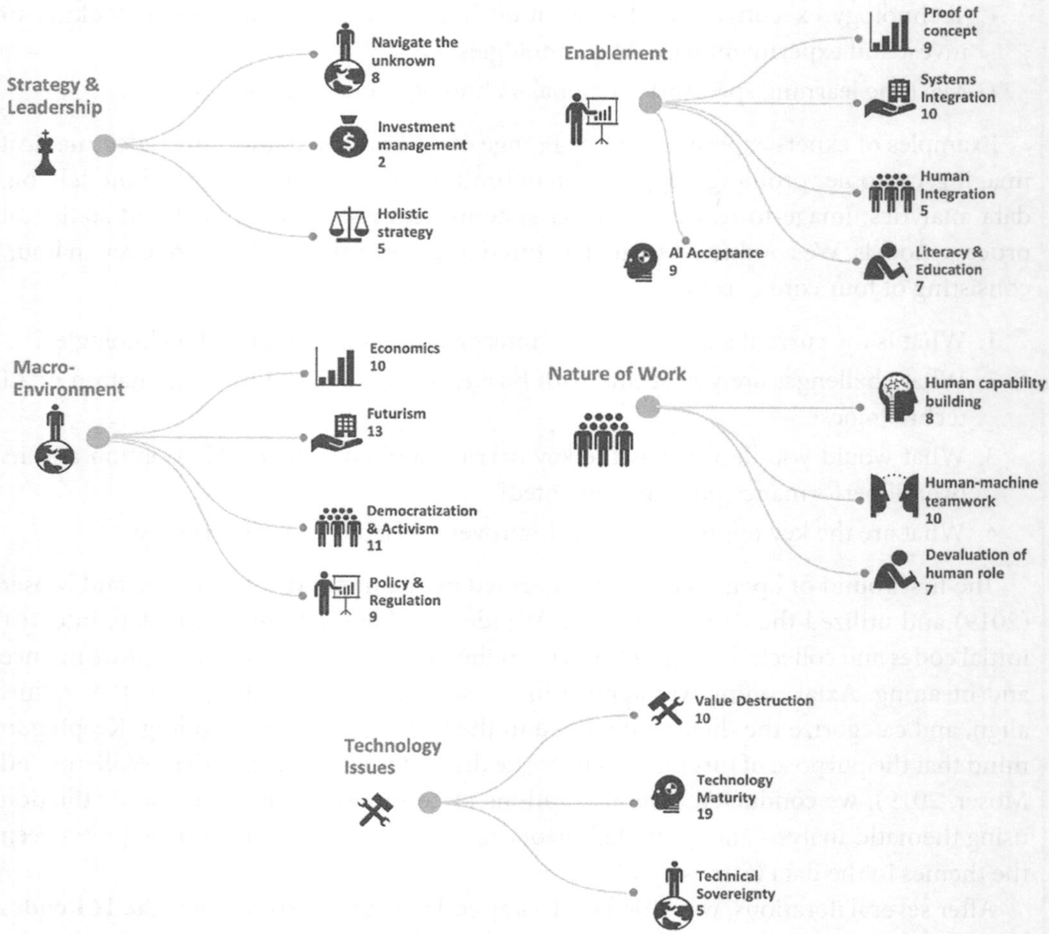

FIGURE 5.1 Five thematic clusters and 18 key code groups.

clear that the "commonly shared knowledge" of our experts as vendors of AI technology solutions was their detailed knowledge of the enablement of their technologies and an awareness of the macro external factors that have an impact on their sales cycles. This had enabled us to condense our initial analysis of subcodes, code groups, and categories while still maintaining the integrity of the story that was unique in this data set. Our final stage was theoretical generalization (Meuser and Nagel 2009), where we represent the research results as empirically generalized findings for this chapter. This was done by referencing our findings to the theoretical foundation of BTF and developing a conceptual framework to guide industry practice and contribution to theory, which is presented later in this chapter.

I have only provided an outline of the detailed methodology and laborious process that was designed and followed for this study. On one hand, you may feel that this is unnecessary; however, I have deliberately left it in this chapter to highlight the level of effort and transparency you should expect of AI strategy research and strategies.

In an industry where many assertions and opinions on AI capability are made, it is important to understand the methodology that was followed to ensure it was sufficiently independent and scientific to be considered by your organization.

KEY FINDINGS ON EXPERT OPINION ON AI ENABLEMENT

We found a complex array of interrelated issues affecting the strategic decision-making and behavior of organizations in relation to AI adoption and implementation. A discussion of the key findings is listed for each of the five key clusters.

Macro Environmental Factors

The macro cluster featured external influences in shaping organizational concerns and decision-making on AI adoption and implementation.

Economic issues such as securing a comparative advantage through improved scale and efficiency are at the forefront for organizations adopting AI. Expert opinion however was divided on the type of impact AI will have on organizations and the global economy. Several noted that it will be a significant disruption with consequences greater than the last industrial revolution. Economic factors were also heavily influenced by the unknown directions of the **regulatory and policy environment**, particularly in relation to the unstable global political environment, geopolitical rivalries, and the influence of a handful of technology companies that were taking place at the time of the interviews.

There is widespread consensus that some regulation is needed to provide guardrails against unethical practices, immature technologies, and malicious actors. However, the majority of experts expressed concerns in four key areas:

1. Too much regulation would stifle innovation,
2. Regulation will negatively impact or slow down industry adoption of AI technologies,
3. Regulation plays into the hands of the largest three to four AI technology companies seeking economic rent by raising barriers to entry for the next tier of technology developers and startups, and
4. Effective AI adoption would be concentrated in large corporations that would be able to resource the new AI compliance requirements relative to smaller businesses.

Democratization and activism featured highly with experts who operated in multiple geographies and were conscious of the unequal distribution of access to AI technologies and their benefits. A key element in these discussions focused on the need to maintain cultural, linguistic, and intellectual diversity, which are potentially threatened by generative AI trained largely on content derived from the English-speaking internet. Several experts mentioned the need for **technical sovereignty in their geopolitical regions,** i.e., the Nordics and India were mentioned here. The ownership and control of key AI technologies were thought to be an area of concern.

Factors in relation to Futurism or anticipation of future trends ranged from a broad range of perspectives: (a) an overestimation of current and future AI capability unduly influenced by business hype and science fiction, (b) the invisibility of future trends which is creating uncertainty or lags in AI investment decision-making, and (c) concerns about the uneven flow of costs and benefits across society, and that this signals a need systemic change and adaptation, but across unknown timelines. The following quotes from the interviews highlight the key concerns over the wider macro external issues that are making organization leaders apprehensive:

- "The future is coming faster and faster, but it's invisible to us. We don't know at what speed it's coming, but we need to change, and leaders need to say ahead of that."
- "There will be a dominance by few players because these companies are bigger than many nation states like Open AI, Google, Microsoft, or Meta. They will definitely dominate, and I think we need a collective effort to keep things in the open, meaning open source."
- "We have to be careful of the impact on different demographics and geographies. If we're not careful, we're going to end up with a new class warfare. China has already raced way ahead of us all, and we don't want to admit it to the wider public."
- "This is making our clients very nervous. The political rhetoric at the moment is not helping; it's just stalling things business-wise."

Technology Factors

Technology factors affecting AI adoption covered three key areas: technology maturity, technical sovereignty, and value destruction.

Technology maturity was the largest category and contained the well-known issues affecting AI efficacy and adoption, such as accuracy, transparency, and trustworthiness, limitations in algorithms for complex, high-cognitive tasks, and the limited fine motor skills in robotics. At the root of many of these immaturities are an outcome of limitations in the availability and appropriateness of data for machine learning and the machine learning models. Experts maintained that the challenges in relation to data are significant and stem from access to good, comprehensive data, which is hampered by difficult data structures and strategy. There was consistent agreement among all the experts that issues and concerns in relation to technology maturity were legitimate; however, it was explained that it was a natural outcome of the evolution and maturity cycle of these emergent technologies that will be improved over time. Experts agreed that the industry needs to understand these limitations and be a proactive part of the development of solutions.

Limitations in **technology design** were mentioned as key issues that affect human–machine augmentation and subsequent value creation. Experts noted that narrow AI systems are often designed standalone and were conscious of the limitations of designing for only one part of a complex organizational system, particularly when human-centered design becomes an afterthought. Experts agreed that technology needs to be better designed to complement human capability and fit within the wider organizational ecosystem. Once again, they viewed these limitations as an outcome of the early stages of development. AI design-related issues became a recurring theme in the interviews.

While AI's known value creation potential is well documented and accepted, experts maintain that there are several potential **value destruction** factors affecting AI adoption. Issues that were mentioned include misinformation and disinformation through the action of bad actors, AI efficacy does not live up to the promise experienced in controlled pilots, through to deliberate misuse of AI systems were users seek to "beat the AI," make the system fail, or where they seek to jump the guardrails.

A final factor mentioned by experts was the perceived need for organizations to maintain their **technical sovereignty** to manage technological risk such as cybersecurity, data security, and leaks. Consistent with expert opinion on the need for **technical sovereignty at the regional level,** the ownership and control of key AI technologies were also thought to be an area of concern at the organizational level. However, experts agreed that the economics of investment in AI infrastructure, data management, and algorithmic training were out of scope for most organizations.

The following quotes illustrate a few of the key technology factors raised by the experts:

- "One of the major prohibiting factors is the actual access to good data. Companies have all these convoluted schemas and terminologies, but the data going in there is still exceptionally difficult to understand."
- "When dealing with neural networks and deep learning, there's an innate randomness to it. So, you always need to be careful with its accuracy and insight. It's not as straightforward as automation."
- "There are data limitation issues which people often do not understand. They build algorithms on American data, and they bring it to India. It will of course not work. It must be built with Indian data to work in India."
- "Here in the Nordics, we don't trust what's happening with AI in the US. Our aim is for technological sovereignty."

Strategy and Leadership

The strategy and leadership cluster focused on three key areas: leading through complexity, needing a holistic approach toward AI adoption, and the need for a long-term investment strategy.

In **leading through complexity**, experts maintain that very often organizational leaders do not know where to start and underestimate how much commitment would be required. Overall, organizational strategic direction on AI tends to be unclear. The reasons were diverse and ranged from

a) divided attention with climate issues, which often take precedence in the minds of leaders,
b) a lack of foresight and forward planning,
c) tend to have a skeptical mindset toward AI but are investigating to not be left behind,
d) lack of strategic objectives, as they're not sure what business problem they're looking to solve.

Consensus among the experts is that the advancement of AI technology is proliferating and the unpredictable directions that are placing pressure on business leaders. Several experts maintain that most businesses are currently in the early investigation stages and still believe adoption of larger-scale AI is too risky, given the large startup costs.

However, experts believe that these positions are uninformed, and the best option for organizations is to form meaningful strategic partnerships to mentor them through these early stages. In terms of holding a **long-term investment strategy,** several experts maintain that organizations operate on inappropriate metrics and time horizons to assess AI performance. There was a unanimous position among the experts that the popular business construct of "return on investment" is inappropriate and sets up the AI investment for failure. The biggest pain point for AI adoption is the investment that starts from an initial startup cost for a pilot, which then progresses to an unknown funding horizon depending on strategic direction, the complexity of the integration, and the required development costs. Experts emphasized that deployment is a one-off cost, but maintenance costs, such as ongoing machine learning, can be significant and must be planned for.

Very often, a parallel transformation in other parts of their organization is required to adequately integrate the AI technology however this was rarely planned for. Many businesses won't continue beyond the experiment or proof of concept due to the magnitude of change that it will require.

In terms of a **holistic approach toward AI adoption**, several experts noted that organizations often made the following mistakes: (a) overfocus on the technical and financial side of AI and less so on the human and systems enablement, (b) little internal organizational dialogue or consultation about an AI strategy, (c) adopting a "set and forget" strategy where businesses adopt AI in one area of the business but do not nurture its growth and ongoing development, or instigate the necessary structural changes in the organization to support it. The following interview quotes illustrate the experts' concerns in relation to strategy and leadership:

- "COVID showed many companies that they did not have a plan. They now realize that if they don't have AI-related technological intervention plan either, it may leave their businesses very exposed."
- "Most businesses don't have a strategic objective; they know that AI is trending and don't want to fall behind their competitors. But they don't really know where to start."
- "There seem to be two types of companies, those who are very interested in their human employees' well-being and their acceptance of the technology. The other type is purely interested in cost and productivity numbers, and that's around 70% of our clients."

Enablement of AI Implementations

Enablement of AI implementation was the largest cluster and comprises five key categories: challenges with technology acceptance, systems integration, human integration, the importance of AI literacy and education, and the development of effective proof of concepts (PoC).

In terms of **AI technology acceptance**, most of the challenges raised focused on the fear and identity loss arising from jobs being altered, devalued, or lost. The second component of AI acceptance was the need for an understanding of how the technology works, and this aligned with classic technology acceptance models. Several experts noted that technology acceptance has significantly improved since the recent introduction of popular consumer-facing generative AI applications such as ChatGPT, Midjourney, and DALL*E, which showed the general public that AI can enable humans to attain highly creative and productive endeavors.

The key learnings of this phenomenon emphasized by the experts are (a) showing evidence to the public of how it enables humans, and not just simply telling them so, and (b) it empowers the individual as opposed to an employer or business.

In terms of **systems integration,** four recurring themes were identified: the challenges of integration with existing legacy systems, the importance of forming strategic partnerships with external AI specialists, the need for systemic change to the organization to accommodate an AI-first operating model, and renewing and upgrading the organization's data strategy.

In terms of **human integration,** experts emphasized the importance of building and integrating advanced technology systems, particularly in areas that require high cognitive function, which need to be designed with the human in the lead with the final analysis or decision-making. The range of terms that were used by the experts includes human oracles, human judges, and humans-in-the-loop. Experts emphasized the need for improving organizational **AI literacy and education** at all levels. The challenges include literacy among the boards and the leadership team at the strategic level. A more concerning observation noted by experts is a reservation among internal technical teams on AI solutions. This can be explained by two factors: their limited experience with AI applications (relative to the depth and scope of experience of the experts on multiple projects) or concerns about perceived technical limitations and cybersecurity risk exposure. The experts maintain that they often have more difficulty in greenlighting a project at this level than at any other. They believe that it is very difficult for an internal technical team to keep their knowledge and skills up to date relative to an external strategic partner, given the current rapid rate of AI advancement.

In terms of effective **proof of concepts (PoC)**, experts discussed the importance of rigorous and methodological design, implementation, and experimentation with PoC, as well as careful mentorship and strategic partnerships throughout the experimentation process. Furthermore, customers need to experiment with different technologies and solutions, and eventually build and experiment with cross-apps that combine multiple systems. Key challenges that are being faced with PoCs include unrealistic metrics and the more common problem of AI applications not working as well in the real world as they did in the pilots.

Often, it's an issue that the AI did not encounter in its training and requires further development to improve reliability. It is at this point that there is a high abandonment rate, where organizations are disappointed with operational improvements or accuracy or reliability and are "not willing to go the extra mile." However, the experts concede that this is not an unrealistic action that organizations take. Finally, they suggest building a tolerance for short-term tradeoffs, such as between efficiency and accuracy. Experts see an important role for organizations to be a more integral part of the future development of AI technologies. The following quotes illustrate expert opinion on enablement factors:

- "Showing an AI proof of concept is very easy. But productizing something that works in the wild is still a Herculean effort."
- "It can be hard to get a direct ROI on AI. They're often not willing to invest if the immediate returns aren't there."
- "Be reasonable, you need to treat AI as a junior employee; you need to nurture them."
- "Honestly, implementation is always extremely hard because companies have existing systems. A PoC can slide right into a brand-new company, as you can set everything up around the AI. But when the AI needs to be set up around other things, such as existing databases, existing data, orchestration tools, and ERPs, you really need an engineer to figure out how everything connects, and then you need a good data digest and machine learning pipelining. And that's MLOps, right? A whole field of machine learning engineering just for that one implementation problem."

Nature of Work

Themes on the nature of work focused on three key areas: overcoming staff feelings of being devalued, the importance of building human capability, and rethinking work design that incorporates reimagined human–machine teamwork.

All the experts identified **staff feelings of being devalued** in their work as a key challenge that organizations are facing. Several experts identified that resistance to AI often stems from what they called an identity problem. However, experts noted that this also occurs in the reverse – many people feel empowered by AI technologies in the workplace. One important observation made by the experts is that *organizations always have a choice* in terms of how this is framed in language and actions to reflect their views of the value of humans over machines; the fault is not in the AI technology but in how organizations use it.

In terms of the importance of **building human capability**, all experts agreed on the importance of ongoing capability, skill, and education development for humans, and that this will need to keep pace with technological developments. Several experts maintain that the onus will be on individuals to drive their capability development, as organizations tend not to keep pace. Mention was again made of generative AI tools like ChatGPT, which became popular on the initiative and drive of individuals who were curious or ambitious.

However, on a general level, the loss of artistic, design, and coding jobs was mentioned as an example of unexpected impacts of AI technologies, as not long ago these jobs were thought to be safe. The framing of capability development was divided in three areas: (a) humans need to now focus their work on partnering with AI and focus on areas tasks where AI is still suboptimal, (b) people need to retrain in another field altogether as less humans will now be required in this space, and (c) AI democratizes these capabilities as it lifts skills in art, design and coding of the average person.

Experts were divided on whether there will be a zero-sum effect (losses of human jobs will be balanced by new jobs created); however, the majority believed that there will be an overall negative effect (more jobs will be lost than created). All maintained however that no one knows for sure, as it is all speculation.

In terms of **reimagined human–machine teamwork,** all the experts agreed about the exciting developments in collaborative work between humans and AI, particularly in areas where AI on its own is unlikely to replace humans over the short to medium term. For example, experts noted that in deploying more complex AI technologies, human oracles are used to supervise certain types of machine learning algorithms that require human judgment, or when dealing with sensitive or incomplete data.

Experts maintained that it's very important to train the human judge or oracle in any given profession on how to work with AI and in understanding how machine learning works. An example was given where a human doctor or air traffic controller needs to have a high-level understanding of the process of machine learning and fitting of data models. Therefore, a certain level of machine learning literacy will become as essential as computer skills were 30 years ago. The overarching points that were made are that the impacts of AI will be significant, but in different intensities and timescales for each industry. A mix of quotes for this cluster is provided below:

- "Certain jobs will be redundant, new ones created, but for a lot of jobs people will feel less important and will have less autonomy – and that includes prestigious jobs like doctors and lawyers that had elitist standings in society."
- "We have all seen the impact on creativity with people using generative AI. You give people a tool and the freedom to do what they want, with just some limits of course, and their creativity and productivity explode."
- "I'll admit that we should be doing a better job when we look at human collaboration with AI, especially wherever human agency is getting compromised. We can put that human more into the center, rather than glorifying a machine-driven decision. We should also start admitting that humans are already working behind the scenes to make AI the success that it is. But frankly, this is not always what the client wants to hear."

The nature of the problems raised by the experts is a symptom of what we discussed in Chapter 2 on the ***perplexity*** of organizations in understanding the nature of the business problems to be solved, the capability of AI, and the cognitive dissonance as the new technology is introduced, but it does not readily meet expectations.

IMPLICATIONS OF THESE RESEARCH FINDINGS

The objective of this research was to investigate organizational experiences with AI technology in response to findings in extant literature of challenges in realizing AI's full potential (Pumplun et al., 2019; Shollo et al., 2022; Mikalef and Gupta, 2021). In this in-depth study, industry experts were asked: What are the current challenges with business adoption and implementation of AI? In this section, we discuss the implications of the experts' insights using the lens of the behavioral theory of the firm (BTF) discussed earlier in this chapter.

Research shows that the prevalence of formidable **macro-external factors** poses significant barriers to more proactive action on AI adoption; an issue that has been understated in the literature we have encountered. While the literature has acknowledged the unstable and rapidly shifting economic, regulatory, and technological landscape (Wagner, 2020; Collins et al., 2021), our interviews show that organizations need to practice more advanced strategic foresight rather than leave the organization vulnerable to the hype. The challenges that this is creating, as explained by BTF as **uncertainty avoidance,** where organizations take a risk-averse approach toward AI adoption in highly uncertain and rapidly changing environments, resulting in the action that is short-term and predictable.

Technology factors identified in the interviews align with the literature in terms of a lack of sufficient technology maturity and value destruction propensity, which create barriers to adoption. Furthermore, AI development is still hampered with critical limitations in transparency, accuracy, reliability, and ethics (Seeber et al., 2020; Fugener et al., 2021). In BTF terms, this has resulted in "firms not optimizing but sufficing" through short-term solutionism, and with many PoC's not extending beyond the experimental stage, inhibiting long-term transformation.

Similarly, **enablement factors** in our research reveal the complexity of issues at create implementation friction across multiple operational areas and are usually where PoCs face major blockages. Through the lens of BTF, this can be explained as organizations affected by a perpetual state of quasi-resolution of conflict between the complex heterogeneity of issues identified in our 18 categories, each with its own unique goals and challenges. This is usually the outcome of organizations not being clear on (a) what problem they are solving, (b) which technology is the right fit, and (c) understanding the consequences of the new technology and the change efforts that will be needed.

Related issues are in relation to the **changing nature of work,** where these challenges are attributed to insufficient attention being paid to human and workplace factors in AI development and implementation (Fügener et al., 2021; Seeber et al., 2020). Management concerns over loss of identity, being devalued, deskilled, while enhancing human capability and reinventing human–machine collaborative systems are an under-explored source of productivity improvement and innovation, as attention tends to be focused on the technology. As one expert mentioned, only 30% of their clients are interested in human issues.

In looking at **conflict resolution between competing business goals,** we found that the complex heterogeneity of issues across our 18 categories, each with its own unique goals and challenges, propels organizations into a *perpetual state of quasi-resolution* of conflict between them. However, our research shows the need for a proactive and decisive strategy and leadership in navigating the unknown long-term impact of AI. Predictable operating environments are now a thing of the past, and unresolved conflicts are becoming prevalent in balancing technical developments with a harmonious workplace, with the expectations of shareholders on ROI.

In terms of **continuous organizational learning and adaptation,** our findings confirm that managerial decision-making on AI adoption and implementation is an adaptive process of organizational learning from performance feedback through the running of proof of concepts. However, evidence suggests that the scope, depth, and process of continuous learning need to be accelerated, pointing to the fact that many do not extend their AI projects beyond PoC stages.

Our final category of **strategy and leadership** appears as the lynchpin among these challenges and is dominated by what appears to be risk-averse, fragmented, and lacking in strategic focus. Our study suggests that an AI-transformed organization requires leadership to be more proactive in navigating complex and ambiguous technical and investment environments. On a tactical level, leadership needs to be more proactive and collaborative in developing a longer-term investment strategy, building strategic foresight, developing expertise over a series of accumulated shorter-term experiments and PoCs for both learning and capability building.

The challenges identified in our study align with extant literature that suggests that there are significant **opportunities for improvement** to better enable the benefits of AI in organizations through focused leadership, capability building, and coordinated enablement that may go beyond the well-known established drivers of digital transformation (Berente et al., 2021; Dwivedi et al., 2021). The findings may also in part explain the mixed AI performance results identified in extant literature (Collins et al. 2021; Mikalef and Gupta, 2021) that are now being reported with more frequency.

In summary, the focus of this chapter was on: *What are the current challenges with business adoption and implementation of AI?* Our research shows that challenges lie in five overlapping clusters: macro-environment issues, technology factors, strategic issues, enablement capability, and adapting the nature of work. There are significant unknowns regarding the future trends of AI technology development that are still hampered by critical limitations in transparency, accuracy, reliability, and ethics.

We posit that low AI adoption rates and low returns on investment appearing in extant literature may be partly explained as an **outcome of the wider contextual issues** that we have identified in our study. A valid case can be made that mixed performance results and low adoption rates are an outcome of risk-averse behavior in a dynamic environment. The impact of digital technologies on corporate strategy and performance is significant, however the magnitude and depth of this impact goes beyond the confines of socio-technical approaches common in information systems research, toward a multidisciplinary approach where consideration needs to be made of AI as an economic actor that has made a complex world even more complex (Menz et al., 2021; Wagner 2020).

PERSPECTIVES AND IMPLICATIONS FOR MANAGEMENT PRACTICE

Given the findings of this study, we offer the following model of the key building blocks in managing and navigating the challenges of organizational AI adoption and implementation.

In this model, we have illustrated the interrelatedness and interdependence of the five key clusters arising from our research, which highlights the ubiquitous influence of macro external factors. As this model is one of emphasizing organizational capability and performance, you can see the integration of organizational dynamic capabilities (Teece, 2007) that was discussed in Chapter 2, underpinning the capabilities required for organizations to be AI-ready.

Briefly again, the dynamic capabilities framework is a strategic management concept that explains how organizations can achieve and sustain competitive advantage in rapidly changing environments by continuously adapting, integrating, and reconfiguring their internal and external resources and competencies. The framework distinguishes *dynamic capabilities* from ordinary operational capabilities, emphasizing that success in turbulent markets depends not just on efficiently managing current operations, but on the ability to innovate, adapt, and transform as circumstances evolve.

This is done through the three enablers: strategic direction, alignment, and organizational microfoundations, as illustrated in Figure 5.2:

1. **Strategic direction** sets the vision, guides capability deployment, and prioritizes opportunities for AI in your organization.
2. **Alignment** integrates organizational assets and prioritizes resource orchestration. Alignment also balances short-term execution with long-term transformation.
3. **Organizational microfoundations** enable the execution of capabilities required to enable AI, build resilience, a culture of leadership, and AI experimentation.

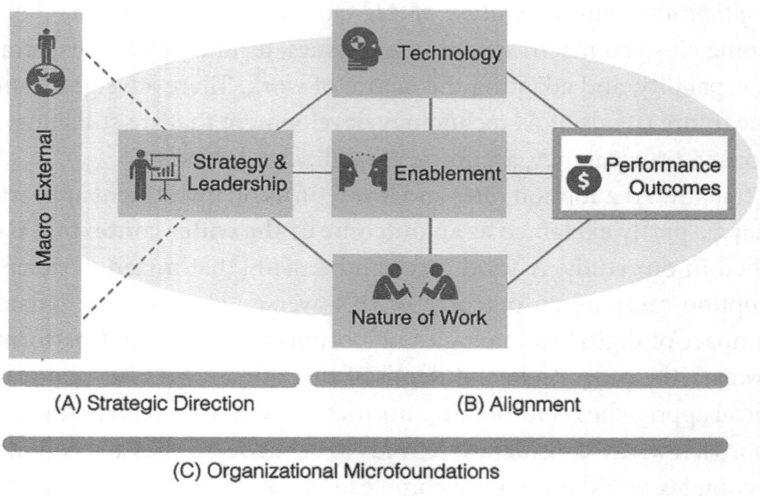

FIGURE 5.2 AI adoption and emblement model.

Digging a little deeper, there are three essential capabilities in organizational microfoundations that help organizations navigate the complexity of their ecosystems, as previously discussed in Chapter 2. As can be seen by the insights and recommendations made by the experts on our research, the following elements need to be embedded into organizational management practices:

- **Sensing**. The ability to scan the environment, interpret signals, and recognize both opportunities and threats that is posed by AI. This requires organizational learning, market intelligence, and the capacity to anticipate changes in the environment and technological progress that is being made.
- **Seizing**. Making timely decisions and allocating resources toward AI investments to capitalize on the opportunities. It may involve new investments, proof of concepts, experiments, business model innovation, or strategic partnerships.
- **Transforming**. The ongoing renewal and reconfiguration of the organization's assets and capabilities to set up AI-enabled technologies for success. This ensures the business remains agile and can adapt to ongoing changes in the external environment in terms of AI capabilities, but also in how they challenge organizational capability and how stakeholders respond.

Dynamic capabilities go beyond routine operational efficiency and need to be tailored to your organization. They are unique to each organization, shaped by its history, leadership, and accumulated knowledge. The framework underscores the importance of **managerial skills in orchestrating resources**, fostering innovation, and ensuring long-term survival and growth in uncertain and volatile markets. That is where your competitive or operational advantage lies, not in the AI technology alone.

To summarize the insights from the AI experts we interviewed, Table 5.1 provides a high-level key action to each of the **18 key themes** to guide leadership teams in the enablement of AI in their organizations.

Many of these factors will be investigated in more detail in Chapters 6 and 7 for a more specialized analysis and deeper strategy recommendations.

The Importance of Ongoing Critical Research into Business Practice

The reasoning behind how organizations make investment decisions to adopt AI technologies and the mechanisms that affect implementation and subsequent performance are wide and varied. **Utilizing the lens of management theories** like the *behavioral theory of the firm* enables us to interpret and potentially predict organizational adoption and implementation of AI in an objective and hype-free environment.

The research in this chapter again finds that organizations need to go beyond focusing on the **AI technology in isolation** and argues that organizational strategic positioning can be of more critical importance (Yun et al., 2019; Haefner et al., 2021). Our findings also align with other researchers in the field, such as Mikalef and Gupta (2021), Shollo et al. (2022), and Pumplun et al. (2019), who call for a deeper investigation into the

TABLE 5.1 High Level Recommendations and Actions by Theme

Key Clusters and Themes	High Level Recommendations
	Macro-External Factors
Democratization and Activism	Participate in active listening to dissenting voices on AI. These people may be among your stakeholders.
Economics Issues	Scaling AI and its efficiencies is challenging most organizations; ongoing experimentation sets you up for greater rates of learning through experimentation.
Futurism and Trends	Proactively engage in future works to strengthen your strategic fitness. Be vigilant of ideological creep into your strategies.
Policy and Regulation	Keep watch on this fluid space to protect your business and your stakeholders. For now, this is likely to remain at high level.
	Technology Factors
Technical Sovereignty	This affects geo-political players; however, your organization may be subject to the capture of sovereign strategies in play.
Technology Maturity	AI is in constant state of becoming, and there are still many flaws and limitations with the tech – keep ahead of these in your risk management.
Value Destruction	AI may create value in one part of your organization but destroy value in other parts. Be aware of dissenting voices and technology limitations, as they are opportunities for risk mitigation.
	Strategy and Leadership Factors
Leading through Complexity	Many leaders don't know where to start or what problem to solve; you are not alone. Seek many sources of information and be aware of the hype machine.
Holistic AI Strategy	Don't overfocus on the technological or financial "priorities" of your AI strategy. You need to set it up for success in solid human and systems enablement and integration strategies.
Investment Management	An "ROI" may not be the appropriate metric. Your timelines need to be carefully constructed and planed as scaling AI requires a spike in financing beyond the initial experiment or PoC.
	Enablement Factors
Systems Integration	Systems integration issues are perennial issues with all digital technologies; AI is no different. Be aware that you may require systemic changes if you're moving toward AI-first model. Listen to your staff regarding difficulties; these are clues.
Human Integration	Concepts such as *humans in the loop* look to using humans to fill in what AI can't do. You need to think in terms of collaboration and integration to get the best out of both human and machine.
Literacy and Education	Renewed literacy and education are required for all to understand how AI and its impact will be different. Make this meaningful for your stakeholders. I have something for you in Chapter 7.
Proof of Concept	PoCs are key learning by experimentation tools. Know their limits. What works in a sandbox may not work in the wild. Build tolerances for short-term tradeoffs to avoid high abandonment rates.
AI Acceptance	There is a high level of acceptance of popular, consumer-facing generative AI. Evidence shows increasing reticence toward more sophisticated forms of AI, so this shift needs to be managed carefully.
	Nature of Work Factors
Devaluation of Work	The human condition seeks meaningful connections with others and through their work. Devaluing the work through AI devalues the human. What kind of organization are you building?
Human Capability	Humans need to be upskilled for new AI capabilities – but they also provide invaluable input on how you can build better AI and AI systems. Partner with collaborators at all levels of deployment.
H-M Teamwork	All chapters so far have spoken to the complexity of human–machine collaboration and entanglements. This is your opportunity to reimagine your business by reframing old ideas.

failure of organizations to realize the potential of AI technologies. An issue that tends to be denied or overlooked by tech companies or even blamed on human and leadership shortcomings as being the source of the problem. It is clear that organizations need to navigate a complex set of heterogeneous factors to enable AI adoption and value creation. Therefore, what is deemed as the "low" AI adoption rates in industry media and the low returns on investment that appear in extant literature may also be partly explained as an outcome of the understated complexity of the operating environment and the wide range of thematic issues that have been identified in our study.

The **significance of external factors** in the macro environment is having a much more significant effect on organizational decision-making than industry cares to admit. From this, we can surmise that activities such as strategic foresight exercises that anticipate a range of potential future trends will be a valuable means to develop strategic fitness in organizations (Kohler, 2021; Gavetti et al., 2012). A more detailed understanding of macro external factors that need to be monitored and contingencies developed is required to help support organizations in developing a better sense of an uncertain future that's driven by the developments in AI.

At a meta level, researchers and practitioners need to **theorize about the phenomenon of AI** beyond it being a traditional technological tool, toward the consideration that AI may in fact be an *economic actor* that has made a complex world and organizational decision-making even more complex (Menz et al., 2021; Wagner, 2020). Multidisciplinary approaches are therefore critical for understanding the complex phenomenon of AI in information systems research and practice (Berente et al., 2021; Dwivedi et al., 2021) and, above all, provide a holistic foundation of understanding the nature of entangled systems without being siloed into the functional silos of academia, business, or government.

CONCLUSIONS

Organizations are currently operating in a time of economic, technical, and social transition that is rife with conflicting information and rapid change, which is framing their decisions to adopt AI technologies. Decision behaviors identified by our experts in this study indicate that organizations are practicing elements of sufficing but not optimizing, making short-term reactionary decisions, and uncertainty avoidance, but are also positively engaged in continuous organizational learning about AI technologies.

However, this behavior can also be seen as a legitimate response to a technological landscape characterized by hype and instability, mixed AI performance results, and critical long-term consequences of AI adoption that need to be negotiated. It is tempting to view these factors as a limitation of current organizational leadership; however, they can also be explained as measured responses in an environment that is becoming increasingly destabilizing and unpredictable despite the expansive potential opportunities for value creation. This places the caliber of strategic decision-making and the skillful enablement of AI technologies as the key differentiators in organizational performance and competitive advantage rather than the AI technology itself.

ACKNOWLEDGMENT

The research undertaken in this chapter has received funding from the European Union's Horizon 2020 research and innovation program under Marie Sklodowska-Curie Grant No 101023024 for *Augmented Humans*.

REFERENCES

Argote, L., and Greve, H. R. (2007). "A Behavioral Theory of the Firm" - 40 years and counting: Introduction and impact. *Organization Science*, *18*(3), 337–349.

Berente, N., Gu, B., Recker, J., and Santhanam, R. (2021). Managing Artificial Intelligence. *MIS Quarterly*, *45*(3) 1433–1450.

Collins, C., Dennehy, D., Conboy, K., and Mikalef, P. (2021). Artificial intelligence in information systems research: A systematic literature review and research agenda. *International Journal of Information Management*, *60*. https://doi.org/10.1016/j.ijinfomgt.2021.102383

Creswell, J. W. and Creswell, J. D. (2018). *Research Design: Qualitative, Quantitative, and Mixed Methods Approaches*. Sage.

Cyert, R. M., and March, J. G. (1963). A behavioral theory of the firm. *Englewood Cliffs, NJ*, *2*(4), 169–187.

Dong, J. Q., Karhade, P., Rai, A., and Xu, S. X. (2013). Dynamic adjustment of information technology, corporate governance, and firm profitability. *Theory, Journal of Management Information Systems*, *38*(1), 29–58.

Dwivedi, Y. K., Hughes, L., Ismagilova, E., Aarts, G., Coombs, C., Crick, T., Duan, Y., Dwivedi, R., … Williams, M. D. (2021). Artificial Intelligence: Multidisciplinary perspectives on emerging challenges, opportunities, and agenda for research, practice and policy. *International Journal of Information Management*, *57*. 101994.

Faraj, S., and Leonardi, P. M. (2022). Strategic organization in the digital age: Rethinking the concept of technology. *Strategic Organization*, *20*(4), 771–785.

Fügener, A., Grahl, J., Gupta, A., and Ketter, W. (2021). Will humans-in-the-loop become borgs? Merits and pitfalls of working with AI. *MIS Quarterly: Management Information Systems*, *45*(3), 1527–1556.

Gavetti, G., Greve, H., Levinthal, D., and Ocasio, W., (2012). The behavioral theory of the firm: Assessment and prospects, *The Academy of Management Annals*, *6*(1), 1–40.

Haefner, N., Wincent, J., Parida, V., and Gassmann, O. (2021). Artificial intelligence and innovation management: A review, framework, and research agenda. *Technological Forecasting and Social Change*, *162*, 120392.

Kohler, K. (2021). Strategic foresight: Knowledge, tools, and methods for the future. *CSS Risk and Resilience Reports*. https://doi.org/10.3929/ethz-b-000505468

Lewellyn, K., and Bao, S., (2015). R&D investment in the global paper products industry: A behavioral theory of the firm and national culture perspective, *Journal of International Management*, *21*(1), 1–17.

Lutz, C., Schöttler, M., and Hoffmann, C. P. (2019). The privacy implications of social robots: Scoping review and expert interviews. *Mobile Media and Communication*, *7*(3), 412–434.

Mahoney, J. T. (2004). *Economic Foundations of Strategy*. Sage Publications.

Menz, M., Kunisch, S., Birkinshaw, J., Collis, D. J. (2021). Corporate strategy and the theory of the firm in the digital age. *Journal of Management Studies*, *58*(7), 1695–1720.

Metcalf, L., Askay, D. A., and Rosenberg, L. B. (2019). Keeping humans in the loop: Pooling knowledge through artificial swarm intelligence to improve business decision making. *California Management Review*, *61*(4), 84–109.

Meuser, M., and Nagel, U. (2009). The expert interview and changes in knowledge production. *Interviewing Experts*, Springer 17–42.

Mikalef, P., and Gupta, M. (2021). Artificial intelligence capability: Conceptualization, measurement calibration, and empirical study on its impact on organizational creativity and firm performance. *Information and Management*, *58*(3), 103434

Pumplun, L., Tauchert, C., and Heidt, M. (2019). A New Organizational Chassis for Artificial Intelligence – Exploring Organizational Readiness Factors. *European Conference on Information Systems*.

Raftopoulos, M., and Hamari, J., (2023). Human-AI collaboration in organizations: A literature review on enabling value creation. *ECIS 2023 Research Papers*.

Seeber, I., Bittner, E., Briggs, R. O., de Vreede, T., de Vreede, G. J., Elkins, A., Maier, R., Merz, A. B., Oeste-Reiß, S., Randrup, N., Schwabe, G., and Söllner, M. (2020). Machines as teammates: A research agenda on AI in team collaboration. *Information and Management*, *57*(2).

Shollo, A., Hopf, K., Thiess, T., and Müller, O. (2022). Shifting ML value creation mechanisms: A process model of ML value creation. *The Journal of Strategic Information Systems*, *31*(3), 101734.

Sohn, K., and Kwon, O. (2020). Technology acceptance theories and factors influencing artificial Intelligence-based products. *Telematics and Informatics*, *47*, 101324.

Strauss, A. L. (1987). *Qualitative Analysis for Social Scientists*. Cambridge University Press.

Surdu, I., Greve, H., and Benito, G., (2021). Back to basics: Behavioral theory and internationalization, *Journal of International Business Studies*, *52*, 1047–1068.

Teece, D. J. (2007). Explicating dynamic capabilities: The nature and microfoundations of (sustainable) enterprise performance. *Strategic management journal*, *28*(13).

Waardenburg, L., and Huysman, M. (2022). From coexistence to co-creation: Blurring boundaries in the age of AI. *Information and Organization*, *32*(4), 100432.

Wagner, D. N. (2020). The nature of the Artificially Intelligent Firm – An economic investigation into changes that AI brings to the firm. *Telecommunications Policy*, *44*(6), 101954.

Williams, M., and Moser, T. (2019). The art of coding and thematic exploration in qualitative research. *International Management Review*, *15*(1), 45–55.

Yun, J. J., Won, D., Park, K., Jeong, E., and Zhao, X. (2019). The role of a business model in market growth: The difference between the converted industry and the emerging industry. *Technological Forecasting and Social Change*, *146*, 534–562.

CHAPTER 6

Threat Avoidance or Opportunity Chasing?

In life, unlike chess, the game continues after checkmate.

—ISAAC ASIMOV

INTRODUCTION

As discussed in previous chapters, artificial intelligence is widely claimed to be driving the advancement of next-generation information systems that will facilitate business performance improvement and innovation (Duan et al. 2019; Dwivedi et al. 2021; Berente et al. 2021). Yet we have a limited understanding of how organizations can translate AI potential into creating business value, with recent studies suggesting that organizations are falling short in realizing business value from AI (Shollo et al., 2022; Pumplun et al., 2019), and at best it was found to have shown inconsistent or mixed results (Langer and Landers, 2021; Cubric, 2020). This chapter explores the possibility that this underperformance may be because we need a deeper understanding of the productive relationships between human systems and machines.

The Technology Acceptance Model (Davis, 1993) and the Unified Theory of Acceptance and Use of Technology (UTAUT) (Venkatesh et al., 2003) are extensively used in existing technology and information systems literature to explain how people accept and adopt new technologies. However, these theories have been in existence for some time, and while they have had success in explaining the adoption of digital technologies, researchers have found that there are limitations inherent in these theories in explaining and predicting the behavioral intentions of users to adopt AI (Gansser and Reich, 2021; Cao et al., 2021). Put simply, traditional theories of technology adoption may not entirely explain the challenges we are currently facing with artificial intelligence.

DOI: 10.1201/9781003616566-9

Given the complexities of AI technologies, acceptance issues go beyond the utility of the technology into complex psycho-social factors that affect human–machine performance. A few of these factors that are commonly cited in the extensive research in this field are as follows:

- Fear of technology (Cabrera-Sánchez et al., 2021).
- AI Anxiety (Oh et al., 2017).
- Algorithm aversion (Dietvorst et al., 2015).
- Mistrust of the technology (Ishowo-Oloko et al., 2019).
- Willful lack of co-operation (Kiesler et al., 1996).

Upon deeper investigation of the extant literature on AI adoption at the individual level, the research emanating under *Augmented Humans* proposes that it's become necessary to extend our understanding of AI technology adoption by considering three-level hierarchy of AI adoption that distinguishes between passive utilitarian *acceptance of AI* (Langer and Landers, 2021) to *active collaboration* (Seeber et al., 2020) and AI *technology co-creation* (Waardenburg and Huysman, 2022).

Not all AIs are the same, as we established in Chapters 1 and 2. Therefore, we need to look deeper into the unique considerations in how humans react to each of these different technologies. For example, a doctor trusting an AI medical imaging diagnostic has a *very different technology acceptance profile* compared to a student trusting the sources cited by ChatGPT for their history essay. Both AI technologies here are subject to hallucination and inaccuracies, but the costs and consequences of both are very different.

The reduced expectation of an all-inclusive technology acceptance theory has largely evolved out of the increasing emergence and maturity of cognitive or smart AI technologies (Ienca, 2019). Given the unique attributes of each of these types of intelligent technologies in the AI technology stack, as discussed in Chapter 1, they are naturally perceived differently by system users. For example, a citizen will embrace an AI that will help them do their job better, but the same citizen will be suspicious of the AI that may eventually take their job or reduce meaningful work. It's now become important to investigate the different groupings of AI separately and comparatively, rather than view AI adoption as a monolithic or homogenous construct.

Two informative theories will be used to frame the research findings at the core of this chapter. **Technology Threat Avoidance Theory (TTAT)** maintains that citizens' "technology adoption" behavior compared to "technology avoidance" behavior is qualitatively different (Liang and Xue, 2009). Where individuals perceive a technology threat, they are engaged in either actively or passively avoiding the perceived threat. This model is largely a legacy of behavioralist theories of human behavior. **Coping Model of User Adoption (CMUA)**, developed by Beaudry and Pinsonneault (2005), explains the cognitive, emotional, and behavioral responses of individuals in coping with significant technology events in their work environment. This model has largely been derived from cognitive theories of human behavior. Both of these important models are discussed in more detail in the next section.

This chapter addresses two key challenges faced by organization leaders in implementing and enabling AI technologies at the individual level:

- What individual factors explain the likelihood of AI acceptance, AI collaboration, and AI co-creation in the workplace?
- What unique factors shape a positive attitude toward the adoption of more sophisticated technologies such as AI collaboration and co-creation?

The purpose of this chapter is primarily to build a deeper understanding of the adoption of AI technology at the individual level to enable organizations and developers to design human-centric AI systems, particularly in more complex areas of human–machine collaboration and AI technology co-design. Furthermore, this work can inform citizens to gain a deeper understanding of their personal frames and mindsets that can shape their approach to improving personal learning and workplace self-efficacy strategies in the adoption and management of AI technologies.

My intention for this chapter is to clarify that it is not sufficient to say "use AI or else" to those who are reticent; in fact, it's terribly naive. You need to get to the crux of the issues to develop a more harmonious and productive workforce that will set up your AI strategy in an environment where it is more likely to succeed.

THE HUMAN-AI RELATIONSHIP AT THE ORGANIZATIONAL LEVEL

As mentioned in the introduction to this chapter, there are three primary conceptual dimensions of AI adoption that are prevalent in research literature. These are: acceptance, collaboration, and co-creation, each representing increasing levels of complexity in terms of human engagement and interaction with artificial intelligence.

Each dimension is characterized by unique human attributes, mindsets, and cognitive that drive the human–machine relationship. An understanding of these unique human attributes in each of the three dimensions may help leaders to (a) accurately predict human behaviors in relation to the introduction of AI in the workplace (Kosinski et al., 2013; Sohn et al., 2025), and (b) design more tailored socio-technical systems that effectively enable productive and trustworthy human–machine relationships (Fügener et al., 2021; Seeber et al., 2020). We offer the following detailed definitions of the three conceptual dimensions of AI adoption that are prevalent in the literature.

AI Acceptance

This refers to the passive use of AI solutions or technologies to improve existing processes or outcomes, where users may not have a direct role in shaping the AI's functionality and only use it as a tool or resource in their job function. Until recently, acceptance of basic AI technologies has been the primary focus of AI research in the information systems domain as it has largely risen out of the early AI implementations that were focused on simpler AI automation technologies (Kaber and Endsley, 2004; Jarrahi, 2018; Dellermann et al., 2019). Therefore, findings and theories based on these base-level technologies will have limited explanatory power when it comes to the more complex forms of AI, which can perform more advanced functions.

For example, **AI in air traffic control** includes automating routine tasks such as AI-driven predictive analytics, which can forecast traffic patterns, weather conditions, and potential conflicts. This enables human air traffic controllers to make more informed decisions and proactively manage traffic flows (Falk, 2024). A case in point is **Traffic Prediction and Management.** This is a critical area of air traffic control where AI helps controllers make proactive decisions by analyzing large amounts of flight data. The most important points of this data include predicting air traffic patterns, optimizing flight routes, and reducing congestion. Combined, this leads to fewer delays and increased safety. Another AI tool is **Weather Forecasting**. Applying AI models to anticipate weather conditions enables controllers to route flights more effectively and minimize situations where bad weather affects air travel (Vaughn College, 2025). At a base level, these AI-enabled technologies help make the air traffic controllers work more effectively and are thus wholeheartedly embraced.

AI Collaboration

AI collaboration involves an interactive relationship between humans and AI, where humans proactively work alongside AI systems in partnership to achieve specific goals. Humans provide input, guidance, and feedback to AI, and AI, in turn, assists and augments human decision-making and tasks (Carroll et al. 2019; Stowers et al. 2021). Collaboration is characterized by interactive communication and cooperation between networked actors that rely on a common vision, strategy, common identity, and joint obligations (Camarinha-Matos and Afsarmanesh, 2008; Smorodinskaya et al., 2017). In most of these human–AI collaborations, AI has replaced some of the traditional roles in any given functions or introduced a new area of task or responsibility. This represents the next level of AI acceptance that requires human acknowledgment of AI as a team member and collaborator that entails a higher skills and capability base for individuals. This is often seen as a requirement of human–machine working relationships in complex and ambiguous operating environments (Hyland-Wood et al., 2019; Fügener et al., 2021), which goes beyond the simpler tasks and functions that can be codified and automated.

Following on with the air traffic control example, AI systems are designed to serve as collaborative tools that provide human air traffic controllers with insights and support. AI systems are designed so that humans retain ultimate authority over decisions; AI augments rather than replaces humans in this workflow. That said, many controller jobs have been reduced to the work being carried out by AI-enabled technologies. However, despite the increasing capabilities of digital systems, air traffic controllers are considered to bring indispensable skills such as judgment, flexibility, and the ability to handle unexpected situations that automated systems currently cannot replicate (Falk, 2024).

An example of one of the more sophisticated collaborative technologies here is **Voice Recognition and Assistance**. This advanced AI-driven voice recognition system helps reduce the controller's functional workload by transcribing and understanding pilot-controller communication. This maximizes efficiency in the tower since automating routine tasks like this allows controllers to focus on more critical matters. Another AI tool is **Automated Conflict Detection.** This system utilizes AI to alert controllers of potential conflicts, while also suggesting maneuvers to prevent collisions by continuously monitoring aircraft positions (Vaughn College, 2025).

AI Co-creation

AI co-creation takes collaboration a step further, where stakeholders actively participate in designing, developing, or evolving AI systems (Waardenburg and Huysman, 2022; Wagner, 2020). This can involve interdisciplinary teams working together to build AI models, customize algorithms, or shape AI solutions according to specific needs. It's a deeper and more involved form of partnership. The concept of co-creation has been around for some time in strategy literature (Ranjan and Read, 2016; Prahalad and Ramaswamy, 2000) and is now an emergent field in AI development. It's been proposed as a solution to overcome limitations in the transparency and explainability of AI algorithms, interfaces, interactions, and recommendations, and to account for the increased blurring of the boundaries between AI use and its development (Waardenburg and Huysman, 2022; Wagner, 2020). The proposition is that if stakeholders were more involved in the design and development process, then current limitations in AI development and performance would be overcome.

There are several different approaches and definitions for co-creation. This study focuses on co-creation as a specific form of collaboration, adapted from Pulkkinen and Hautamaki (2019) and Liwång (2022), where activities and resources of organizations are systematically integrated to produce results that would not have been possible without a joint approach. The view of co-creation in this chapter is that cooperation between stakeholders creates a shared responsibility for system development, promotes fruitful dialog on central capability aspects and challenges, and promotes the exchange of results from research. For example, consider a case study by Andersson (2018) on the development of two military concept development projects, a combat vehicle and a naval vessel, with the close co-operation between demonstrators, research, government agencies, and industry organizations. Using the air traffic control example, many studies have been conducted on fully automating air traffic control with AI. However, given the unpredictable and complex nature of the work, it is unlikely that autonomous systems will replace the air traffic control function, but they will remain as an ever-improving, important, and intelligent teammate (Kerstholt et al., 2018).

In the following sections, we build a case for how and why citizens respond differently to increasingly sophisticated AI and what this means for organizational leaders – and you as a citizen.

DEEP DIVE INTO THREAT AVOIDANCE AND OPPORTUNITY CHASING

Most theories that help us frame and understand citizen adoption of technology present us with dichotomies, such as avoiding threat or chasing an opportunity. The reality is that the human response to technology is more nuanced and will only respond in this way if the technical system has been designed to force an either/or decision from citizens. This is a critically important point to keep in mind as we delve into the research presented below.

The Influence of Behavioralism and Persuasive Design

The foundational beliefs of traditional human motivation theories are that people seek pleasure and avoid pain. This has been the basis of behavioralist theories that go back to Freud, Pavlov, Skinner, and many others (Braat et al., 2020). These behavioralist theories have their logical foundations in biological systems, which were heavily influenced by research in laboratory animals (Fullana et al., 2020). The fundamental premise is that all human behaviors are acquired through conditioning, which is a process of reinforcement and punishment. This is essentially a reductionist view of humanity.

Behaviorist theories became popular in Silicon Valley in the 1990s popularized by the seminal work undertaken at Stanford University on persuasive design (Fogg, 2002) and enabled by the rise of the internet, computing, and mass data collection. The fundamental idea was that computers can be used to influence citizens by persuading them to change their attitudes, motivations, compliance, and behavior (Nass et al., 1996; Fogg and Hreha, 2012). Despite the moral outrage at the time, and evidence that it can be used unethically, persuasive design took hold due to its ability to facilitate persuasion that enabled businesses to improve their profits and even promote positive social goals. This occurred around the same time when web-based businesses grew exponentially, as did the need to convince "users" to press those buttons or click those links or keep playing those digital games.

For example, the significant growth in the games industry, particularly for massive multiplayer online role-playing games (MMORPGs) started around this time, like Warcraft in 1994, Ever Quest in 1999, and World of Warcraft in 2004. This was made possible through significant advancements in data harvesting, game AI, user experience (UX), and user interface (UI) design. Design principles of behavioralist or persuasive design, such as operant conditioning, reward systems, progression schedules, and positive reinforcement, enabled massive market popularity and the growth of a multi-billion-dollar industry.

More recently, persuasive design has been adopted into the business lexicon as the less emotionally charged term, *behavioral economics*. The appeal of persuasive design or behavioral economics to technologists, and to the clients who purchased their systems, is that with the assistance of big data, data analytics, and mathematical models, technology systems can be designed to frame consumer choices to deliberately influence and nudge optimal purchase outcomes, often under an illusion of choice. This technological nudging extended to the development of learning software, which was critiqued as "learnification" (Knox et al., 2019) and in consumer markets and business processes as "gamification."

While there are some positive benefits to "nudge" or motivate citizens toward certain behaviors (for example, in healthcare), often dark design patterns are used to subliminally influence citizens toward optimizing company profit over their welfare. For example, the most devastating outcomes of algorithmically driven behavioral design have been the shaping, influencing, and nudging that take place in AI-enabled social media applications to influence public opinion and politics (Penney, 2017).

Remember, AI is not neutral.

I remember when I signed up to attend a three-day intensive course on persuasive design for digital products designed for technology executives in San Francisco over a decade ago. The required reading was a prescribed book on dog training. I read it as if looking for clues to a puzzle, but no, it was just a book on dog training full of rewards, punishments, and withholding tactics. When I asked why this book was in the first 10 minutes of the course, he said quite bluntly that **training humans is the same as training dogs.** The mental model and worldview of this statement were quite clear. When I asked, rather incredulously, what about drive for learning, self-actualization, connection to community, and purpose? He just sighed and said, "Oh, you're one of those…"

Technology is not neutral. It never has been or ever will.

FOUNDATIONAL THEORIES FOR THIS CHAPTER

We take a deep dive into technology threat avoidance theory (TTAT) and the Coping Model of User Adaptation (CPUA), given their influence in shaping modern management practices with regard to technology and information systems. The central tenet of the TTAT for citizens in the workplace is that technology adoption and technology avoidance are qualitatively different behaviors (Liang and Xue, 2009). Where users perceive a new technology as a threat, they view it as malicious, and this activates different emotional and neurological responses than do opportunities. A **malicious technology** is defined as a system perceived by users to be "repulsive" and to cause negative outcomes for them; citizens will therefore avoid it. A **virtuous technology** is perceived by users to be attractive as it creates positive outcomes through its use; citizens would therefore be happy to adopt it. When a citizen views a technology as malicious or a threat, they engage in either (a) actively avoiding the threat by engaging in *safeguarding measures* or (b) passively avoiding the threat by taking *emotion-focused coping behaviors*.

According to Liang and Xue (2009), human perceptions of whether a technology is considered "malicious" or "virtuous" are based on either the *designer's intention* or the *perception of the user*. In terms of *design intention*, a deep fake video created to spread misinformation is clearly viewed as malicious. In terms of *user perception*, GPT models such as Perplexity, Claude, and ChatGPT are considered virtuous by students and knowledge workers as they can undertake research and writing tasks in shorter periods of time than they have in the past. Be mindful of this either/or dichotomy, as later we will see that there was never a concern in these theories that the technology was at "fault" but just a weakness in the human.

Key challenges, according to TTAT, arise where a technology has been designed to be virtuous but is perceived to be malicious. This arises out of a citizen's contextual situation or through conflicts of interest and will therefore engage in threat avoidance. In this category, we can use the example of text-to-image LLMs such as DALL-E or Midjourney. Developers sincerely believed they were creating a virtuous AI technology to help democratize the art-making process. However, a sizeable cohort of the artistic community believes that this technology carries the characteristics of a malicious technology for the harm it does to artists. For example, they consider these LLMs as a threat as their artwork has been stolen without payment or recognition to train AI models, which in turn takes over their jobs and businesses.

Coping Model of User Adaptation (CMUA) developed by Beaudry and Pinsonneault (2005) maintains that users adapt to a major technology event such as the introduction of AI in the workplace by employing a wide range of responses to restore emotional stability, modify tasks, adapt the technology, or even resist it. A key tenet of CMUA is that how people cope with a significant technological event in their workplace is largely determined by the resources that are available to them, and this includes financial, material, physical, psychological, cognitive, and social. All these factors play a significant role in workplace acceptance of AI technologies, which have implications for business outcomes. Unless these contextual aspects are managed, leaders face challenges in implementing sophisticated AI in the workplace. As illustrated in Figure 6.1, there are three key elements to understanding how citizens cope when confronted by a new technology.

The model begins with the *initial element* of "technology perception" or how the citizen perceives the AI that is being introduced, as either malicious or virtuous. This is an emotional or neurological response as the brain's synapses instantly respond. The *second element* requires a logical processing in the brain and depends on the citizen's "personal situation" in terms of how much personal control or power they have over how and where the technology is introduced; this is either high or low levels of control. The *third element* is when the brain kicks into response mode; the actions or responses range from self-preservation behavior for citizens with low levels of control or power to maximizing personal benefit for those citizens with higher levels of control or power. For example, consider the following scenarios where AI-enabled robots are introduced by an automobile manufacturer:

- **Threat perception**: A citizen on the production line of the factory (which has banned unions and does not offer staff retraining to factory workers) feels they have low levels of personal control or power. This citizen will consider the technology malicious and will engage in self-preservation behavior against the AI threat perception. CMUA theory suggests that this citizen, *depending on their levels of personal power and resources*, will attempt to either:

  - **Modify their tasks.** Citizens may work with their union and employer to alter their roles and responsibilities to accommodate the work to be done by the robot.

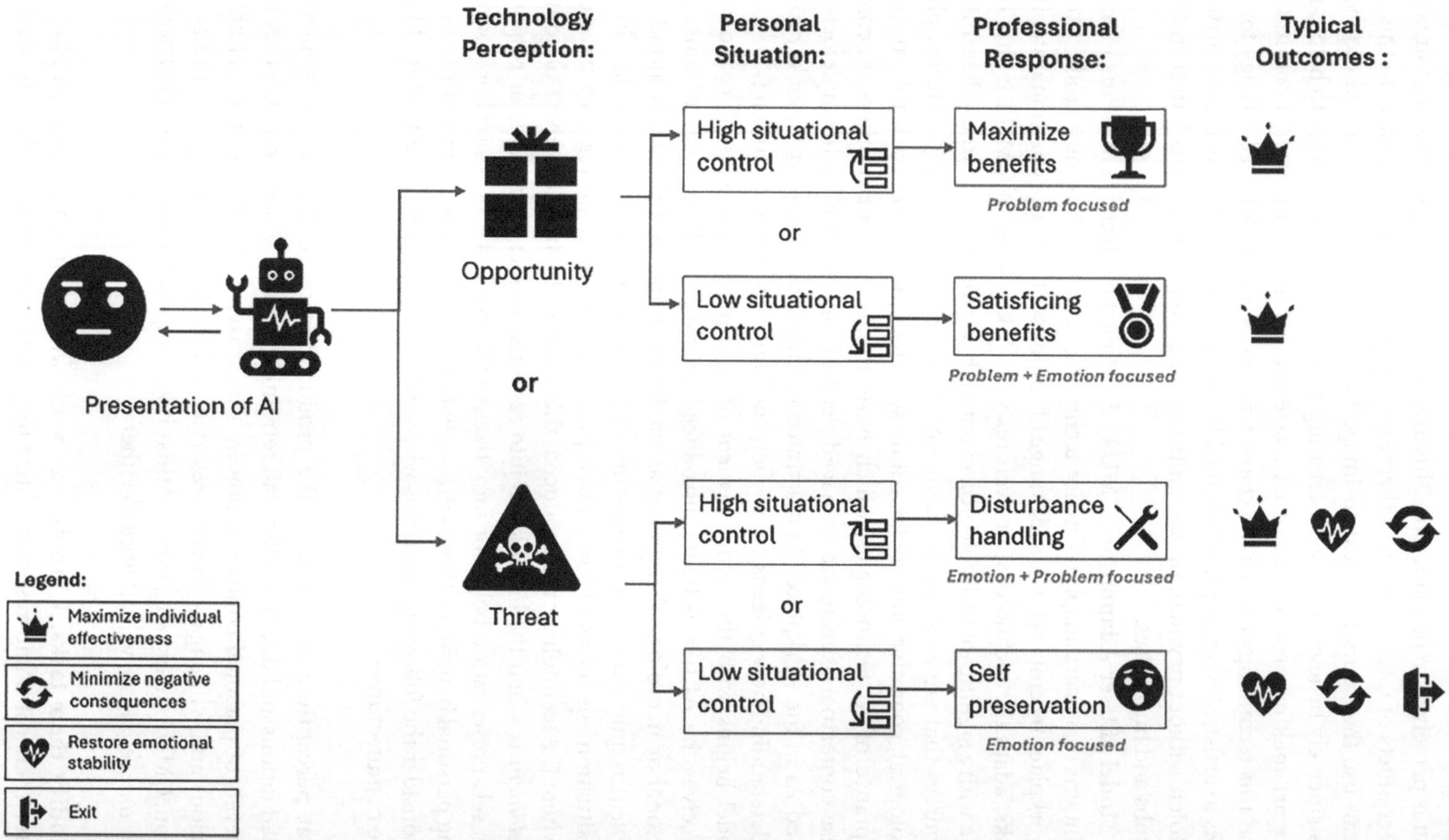

FIGURE 6.1 Coping model of user adaption decision tree.

Source: Adapted from Beaudry and Pinsonneault (2005) by the author.

    - **Adapt the technology**. Look to retrain themselves to work productively alongside the robots or even suggest how the robot can be modified or better integrated to more effectively, primarily to protect their jobs.
    - **Resist**. The citizen may refuse to work with robots, which will result in an exit from their position.
- **Opportunity perception**: A citizen who works as a software engineer in this plant (who has generous training benefits and company share options) feels they have high levels of personal control as they feel that they will gain meaningful work in working with developers to maintain these robots. This citizen will consider the technology as an opportunity and engage in benefit-maximizing behavior.

CMUA and TTAT both provide an important theoretical lens to help us place AI adoption and adaptation in perspective, given the widely reported phenomenon of fear and concern about the impact of AI technologies on job losses and loss of autonomy and opportunity at work (Mirbabaie et al., 2021; Gansser and Reich, 2021). It is clear from the research that the incidence of technology threat avoidance behavior will accelerate as AI technologies become more sophisticated, as depicted in our model of the three levels of adoption – acceptance, collaboration, and co-creation.

Perceptions of opportunity or threat are formed by the personal situation of citizens. A citizen's perception of a technology threat influences their adoption behavior. Threat perceptions are determined by the perceived probability of the threat's occurrence and the perceived severity of the threat's negative consequences. It is also well-regarded in other research examining AI technologies, such as Cao et al. (2021), Duan et al. (2019), Dwivedi et al. (2021), O'Neil (2018) and Ransbotham et al. (2018).

This is also supported by other theoretical perspectives, such as **social identity theory** (Hogg, 2016), which identifies that human perception of self is significantly derived from work roles, and a potential destabilization of that may affect human behaviors toward AI technology.

In the following sections of this chapter, our results show decreasing support for increasing levels of sophistication of AI technologies. Our survey respondents report increasing perceptions of threat and vulnerability, and intentions to engage in increasing threat avoidance behavior at higher levels of AI technology sophistication.

BEHAVIORAL INTENTION TO ADOPT INCREASINGLY SOPHISTICATED AI

The original research for this work (Raftopoulos, 2025) surveyed 305 professionals in Europe, and then this research was extended to include 309 professionals from the USA and another 316 from India. Survey participants were recruited from the *prolific.com* platform, screened for professionals residing in either Europe, USA or India with full-time employment and who use a high amount of technology at work. This was a purposive sample (Etikan et al., 2016) in terms of selecting candidates who would most likely be open to technology collaboration and co-creation, so we could investigate the upper limits of perceptions toward adoption of sophisticated AI technologies. This was a key factor in this study, as it was on professionals *already comfortable* with AI and technology in general in three distinct geographies.

The results of the initial study of European professionals showed strong results in terms of increasing reluctance to accept increasing levels of AI sophistication, so we replicated the study in the USA and India to compare the results. We found that similar trendlines and qualitative factors emerged in all three segments, which gives us confidence that the factors presented in this chapter are universal to AI adoption.

The measures of the behavioral intentions on the willingness to adopt AI technology at increasing levels of sophistication were based on the work of Araujo et al. (2020) and Adell (2010). We theorized that the most effective way to measure these variables is to present different scenarios to survey participants on AI adoption, collaboration, and co-creation, with each depicting increasing levels of complexity with human–AI interaction. For example, Adell (2010) presented scenario-based questions by asking respondents to imagine a stated situation in the adoption of intelligent transport systems, and Araujo et al. (2020) on perceptions on algorithmic management.

We based our scenarios on a brief outline and allowed respondents to derive meaning from each statement. Given that the AI domain is constantly changing and is dominated by fragmented definitions, interpretations, and siloed technologies, we didn't pursue the need to determine respondents' understanding of the technical meanings of each level due to the lack of common industry agreement and standards (Cubric 2020; Collins et al., 2021).

Furthermore, our rationale was that this survey was not a test of technical knowledge, but one of identifying the psycho-social and threat and opportunity responses of respondents to the rise of AI technology capability. We came to this position by forming and consulting with a panel of five academic and AI practitioner experts that we established to check for the adequacy of our definitions and refine the questions. After several reviews and iterations, we agreed that this approach would meet our stated research objectives. We also ran a pilot survey with 50 respondents, and we were satisfied with how respondents interpreted and answered the survey. The three scenario-based questions used in the final survey are as follows:

- **AI Acceptance scenario (AIA):** "Imagine your organization is introducing a basic AI technology that would make some of your work tasks easier and more effective."
- **AI Collaboration scenario (AIC):** "Imagine your organization is introducing a sophisticated AI technology that performs half of your work tasks, and you would need to team or collaborate with it to do your work effectively."
- **AI Co-creation scenario (AICC):** "Imagine your organization is planning to develop a highly sophisticated AI technology in your area of expertise and they have asked you to allocate dedicated time over the next 6-12 months to work with the developers on its design, training, and implementation."

For each scenario, two questions with a five-point Likert scale were asked: (1) Whether they would be happy to work with the AI and (2) an open-ended question asking for an explanation of their reasoning for their answers to each scenario.

We ran comparative tests to examine the mean difference of the latent constructs, which included an independent sample T-test for gender and one-way ANOVA tests for variables of age and qualification. The results of the independent sample t-test indicated that there are no significant statistical differences in the mean values of the constructs between males, females, and non-binary. The results of the one-way ANOVA indicated that there are no significant statistical differences in the mean values of the constructs between groups of age and levels of educational qualifications.

A broad range of AI technologies and use cases were reported by respondents. Most of the core functional areas where AI technologies were implemented were in information technology (16% of total respondents), information systems (13%), marketing and sales (18%), human resources (9%), and finance (9%). In terms of the key functional roles performed by AI technologies, they concentrated in the areas of customer service (21%), business analytics (18%), forecasting and prediction (17%), and optimization and automation (16%).

The AI technology stack included a range of different technologies for each application, for example, combining machine learning, computer vision, and virtual assistants. In answering the technology stack question, over half of respondents mentioned (without prompting) the use of the top-tier AI technology providers in the development of their AI applications, such as Oracle, SAP, IBM, Accenture, and AWS, as well as other smaller solutions providers.

Less than 10% of respondents mentioned the use of popular generative AI technologies or tools in their work. This may be because we had screened for professionals working with high levels of technology in large organizations; therefore, these respondents may be focused on more significant enterprise-level AI technology investments such as machine learning, data analytics, optimization, forecasting, prediction, and automation.

THE THREE LEVELS OF AI ADOPTION

In the first study, the behavioral intention of professionals to accept, collaborate, or co-create artificial intelligence steadily declines at increased levels of technological sophistication. In Europe, positive attitudes toward the adoption of AI (those who selected Strongly Agree or Agree) started at 86% for scenario 1 for acceptance of basic AI, then dropped to 63% for scenario 2 on collaborative AI, and down to 59% for scenario 3 for co-creating AI (Raftopoulos, 2025). Intrigued by these results, we ran the same survey in the USA and in India for comparison to investigate whether this trend is similar to the perceptions in other geographies. The results showed similar trendlines of declining support of increasingly sophisticated AI for both USA and India, as depicted in Figure 6.2.

It was interesting to note that for each scenario, there seemed to be a higher rate of acceptance of AI technologies in Europe compared to the USA and India. For example, for adopting basic AI technologies, 86% of Europeans agreed, compared to 79% of Americans and 54% of Indians. We explore the reasons behind the reluctance to adopt

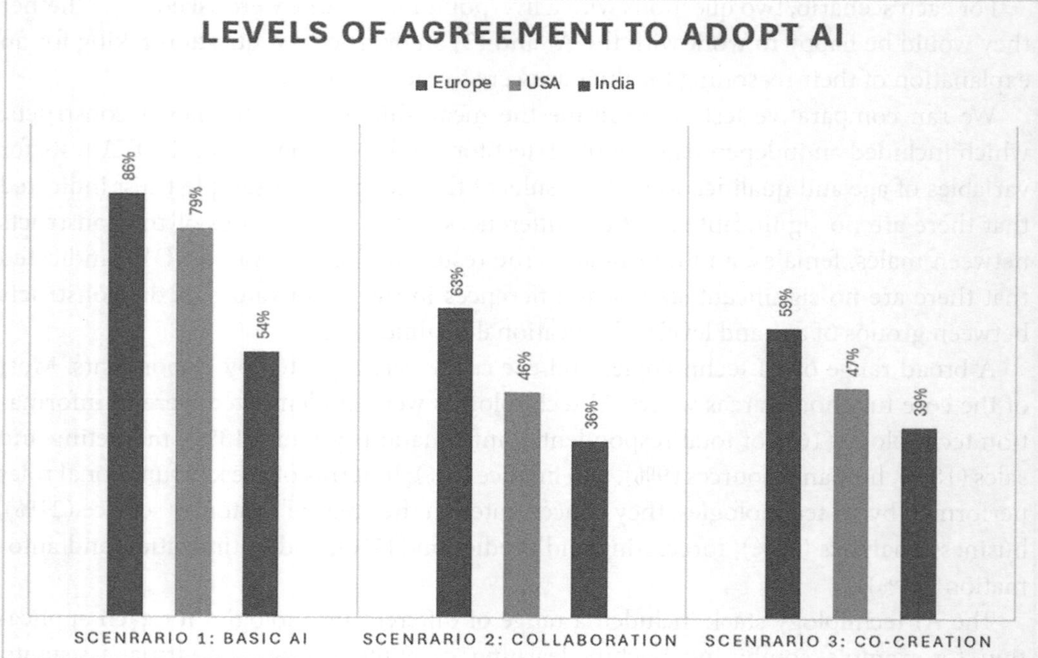

FIGURE 6.2 Levels of agreement to adopt AI.

increasingly sophisticated AI at the individual level in the next section; however, it is unclear why the geographic differences exist in each scenario. Given the results of the qualitative analysis based on fears and concerns in adopting AI, we hypothesize that the geographic differences in the results may be attributed to the lower socio-economic safety net in the USA and India compared to Europe. However, this is yet untested,

Evaluation of Attitudes toward Sophisticated AI

The qualitative responses to the open-ended questions were uploaded into specialized qualitative software *Atlas.ti* and were coded in detail using a codebook we developed for the study. We also ran a comparative analysis utilizing *Atlas.ti's* AI-generated code feature (which was currently still in beta at the time of the analysis). However, even though the software's AI codes were significant in number and generated at speed, we did not find that it provided any material differences or additions to our insights from the data compared to us running the software without their AI coding.

From the data, a total of 223 thematic codes were generated to capture the full range and nuances of the different views and attitudes toward increasingly sophisticated AI at work. We aggregated the 223 codes into three core clusters according to how the respondents answered their likelihood of adopting the AI technology for each scenario:

a) **Positive cluster:** these were those who answered Strongly Agree or Agree in adopting AI.
b) **Neutral cluster:** these were those who answered Neutral.

c) **Negative cluster:** these were those who answered Disagree or Strongly Disagree.

Using a grounded approach, we continued to segment the codes to derive a set of key thematic categories for each cluster. The final set of three clusters and their categories are as follows:

Positive cluster: Five thematic categories were derived from 109 codes as outlined in Table 6.1. It should be noted that respondents who answered Strongly Agree or Agree to the scenario questions only wrote positive responses in the open-ended questions. Interestingly, no negative or downside qualifiers were mentioned in their responses.

Neutral cluster: Seven thematic categories were derived from 65 codes as outlined in Table 6.1. Note that those who answered neutral mentioned many of the positive themes already recorded in the positive cluster, but in addition to these, neutral respondents added a negative statement or qualifier in their responses.

Negative cluster: Seven thematic categories were derived from 49 codes as outlined in Table 6.1. Those who answered Disagree or Strongly Disagree in the scenario

TABLE 6.1 Thematic Clusters and Categories

Thematic Categories and Clusters		Codes Generated	
Positive Cluster: 5 Categories		%	n
1	Making a contribution and future thinking	26.0	28
2	Desire for influence and control	22.6	25
3	Excitement, desire, and challenge	18.5	20
4	Workplace and organizational benefits	17.1	19
5	Professional development, growth, and job security	15.8	17
	Total:	**100**	**109**
Negative Cluster: 7 Categories		%	n
1	Concern for job loss	21.6	11
2	Not interested	17.1	8
3	Not my job	17.0	8
4	Resistance	15.9	8
5	Lack of confidence	11.4	6
6	Emotion, fear, scared	9.0	4
7	Skepticism, AI not ready	8.0	4
	Total:	**100**	**49**
Neutral Cluster: 7 Categories		%	n
1	Implementation issues	25.8	17
2	Concern for job loss	20.7	13
3	Human touch needed	13.8	9
4	AI not ready	12.1	8
5	Disruption to business	12.1	8
6	Guarantee or reward expectation	8.6	6
7	Don't know/unsure/confused	6.9	4
	Total:	**100**	**65**
	Total number of thematic codes:		**223**

questions tended to only write negative or downside statements in their open-ended responses.

While there was some overlap with the negative or qualifier statements made by the neutral cluster (for example, job losses) the responses tended to be unique to this cluster. For example, many neutral respondents focused on implementation challenges, whereas negative respondents did not. Many negative respondents mentioned a lack of confidence, emotion, or outright resistance, whereas the neutral cluster did not.

The thematic clusters derived from our research suggest that there are very distinct positions held by professionals working with AI-enabled technologies. There are key implications for AI technology threat avoidance and coping adaptation unique at each level of AI adoption. First, let us examine each cluster.

Positive cluster: The positive cluster exhibited unique characteristics in terms of its motivations and cognitive frames. As can be seen in Table 6.1, it is notable that motivations are centered on higher-order, personal benefits from adopting increasingly sophisticated AI. For example, 58% of reasons centered on notions of making a personal contribution, desire to be more influential in the organization, and excitement and challenge. A smaller percentage is focused on the economics of more tangible benefits, such as economic benefits and job security, in working with sophisticated AI. Notable as well is that no mention was made of implementation challenges for the organization (which was dominant in the neutral cluster) or for fear of job losses which dominated in the negative cluster.

Quotes by respondents in their own words to illustrate the depth of their convictions are as follows:

- "I currently work on the development of new AI technologies, and it is what I intend to do the rest of my work life. Therefore, dedicating my time to developing an AI technology is the way I want to live."
- "Collaborating with a team on the development and implementation of AI technologies could prove extremely valuable for my professional development."
- "This scenario, while being demanding, would have a very high return, both in terms of productivity and business health, but also in terms of the fact that if I helped design this AI, this would enhance my resume, and my know-how and people would identify me and the AI and even at work it. It would improve my network, and the consideration others have of me."

Implications of these findings are that organizations will need to manage the expectations of this group of employees; otherwise, the positivity may start to wane. These challenges are amplified given that, industry hype aside, it is unclear if AI technologies will provide this level of opportunity. In all likelihood, this group of individuals may be from professions that currently do not feel vulnerable as AI advances. Thought needs to be made as to how this group is managed when new AI technologies emerge, which may challenge their personal situations and professions.

Neutral cluster: The perceptions of the neutral cluster also exhibited unique characteristics in terms of respondent motivations and cognitive frames. While respondents also expressed many of the positive perceptions mentioned in the positive cluster, they also reported parallel negative statements or drawbacks. As can be seen from the thematic categories in Table 6.1 it is notable that this cluster expressed major concerns with implementation challenges that included the need for the human touch in technical systems, AI not being ready to perform more challenging work, and overall disruptions to business that need to be addressed; these implementation challenges took up 51.7% of responses. This was followed by 20.7% being concerned about job losses and 8.6% about expectations for some form of guarantee about their position or reward if they were to work with developers in the co-creation of more sophisticated AI in their field. Interestingly, while the positive cluster was overwhelmingly eager to adopt AI, they did not express concerns about the business challenges of AI implementation, as per the neutral cluster.

Quotes by neutral respondents in their own words to illustrate the depth of the complexity of their attitudes are as follows:

- "I would find it interesting to design, train, and implement the AI technology, so I will be an expert about it. But I am still concerned about how this AI technology will affect the business and the employees in the future."
- "AI is not yet at a level of confidence or capability to be helpful or trustworthy enough in our business."
- "I find AI fascinating so I would love to work on implementing one in a real use-case, but I'd be scared that the AI could replace me one day."
- "Highly sophisticated AI technology could be disruptive and could take too much control of the company business, making us too dependent on the AI technology. This technology could be harmful both for employees and for the employer."

These findings imply that the unique expectations and concerns of the neutral group will need to be actively managed by organizations to avoid a loss of positivity from this group that may even recede into more negativity if the concerns are not adequately addressed. In addition to the positive expectations covered above, managing the negative perceptions of loss of autonomy and job losses, new social contracts will need to be developed commensurate with the alteration of the nature of work and employment brought about by increasingly sophisticated AI.

Organizations need to question what more can be done to ease the impact on employees, and how they can differentiate themselves from other organizations to attract and retain the best talent. Most importantly, consideration needs to be made of the implementation challenges raised by this group. These concerns are consistent with the issues raised in extant literature (Fügener, et al., 2021; Newlands, 2021) and in our other work

(Raftopoulos and Hamari, 2023; Raftopoulos and Hamari, 2024) and in Chapters 1 and 2 of this book, where both solution providers and employees have identified how these technical and implementation challenges have been ignored and have consequently resulted in sub-optimal AI performance.

Negative cluster: The perceptions of the negative cluster were unique compared to the other two. Concerns over job losses were highly rated in this cluster; however, there was a sizeable proportion of disinterest in adopting AI that ranged from no interest to feelings that "it's not my job" to active and passive resistance. There was some emotion also mentioned in terms of a lack of personal and professional confidence for the job of working with increasingly sophisticated AI, to feelings of fear and being scared. A small percentage also expressed skepticism that AI was not ready to take on more advanced work compared to what humans can do.

Quotes of respondents in their own words to better understand the depth of concerns:

- Many short rejection statements were made, such as: "It's not my job." "I'm not interested in this." "I don't feel competent, educated, and qualified for this." "I will sabotage."
- "I will cooperate with my colleagues to develop this technology, but I would have great concerns about my future since AI may replace me. So, I probably would contribute to the development of this technology unwillingly."
- "The difference here is I'm working on the AI tool that will be so sophisticated it's outside of the 'co-worker' range and everyone knows it. Either you work for me or you blow us all away, I don't want AI to be similar to Fred from the next desk, that feels off."

Organizations will need to manage the perceptions and concerns of this group of employees as they engage in what TTAT calls threat avoidance behavior. Otherwise, organizations may see a continued decline in staff motivation and morale exacerbated by increasingly sophisticated AI. In addition to the discussion presented in the positive and neutral clusters above, organizations need to be cognizant of the reality of AI-induced loss of autonomy and job losses, and how this affects the entire organization.

Perhaps more work needs to be done for this cluster of employees that is beyond the scope of an organization – it may require industry effort or at the policy level, which are prevalent notions in extant literature that range from public policy initiatives, curtail the deployment of AI, industry-wide training and development, to universal basic income (Tschang and Almirall, 2021). However, as public policy is slow to respond, this presents an opportunity for business leaders to be more proactive in strengthening their organizations. Leaders also need to remember that these citizens are among their customers, stakeholders, and service providers.

Citizens with "negative" perceptions may already feel vulnerable to job insecurity as AI advances, compared to those in the positive cluster. It is worth noting that, given the deliberate sampling of our respondents, these citizens are also highly skilled, highly educated employees who have a high usage of technology at work. Therefore, it is advisable not to make simple or convenient assumptions about citizen attitudes toward sophisticated AI.

Many of the responses in this cluster are consistent with what CMUA describes as an *emotional response to perceived threats* brought on by technology through avoidance and resistance, usually by individuals who have little or no personal power and resources to cope (Beaudry and Pinsonneault, 2005). As our research shows, such deep fears or even misconceptions may lead to behavior that passively or actively resists AI adoption in the workplace or compromise its effectiveness once the technology is implemented. For example, in their work on AI identity threat, Mirbabaie et al. (2021) identified loss of status position, changes to work, and AI identity as significant predictors influencing AI identity threat to employees with AI experience in the workplace.

IMPLICATIONS FOR MANAGING OPPORTUNITY AND THREAT PERCEPTIONS

These findings imply that organizations looking to implement increasingly sophisticated AI technologies will be challenged with three key factors:

a) Meeting or managing the ambitious expectations of 58% of its workforce, which has positive and enthusiastic attitudes toward what they expect from working with increasingly sophisticated AI. For their optimal performance, their expectations include personal and material gains in:

- Making a contribution and future thinking of the organization.
- Desire for increased influence and control in the organization.
- Desire for more excitement and challenge in working with AI in their jobs.
- Increased workplace and organizational benefits to be earned.
- Increased professional development, growth, and job security.

b) Managing the implementation and technical challenges raised by concerned "neutral" employees who are around 23% of the workforce. These concerns include proactive management of:

- Structured plans for approaching implementation issues.
- Concerns for job loss, loss of autonomy, or meaningful work.
- Incorporate a humanness in company products and services so they don't feel robotic or lifeless.
- Ongoing plan audit to ensure AI maturity and readiness.
- Manage disruption to business and workplace relations and business continuity.

- Additional guarantee or reward expectation for effort negotiated with workers.
- Those who claim that they don't know or are unsure how they feel about sophisticated AI may have mixed feelings or be confused, which dampens motivation.

c) Managing the negative attitudes of a critical and distrusting 18% of the workforce. Leaders will need to find more collegiate and constructive approaches to manage the concerns of this cluster. Their concerns include:

- Fear of job losses.
- Not interested in AI.
- Not their job to make AI work.
- Active resistance to introducing sophisticated AI.
- Lack of personal confidence in working with AI.
- Emotion, fear, or being scared.
- Skepticism that AI is not yet ready.

Let's be blunt about what this means (Figure 6.3). Out of every ten of your employees, six are enthusiastic and expect rewards and recognition, two are neutral because of concerns over the implementation work that needs to be done and the disruption that will be experienced, and two are negative and need cajoling. In the current global economy, you really need ten out of ten employees on board. The big tech companies don't have the answer for you; they just want to sell you the tech. You need to do the work.

The challenge for all organizations, AI developers, and solution providers is to identify the veracity and potential consequences of employee attitudes, perceptions, and intended behaviors toward sophisticated AI (whether they are real, probable, or misinformed) and develop corrective or supportive strategies accordingly. This is an exercise in rebuilding your organization to be future-ready.

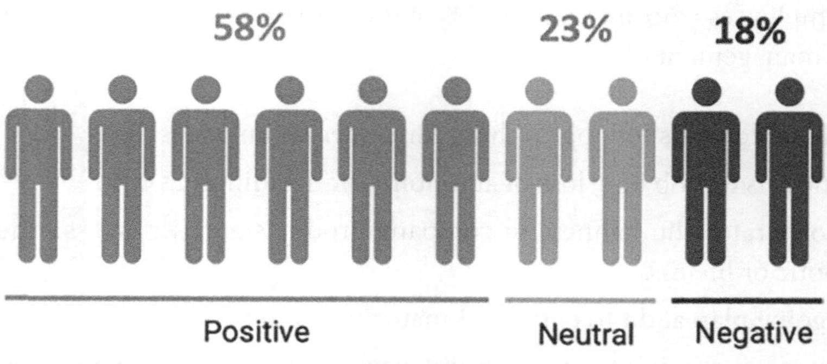

FIGURE 6.3 How many employees are on board with your AI strategy?

A final note on this is that you shouldn't be disappointed in your four employees who may not be as enthusiastic as the other six. These four employees are citizens. They may be reflecting what your customers and stakeholders are also thinking. They may be reflecting the kind of leader you are. They may be signaling how effective your organization really is. They may have information that you need to carefully listen to. AI technologies will only amplify what already doesn't work in your organization.

In closing this section, here are some questions that should keep you up at night:

- Focus on the 6/10 positive: How do you ensure their needs are met and the opportunities that are expected to materialize? How do you make them advocates for change? Do they really have your organization's best interests at heart?
- Focus on the 2/10 neutral: What is this group trying to tell you about the technology that you don't want to hear? What are they telling you about your organization and your leadership? Are you shooting the messenger?
- Focus on the 6/10 negative: Is it time to let these people go? Could they be your smartest people? How can you turn their perceived negatives into positives? What can you learn from them?

IMPLICATIONS FOR LEADING AI TRANSFORMATION

Extant literature on human adoption of AI technology is still emergent and is often absent and inconclusive on the complex psycho-social drivers affecting adoption and adaptation. Our model of the three levels of AI technology adoption is supported, given the levels of definitive rating in (a) their mean average scores on their likelihood to adopt and (b) the distinct and nuanced explanations given by our survey respondents on why they would or would not adopt increasingly sophisticated AI technologies. What applies in working with basic AI may not apply to more sophisticated AI.

The most significant finding in this research is that the attitudes toward adopting increasingly sophisticated AI technologies **appear to be universal**. The results of the comparative tests indicated that there are no significant differences in the mean values of the constructs between genders, between age groups, and education qualifications or international geographies. Similar results can be seen in Araujo et al. (2020), where they found inconclusive or mixed results when it comes to demographic characteristics as predictors of user perceptions and adoption of AI technologies. This suggests that there are deeper socio-cognitive-emotive factors at play that cannot be simply reduced to gender, education, culture, and age-related factors. This is the human condition. This is the nature of our deep entanglements coming to the surface in troubled times.

AI technologies in the workplace have **implications for meaningful work** and human flourishing (Bankins and Formosa, 2023; Bailey et al., 2019) that are still underserved in technology adoption literature. As business leaders and technology researchers, we tend to ignore the importance of humanness, what it means to be human, and the importance of meaning and connection when designing and implementing technologies. This is despite the proven research that human well-being and flourishing are vital for organizational and social creativity, innovation, and productivity. We are now paying the price of that oversight on the effect that AI technologies are having on our social systems, when potentially 40% of the workplace has doubts and concerns.

Looking at the data, while the **positive cluster** appears to be enthusiastic and supportive of adopting increasingly sophisticated AI, it is coming from a place of personal gain, and not necessarily mindful of the full impacts on the business. This group may potentially have more personal power and influence in the workplace and will seek more of it with AI.

Conversely, the **negative cluster** is predominantly focused on concern and fear, and even expressed both passive and active resistance to AI adoption. This group may perceive themselves to currently have limited or no personal power and influence in their roles and stand to lose more with increasingly sophisticated AI. The **neutral cluster** straddles the middle; they see both the positives and the negatives but tend to be predominantly concerned with the impact AI technology will have on the business in terms of technology enablement, questioning technology readiness, as well as the impacts on business disruption.

A deep understanding of how citizens process potential threats or opportunities is important to help set up your AI project for success. In Figure 6.4, we outline the CMUA factors that contribute to the primary and secondary appraisals process that citizens process when confronted by a new AI technology:

1. The initial or **primary appraisal** of threat or opportunity from the introduction of AI, citizen will assess the impact on their work autonomy, the characteristics of the technology, the resources available for them to learn and adapt, and establish or renew their self-confidence, and be safe.
2. This is followed by **the secondary appraisal** of the adaptation response which is based on their assessment of their personal power and control over the situation. This includes elements on the citizen's prior experience with the technology, the views of their peers and supervisors, the usefulness of the technology, and the organization culture.

The outcomes of a citizen's chosen adaptation strategy, as depicted in Figure 6.4, are based on maximizing benefit and personal efficiency and effectiveness (the positive cluster from our research), to the self-preservation mode of the negative group which focuses on restoring emotional stability or exit.

Each of the items in this diagram is also your potential leverage point to integrate and enable positive perceptions toward AI through meaningful action on your part.

The differences in the views and perceptions of each cluster of positive, negative, and neutral also represent different challenges for AI developers and solution providers of AI technologies. The current business model of AI technology development is modular, fragmented, and difficult for developers to trace responsibility and accountability (Widder and Nafus, 2023). Raisch and Krakowski (2021) claim that technical solutions to

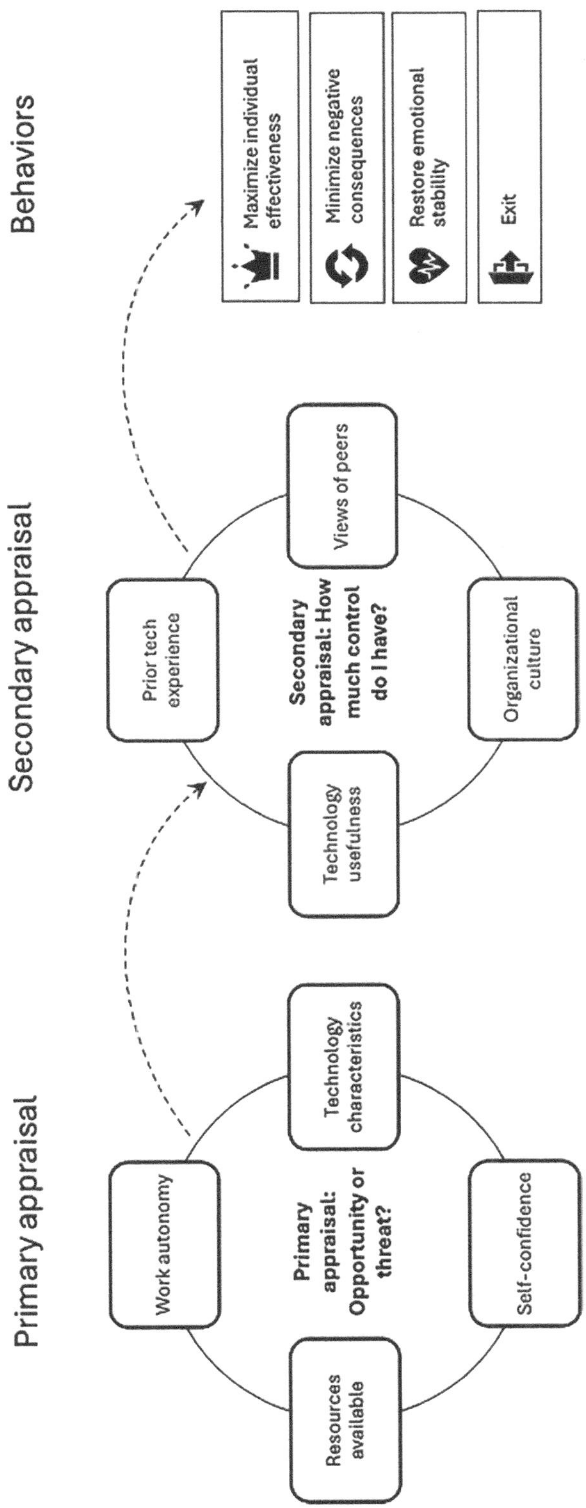

FIGURE 6.4 Primary and secondary appraisals of AI threat or opportunity.

building business systems seldom consider the complexity of socio-technical interactions between stakeholders, yet these interactions have considerable impacts on organizations and society. Consideration needs to be made of the adequacy of the AI development models moving forward; however, researchers believe that the current system of AI software development is unlikely to change any time soon (Widder and Nafus, 2023).

Our concluding remarks are that the adoption of and adaptation to increasingly sophisticated AI is challenged on several fronts – user threat avoidance versus opportunity chasing, organizational strategic capability to manage expectations and threat avoidance behavior, and AI developers' capability to engage users in meaningful co-creation of socio-technical systems.

The need to pay attention to this is clear, given research that claims that AI technologies may inadvertently reinforce existing power structures and mental models (Birhane et al., 2021; Bender et al., 2021), which becomes an obstacle for future-focused business innovation if algorithms are anchored in past assumptions and practices. This is how current technological design has become entangled with the human mental models of the past, and changing its trajectory requires conscious effort to disentangle these ties.

IMPLICATIONS FOR HUMAN-AI RESEARCH

This chapter identifies three broad categories of employees in terms of how they respond to working with increasingly sophisticated AI. The positive cluster believes AI offers opportunities, the neutral group is positive but has reservations, and the negative group focuses on the downside. Our work supports TTAT, as we found that individuals clearly distinguish between *malicious* and *virtuous* AI. According to TTAT, a virtuous technology is perceived by users to be attractive as it creates positive outcomes through its use (Liang and Xue, 2009), and this is a key finding in our study concerning the characteristics of our "positive cluster" who engaged in opportunity chasing. The 18% of respondents in our "negative cluster" is consistent with what Liang and Xue call threat avoidance behavior.

However, our research shows that there is a middle ground not directly addressed by TTAT or CMUA that is prevalent in our neutral cluster. TTAT and CMUA are defined by dichotomies: *either* virtuous *or* malicious. Users are *either* actively or passively avoiding threats. AI presents *either an opportunity or a threat.* The smart approach to viewing the different positions held by citizens is not as dichotomies but as sitting on a spectrum. The attitudes shared by citizens in this survey are not fixed positions but dynamic and are largely influenced by the presence of proactive leadership and organizational strategy – or a lack thereof.

The final key critical insight is that there is an implied or indirect assumption in both TTAT and CMUA theories on the robustness of the technological functionality and that it is fit for purpose. As these theories were originally based on mature technology architectures, we propose that they did not account for the level of immaturity of emergent AI technologies that have perhaps gone to market much earlier than technologies in the past.

The current generation of AI technologies is still young and underdeveloped, and the industry is rife with hype and overselling of capabilities and the promise of returns on investment that are struggling to materialize (Birhane et al., 2021; Newlands, 2021; Bender et al., 2021). Furthermore, AI technologies are introducing systemic challenges of product market concentration, inequities, and ethical problems compared to previous waves of automation and robotization (Ernst et al., 2019). These are conditions that can trigger emotions of perceived AI technology "maliciousness" or a threat to a level that may not have been accounted for in TTAT and CMLA in the past.

TTAT arose on the premise that IT acceptance theories could not fully explain citizen IT threat avoidance behavior and developed a new theory to explain threat avoidance behavior (Liang and Xue, 2009; Cao et al., 2021). We believe the opportunity has now presented itself to further adapt TTAT to consider a third phenomenon, where individuals engage in threat avoidance behavior when the maturity of the technology is compromised due to its technical limitations and its ability to cause unintended harm to organizations, workplaces, and society in general.

IMPLICATIONS FOR PRACTICE

The implications for practice are considerable for both organizations investing in and implementing AI technologies and solution providers that are developing and assisting clients in AI implementations. Organizations will need to be mindful of the attitudes, perceptions, and potential behaviors unique to each of the three key categories of employees when looking to invest in increasingly sophisticated AI technologies. It is widely accepted that the successful adoption of an information system depends to a great extent on users' perceptions of the information system, as we have identified in our research.

We have identified that individual cognitive frames are a key factor in managing the adoption of information systems, consistent with the findings of Lin and Silva (2005) and Davidson (2008), where the three different levels of AI sophistication trigger different responses in individuals. The additional challenge here is that individual cognitive frames are dynamic and highly situational (Orlikowski and Gash, 1994). This leaves an open question of how organizations continually adapt their workplace and managerial practices in tandem with the constant changes in AI progression and advancement. AI technologies require a more sophisticated approach to organizational design and digital transformation than have been offered by the conventional frameworks of the past (Hanelt et al., 2021).

The adoption of AI depends not only on the intrinsic qualities of the information system but also on the changing contexts in which the information system is evaluated. Lin and Silva (2005) argue that the management of information systems adoption is a social and political process in which stakeholders constantly frame and reframe their perceptions of that system. This implies that organizations may need to develop more ongoing, dynamic, and consultative practices with their employees and stakeholders with AI development and enablement.

Transformational leadership is needed to avert technophobia (Khasawneh, 2020; McClure, 2018) and technostress (Tarafdar et al., 2007) emerging from workplace concerns over job losses, underemployment, anxiety, burnout, and surveillance that are fueled for many by artificial intelligence. The importance of this cannot be underestimated, as creating business value from AI technologies still requires that humans and machines work together collaboratively at this early stage of AI technology development.

CONCLUSIONS

The findings of our research show declining support for AI adoption at increased levels of technological sophistication. There is a complex heterogeneity of issues reported by our respondents regarding the adoption of increasingly sophisticated AI, which raises issues for practice for organizations investing in AI as well as for AI developers and solution providers.

Technology threat avoidance theory can partially explain user reticence to adopt more sophisticated technologies, as it's unclear whether AI threat avoidance may in part be attributed to genuine concern with the limitations inherent in the AI technology, the veracity of organizational workplace implementations, or its ability to provide for secure or meaningful work.

The implications of this research are that if current industry challenges regarding limited returns on investment from AI technologies are prevalent today, then this may be exacerbated with the introduction of more sophisticated AI technologies in the future.

Individual cognitive and behavioral responses, such as threat avoidance and opportunity chasing, are shaped by a perception of personal power and resources. An understanding of these drivers will enable organizations and developers to recalibrate their processes to produce improved and effective socio-technical systems and practices, and better outcomes for society as a whole.

ACKNOWLEDGMENTS

The author wishes to thank Professor Juho Hamari for his feedback on the early stages of this research. This project has received funding from the European Union's Horizon 2020 research and innovation program under the Marie Sklodowska-Curie Grant Agreement No 101023024 for Augmented Humans.

REFERENCES

Adell, E. (2010, April). Acceptance of driver support systems. In *Proceedings of the European Conference on Human Centred Design for Intelligent Transport Systems* (Vol. 2, pp. 475–486). Humanist VCE: Ifsttar—Lyon-Bron, Berlin, Germany.

Andersson, K. E. (2018). Key requirements in the procurement of future low observable combat vehicles: a European perspective. *Systems Engineering*, *21*(1), 3–15.

Araujo, T., Helberger, N., Kruikemeier, S., and De Vreese, C. H. (2020). In AI we trust? Perceptions about automated decision-making by artificial intelligence. *AI & Society*, *35*, 611–623.

Bailey, C., Yeoman, R., Madden, A., Thompson, M., and Kerridge, G. (2019). A review of the empirical literature on meaningful work: Progress and research agenda. *Human Resource Development Review*, *18*(1), 83–113.

Bankins, S., and Formosa, P. (2023). The ethical implications of artificial intelligence (AI) for meaningful work. *Journal of Business Ethics*, *185*(4), 725–740.

Beaudry, A., and Pinsonneault, A. (2005). Understanding user responses to information technology: A coping model of user adaptation. *MIS Quarterly*, *29*(3), 493–524.

Bender, E. M., Gebru, T., McMillan-Major, A., and Shmitchell, S. (2021). On the dangers of stochastic parrots: Can language models be too big? In *Proceedings of the 2021 ACM Conference on Fairness, Accountability, and Transparency* (pp. 610–623).

Berente, N., Gu, B., Recker, J., and Santhanam, R. (2021). Managing Artificial Intelligence. *MIS Quarterly*, *45*(3), 1433–1450.

Birhane, A., Kalluri, P., Card, D., Agnew, W., Dotan, R., and Bao, M. 2021. *The Values Encoded in Machine Learning Research*. http://arxiv.org/abs/2106.15590

Braat, M., Engelen, J., van Gemert, T., and Verhaegh, S. (2020). The rise and fall of behaviorism: The narrative and the numbers. *History of Psychology*, *23*(3), 252.

Cabrera-Sánchez, J. P., Villarejo-Ramos, Á. F., Liébana-Cabanillas, F., and Shaikh, A. A. (2021). Identifying relevant segments of AI applications adopters – Expanding the UTAUT2's variables. *Telematics and Informatics*, *58*, 101529.

Camarinha-Matos, L. M., and Afsarmanesh, H. (2008). On reference models for collaborative networked organizations. *International Journal of Production Research*, 46(9), 2453–2469.

Cao, G., Duan, Y., Edwards, J. S., and Dwivedi, Y. K. (2021). Understanding managers' attitudes and behavioral intentions towards using artificial intelligence for organizational decision-making. *Technovation*, *106*, 102312.

Carroll, M., Shah, R., Ho, M. K., Griffiths, T. L., Seshia, S. A., Abbeel, P., and Dragan, A. (2019). *On the Utility of Learning about Humans for Human-AI Coordination*. http://arxiv.org/abs/1910.05789

Collins, C., Dennehy, D., Conboy, K., and Mikalef, P. (2021). Artificial intelligence in information systems research: A systematic literature review and research agenda. *International Journal of Information Management*, *60*, 102383.

Cubric, M. (2020). Drivers, barriers and social considerations for AI adoption in business and management: A tertiary study. *Technology in Society*, *62*, 101257.

Davidson, E. J. (2002). Technology frames and framing: A socio-cognitive investigation of requirements determination. *MIS Quarterly*, *26*(4), 329–358.

Davis, F. D. (1993). User acceptance of information technology: System characteristics, user perceptions and behavioral impacts. *International journal of Man-Machine Studies*, 38(3), 475–487.

Dellermann, D., Calma, A., and Lipusch, N. (2019). The future of human-AI collaboration: A taxonomy of design knowledge for hybrid intelligence systems. *arXiv preprint arXiv:2105.03354*.

Dietvorst, B. J., Simmons, J. P., and Massey, C. (2015). Algorithm aversion: People erroneously avoid algorithms after seeing them err. *Journal of Experimental Psychology: General*, *144*(1), 114.

Duan, Y., Edwards, J. S., and Dwivedi, Y. K. (2019). Artificial intelligence for decision making in the era of Big Data – evolution, challenges and research agenda. *International Journal of Information Management*, *48*, 63–71.

Dwivedi, Y. K., Hughes, L., Ismagilova, E., … Williams, M. D. (2021). Artificial Intelligence (AI): Multidisciplinary perspectives on emerging challenges, opportunities, and agenda for research, practice and policy. *International Journal of Information Management*, *57*, 101994.

Ernst, E., Merola, R., and Samaan, D. (2019). Economics of artificial intelligence: Implications for the future of work. *IZA Journal of Labor Policy*, *9*(1), 1–35.

Etikan, I., Musa, S. A., and Alkassim, R. S. (2016). Comparison of convenience sampling and purposive sampling. *American Journal of Theoretical and Applied Statistics*, *5*(1), 1–4.

Falk, Helena Sjöström, (2024). *Digitalisation and AI in Air Traffic Control: Balancing Innovation with the Human Element*. Eurocontrol, EU.

Fogg, B. J. (2002). Persuasive technology: Using computers to change what we think and do. *Ubiquity*, *2002* (December), 2.

Fogg, B. J., and Hreha, J. (2012). Persuasive technology. In *Using Computers to Change What We Think and Do*. Elsevier. https://doi.org/10.1016/B978-1-55860-643-2.X5000-8

Fügener, A., Grahl, J., Gupta, A., and Ketter, W. (2021). Will humans-in-the-loop become borgs? Merits and pitfalls of working with AI. *MIS Quarterly: Management Information Systems*, *45*(3), 1527–1556.

Fullana, M. A., Dunsmoor, J. E., Schruers, K. R. J., Savage, H. S., Bach, D. R., and Harrison, B. J. (2020). Human fear conditioning: From neuroscience to the clinic. *Behaviour Research and Therapy*, *124*, 103528.

Gansser, O. A., and Reich, C. S. (2021). A new acceptance model for artificial intelligence with extensions to UTAUT2: An empirical study in three segments of application. *Technology in Society*, *65*, 101535.

Hanelt, A., Bohnsack, R., Marz, D., and Antunes Marante, C. (2021). A systematic review of the literature on digital transformation: Insights and implications for strategy and organizational change. *Journal of Management Studies*, *58*(5), 1159–1197.

Hogg, M. A. (2016). *Social Identity Theory* (pp. 3–17). Springer International Publishing.

Hyland-Wood, D., Harrison, A., and Kolera, B. (2019). Righting writing's wrongs: Toward effective writing partnerships between humans and AI. *Universal Journal of Educational Research*, *7*(5), 1306–1318.

Ienca, M. (2019). Democratizing cognitive technology: A proactive approach. *Ethics and Information Technology*, *21*(4), 267–280.

Ishowo-Oloko, F., Bonnefon, J. -F., Soroye, Z., Crandall, J., Rahwan, I., and Rahwan, T. (2019). Behavioural evidence for a transparency–efficiency tradeoff in human–machine cooperation. *Nature Machine Intelligence*, *1*(11), 517–521.

Jarrahi, M. H. (2018). Artificial intelligence and the future of work: Human-AI symbiosis in organizational decision making. *Business Horizons*, *61*(4), 577–586.

Kaber, D. B., and Endsley, M. R. (2004). The effects of level of automation and adaptive automation on human performance, situation awareness and workload in a dynamic control task. *Theoretical Issues in Ergonomics Science*, *5*(2), 113–153.

Kerstholt, J., Barnhoorn, J., Hueting, T., and Schuilenborg, L. (2018). Automation as an intelligent teammate: Social psychological implications. In *NATO-HAT Symposium on Human Autonomy Teaming*. NATO Publications.

Khasawneh, O. Y. (2020). Transformational leaders help their employees overcome their technophobia. *International Journal of Technology and Human Interaction (IJTHI)*, *16*(3), 70–85.

Kiesler, S., Sproull, L., and Waters, K. (1996). A prisoner's dilemma experiment on cooperation with people and human-like computers. *Journal of Personality and Social Psychology*, 70(1), 47.

Knox, J., Williamson, B., and Bayne, S. (2019). Machine behaviourism: Future visions of "learnification" and "datafication" across humans and digital technologies. *Learning, Media and Technology*, *45*(1), 31–45. https://doi.org/10.1080/17439884.2019.1623251

Kosinski, M., Stillwell, D., and Graepel, T. (2013). Private traits and attributes are predictable from digital records of human behavior. *Proceedings of the National Academy of Sciences*, *110*(15), 5802–5805.

Langer, M., and Landers, R. N. (2021). The future of artificial intelligence at work: A review on effects of decision automation and augmentation on workers targeted by algorithms and third-party observers. *Computers in Human Behavior*, *123*, 106878.

Liang, H., and Xue, Y. (2009). Avoidance of information technology threats: A theoretical perspective. *MIS Quarterly*, *33*(1), 71–90.

Lin, A., and Silva, L. (2005). The social and political construction of technological frames. *European Journal of Information Systems, 14*, 49–59.

Liwång, H. (2022). Defense development: The role of co-creation in filling the gap between policy-makers and technology development. *Technology in Society, 68*, 101913.

McClure, P. K. (2018). "You're fired," says the robot: The rise of automation in the workplace, technophobes, and fears of unemployment. *Social Science Computer Review, 36*(2), 139–156.

Mirbabaie, M., Stieglitz, S., Brünker, F., Hofeditz, L., Ross, B., and Frick, N. R. (2021). Understanding collaboration with virtual assistants – the role of social identity and the extended self. *Business & Information Systems Engineering, 63*, 21–37.

Nass, C., Fogg, B. J., and Moon, Y. (1996). Can computers be teammates? *International Journal of Human-Computer Studies, 45*(6), 669–678.

Newlands, G. (2021). Lifting the curtain: Strategic visibility of human labour in AI-as-a-Service. *Big Data and Society, 8*(1), 20539517211016026.

Oh, C., Lee, T., Kim, Y., Park, S. H., Kwon, S., and Suh, B. (2017). Us vs. them: Understanding artificial intelligence technophobia over the Google DeepMind Challenge Match. *Conference on Human Factors in Computing Systems – Proceedings, 2017-May*, 2523–2534.

O'Neil, C. (2016). *Weapons of Math Destruction: How Big Data Increases Inequality and Threatens Democracy*. Crown Publishing Group, USA.

Orlikowski, W. J., and Gash, D. C. (1994). Technological frames: Making sense of information technology in organizations. *ACM Transactions on Information Systems (TOIS), 12*(2), 174–207.

Penney, J. (2017). *The Citizen Marketer: Promoting Political Opinion in the Social Media Age*. Oxford University Press.

Prahalad, C. K., and Ramaswamy, V. (2000). Co-opting customer competence. *Harvard Business Review, 78*(1), 79–90.

Pulkkinen, K., and Hautamäki, A. (2019). Co-creation with companies: A means to enhance societal impact of university researchers? In Sørensen, M. P., Geschwind, L., Kekäle, J., and Pinheiro, R., (eds.), *The Responsible University: Exploring the Nordic Context and Beyond* (pp. 145–172). Springer International Publishing.

Pumplun, L., Tauchert, C., and Heidt, M. (2019). *A New Organizational Chassis for Artificial Intelligence – Exploring Organizational Readiness Factors*. European Conference on Information Systems. Stockholm-Uppsala, Sweden.

Raftopoulos, M., and Hamari, J., (2023). *Artificial Intelligence in the Workplace: Implementation Challenges and Opportunities*. The Americas' Conference on Information Systems (AMCIS) 2023, Panama City, Panama.

Raftopoulos, M., and Hamari, J. (2024). *Organizational Challenges in Adoption and Implementation of Artificial Intelligence*. Hawaii International Conference on System Sciences (HICSS) 2024, Waikiki, Hawaii, USA.

Raftopoulos, M. (2025). Threat avoidance or opportunity chasing? In Leibowitz, J. and McAlidon, P. (eds.), *Leveraging AI for Business Innovation*. World Scientific Publishing. https://doi.org/10.1142/14397

Raisch, S., and Krakowski, S. (2021). Artificial intelligence and management: The automation–augmentation paradox. *Academy of Management Review, 46*(1), 192–210.

Ransbotham, S., Candelon, F., Kiron, D., LaFountain, B., and Khodabandeh, S. (2021). The cultural benefits of artificial intelligence in the enterprise. *MIT Sloan Management Review*, 1–19. https://digitalrosh.com/wp-content/uploads/2023/03/MITSloan-Cultural-benefits-of-AI.pdf Accessed 13 November 2025

Ranjan, K. R., and Read, S. (2016). Value co-creation: Concept and measurement, *Journal of the Academy of Marketing Science*, *44*(3), 290–315.

Seeber, I., Bittner, E., Briggs, R. O., de Vreede, T., de Vreede, G. J., Elkins, A., Maier, R., Merz, A. B., Oeste-Reiß, S., Randrup, N., Schwabe, G., and Söllner, M. (2020). Machines as teammates: A research agenda on AI in team collaboration. *Information and Management*, *57*(2), 103174.

Shollo, A., Hopf, K., Thiess, T., and Müller, O. (2022). Shifting ML value creation mechanisms: A process model of ML value creation. *The Journal of Strategic Information Systems*, *31*(3), 101734.

Smorodinskaya, N., Russell, M. G., Katukov, D., and Still, K. (2017). Innovation ecosystems vs. innovation systems in terms of collaboration and co-creation of value. In *Proceedings of the 50th Hawaii International Conference on System Sciences* (pp. 5245–5254). HICSS.

Sohn, Y., Kwak, D., Son, S., Kang, C., and Lim, Y. K. (2025). Driving with algorithms beyond gig work: Investigating how algorithmic management affects workers' practices in an on-demand ride-pooling service. In *Proceedings of the 2025 ACM Designing Interactive Systems Conference* (pp. 2117–2129). ACM.

Stowers, K., Brady, L. L., MacLellan, C., Wohleber, R., and Salas, E. (2021). Improving teamwork competencies in human-machine teams: Perspectives from team science. *Frontiers in Psychology*, *12*, 590290.

Tarafdar, M., Tu, Q., Ragu-Nathan, B. S., and Ragu-Nathan, T. S. (2007). The impact of technostress on role stress and productivity. *Journal of Management Information Systems*, *24*(1), 301–328.

Tschang, F. T., and Almirall, E. (2021). Artificial intelligence as augmenting automation: Implications for employment. *Academy of Management Perspectives*, *35*(4), 642–659.

Vaughn College (2025). www.vaughn.edu/blog/ai-driven-technology-takes-air-traffic-control-to-the-next-level/ accessed Tuesday 4 March 2025, 3:11pm.

Venkatesh, V., Morris, M. G., Davis, G. B., and Davis, F. D. (2003). User acceptance of information technology: Toward a unified view. *MIS Quarterly*, *27*(3), 425–478.

Waardenburg, L., and Huysman, M. (2022). From coexistence to co-creation: Blurring boundaries in the age of AI. *Information and Organization*, *32*(4), 100432.

Wagner, D. N. (2020). The nature of the Artificially Intelligent Firm – An economic investigation into changes that AI brings to the firm. *Telecommunications Policy*, *44*(6), 101954.

Widder, D. G., and Nafus, D. (2023). Dislocated accountabilities in the "AI supply chain": Modularity and developers' notions of responsibility. *Big Data and Society*, *10*(1), 205395172311.

IV

Flourishing

CHAPTER 7

Collaborative AI Systems Design

The Three Laws of Robotics:

1. A robot may not injure a human being or, through inaction, allow a human being to come to harm.

2. A robot must obey the orders given it by human beings except where such orders would conflict with the First Law.

3. A robot must protect its own existence as long as such protection does not conflict with the First or Second Law.

The Zeroth Law: A robot may not harm humanity, or, by inaction, allow humanity to come to harm.

—ISAAC ASIMOV

THE SCIENCE BEHIND COLLABORATIVE AI SYSTEMS DESIGN

Artificial intelligence is reshaping workplaces and is reconfiguring the design of work processes, information systems, and human–machine–algorithm interaction. However, despite the tsunami of potential opportunities presented by artificial intelligence (AI), the industry is ill-prepared, and little is known about the factors that contribute to its sustainable value creation potential (Pumplun et al., 2019; Shollo et al., 2022; Mikalef and Gupta, 2021). As presented in previous chapters, recent studies suggest that many organizations are falling short of creating tangible business value through AI (Shollo et al., 2022) and that returns on AI investment are below expectations (Mikalef and Gupta, 2021). The failure to realize the potential of AI-enabled technologies is largely attributed to an array of technology design and implementation challenges that can be averted with more

DOI: 10.1201/9781003616566-11

inclusive collaboration with users as stakeholders in system design (Raftopoulos and Hamari, 2023).

As discussed in Chapter 6, the blurred boundaries between AI technology development and its use make it necessary to theorize beyond narrow approaches dominated by traditional theories on technology adoption and by digital transformation models of the past. Organizations today need tools to more accurately reflect current and future challenges brought on by AI, and this points to a need to consider stakeholder co-creation approaches (Waardenburg et al., 2022; Wagner, 2020). This is notwithstanding the fact that the pervasive human–technology entanglements, as discussed in Chapters 3 and 4, have an invisible and subconscious hold over us as individuals, organizations, and society.

Value creation from AI or intelligent technologies represents unique challenges due to the complex interactions (and changing nature) between technology, systems, tasks, and processes (Spies et al., 2020). Furthermore, human–machine systems based on AI technologies require a more sophisticated approach to organizational design and digital transformation than have been offered by the conventional frameworks of the past (Hanelt et al., 2021), as well as the design of task and technology alignment in workplace and functional designs (Goodhue and Thompson, 1995).

As established in Chapter 6, stakeholder perceptions of AI are a key factor in influencing effective acceptance and workplace implementations of AI technologies (Cao et al., 2021; Dwivedi et al., 2021), while established technology acceptance theories (Venkatesh et al., 2003) address the utilitarian aspects of AI technology acceptance, they cannot fully explain technology threat avoidance behavior driven by complex psychosocial factors (Liang and Xue, 2009) which may be contributing to sub-optimal AI technology design and implementation.

The most effective means of approaching these complex challenges is by working together with stakeholders using collaborative and participatory methods (Crisan et al, 2022; Ghajargar and Bardzell, 2022). We used a design science approach (Hevner et al., 2004) and grounded theory (Corbin and Strauss, 2008; Muller, 2014) to develop and test prototype interactive design tools. . These tools presented in this chapter can support researchers, project managers, organizational leadership teams, and technology developers in three areas:

a. Onboarding workplaces on designing AI-enabled information systems that are human-centered and value-conscious.
b. Offers empirically tested participatory approaches for potential stakeholder consultation and co-creation of more effective human–machine systems design.
c. Engage stakeholders with playful approaches to enhance AI literacy.

These tools will help facilitate high-level approaches for examining the underlying assumptions, expectations, and knowledge that management and technical stakeholders hold about AI technology in their organizations. Consistent with design science approaches, we researched, developed, and tested three sets of tools ready for use by researchers and practitioners:

- **A set of conversational design cards** that explore the three core topics of (a) AI functional design concepts, (b) provocations on the dark side of AI, and (c) human flourishing in the age of AI. A fourth set of cards was also developed on the nine *AI design archetypes or personas* to engage citizens in expressing their innate fears and ambitions in using AI.
- **A design card game** called *Designing Tiny Robots* that engages stakeholders in creating rapid prototypes of AI systems using three design challenge cards of Technology, Touchpoints, and Experience. An additional three sets of cards are played to test the initial design assumptions in the form of bugs, cyber threats, and ethics.
- **A design sprint process and design canvases** that utilize the conversation cards and the Tiny Robots design card game in a participatory workshop environment.

Design-science research addresses *unsolved problems in unique or innovative ways* (Hevner et al., 2004) and encourages researchers to take different or unique approaches to design. The design-science approach works best when requisite knowledge in a field is nonexistent, there is a reliance on creativity to find the truth, and where there is an element of trial-and-error that is required in the research effort in tackling a "wicked problem" (Hevner et al., 2004). These methods were adopted as they're an ideal fit for navigating the complex and fast-evolving nature of AI technologies that organizations are grappling with.

In the remainder of this chapter, we present the findings of the development and testing of these AI design tools that meet our core challenge: ***How might we make AI systems design and development tangible, engaging, and understandable to engage stakeholders in a process of co-creation?*** These tools have been rigorously researched, tested, and refined, and are ready for your immediate use with your stakeholders. The key message in this chapter is: ***Get Creative.***

BACKGROUND TO COLLABORATIVE DESIGN AND THE ART OF BEING PLAYFUL

I know you're keen to get started on these tools (I did tell you to *get creative*), but some background on the science is not a bad thing. As I emphasized in previous chapters, understanding the methodology is key in getting to the source of truth of any recommended insights and actions.

The development and implementation of AI-enabled technologies have seen a proliferation of a variety of approaches to ensure human-centered and ethical design principles are melded into technology development. This has largely been in response to widespread industry criticism of unethical practices and unintended negative consequences of "black box" algorithmic decision-making. In their research on conceptualizing AI literacy,

Ng et al. (2021) emphasized the importance of integrating "unplugged" or alternative learning tools to engage the public in learning about AI, such as role-playing, storytelling, and public art, which the authors consider viable approaches to establish a collaborative, robust, and safe society. This is also an important method of disentangling systems to understand their component parts.

In industry design practice, a plethora of tangible design tools and methods have been developed with a similar purpose (Ng et al., 2021). For example, Ghajargar and Bardzell (2022) developed a set of ten concept cards to improve the AI literacy of human–computer interaction (HCI) for researchers and practitioners. This method has been found to enable creative and tangible means to explore explainable AI and gain new design perspectives for HCI (Ghajargar and Bardzell, 2022).

Several AI design canvases have been developed and included in our work (Kerzel, 2021) as practical tools to facilitate public awareness and knowledge of AI capability, and as frameworks for how stakeholders might work with these technologies to create business value and minimize harms. These works on AI design canvases have been modelled on the Business Model Canvas, which was originally developed and popularized by Osterwalder and Pigneur (2010).

On a more technical level, AI model cards for software developers have also been developed over the last few years, spearheaded by Mitchell et al. (2019) as a method for documenting technical design guidelines and increasing the transparency of responsible machine learning and AI models. AI model cards have now been adopted by several large technological companies, such as Hugging Face, Open AI, Google, and Salesforce, for increased AI transparency and governance. For example, Crisan et al. (2022) have extended AI model cards using a human-centered approach to model documentation for large language models for non-technical stakeholders.

Design methods such as ECCOLA were developed by Vakkuri et al. (2021) as a method for implementing AI ethics using a deck of 21 design cards divided into eight different AI ethics themes that are utilized in a sprint process designed to facilitate critical thinking about AI systems development. Model cards are live models; hence, they are in constant development and refinement and open to the public for full transparency.

The method and approach for the development of the AI design tools in this chapter has taken inspiration from this work and has also been further enhanced by the field of design games (Brandt and Messeter, 2004; Hornecker, 2010; Mueller et al., 2014) and design card methodologies (Flanagan and Nissenbaum, 2007; Friedman and Hendry, 2012; IDEO, 2003; Schell, 2008). Research shows that the use of card-based methods provides tools for brainstorming exercises during design workshops that facilitate creative dialogue (Hornecker, 2010). They also assist in creating an environment for a better understanding of the systems that are being designed and the user interactions and experiences that are being created.

Physical objects such as design cards also make tensions and disagreements between workshop participants more tangible and less personal. They can also speed up the design process by helping participants focus on the task and create common ground product or design features, while also allowing room for divergent interpretation (Hornecker, 2010). Playfulness is deeply rooted in human culture, and any activity can potentially be designed with a playful approach to make the task more motivating and engaging. This is not only to provide an enjoyable experience for participants but also to facilitate the creation of practical design outcomes (Arrasvuori et al., 2011; Lucero and Arrasvuori, 2010).

The rising popularity of using cards as design tools across many domains, such as service, product, and technology design, lies in the fact that they are tangible representations of abstract concepts and are simple to use and easy to manipulate when non-technical stakeholders are involved in the process (Wölfel and Merritt, 2013). This helps to make the design process more visible and less abstract (Hornecker, 2010; Lucero and Arrasvuori, 2010) and provides a process to reason and justify design decisions as well as facilitate a creative ideation process (Mueller et al., 2014).

AI technologies offer many positive benefits to both citizens and organizations; however, there is also a parallel disruption that poses largely unknown systemic impacts on our social, economic, ethical, and political systems and the potential harms they may cause (Marcus, 2022; Birhane et al., 2021; Bender et al., 2021). The democratization of decision-making on AI design and development is emerging in extant literature and in practice as a possible solution to these emerging problems. This includes the involvement of a wide range of stakeholders and using different methods of engagement that will lift public AI literacy and capability, as well as engaging stakeholders in the co-creation of responsible and effective AI technologies (Ng et al., 2021; Crisan et al., 2022; Vakkuri et al., 2021). Publicly available methods and practices in engaging stakeholders in collaborative AI systems design are currently limited and highly technical. Our work contributes to addressing this gap.

Citizen participation and mutual learning underpin the epistemology of our research in developing these tools, which are key criteria of ensuring rigor and relevancy (Farrow, 2021). The scientific methodology used to collect data needed to develop the tools was based on Torbert's (1998) "first, second, and third person" framework that closely integrates research and practice. This methodology incorporates opportunities for individual participant reflection, participation, and collective insight generation. A summary of the collaborative design activities that were developed using this method is illustrated in Figure 7.1.

According to Torbert, methods need to take teams on a journey that helps them go beyond deeply ingrained defense mechanisms to create new possibilities for action. The experiential phases include:

- The "First Person" phase that builds an "enquiring approach" so participants may proceed with enhanced awareness. We built this enquiring approach into our opening *Initiation* phase using conversation cards.
- The "Second Person" analysis comes through dialogue and the development of "communities of inquiry and learning organizations." We built this into our second phase of *Teambuilding*.

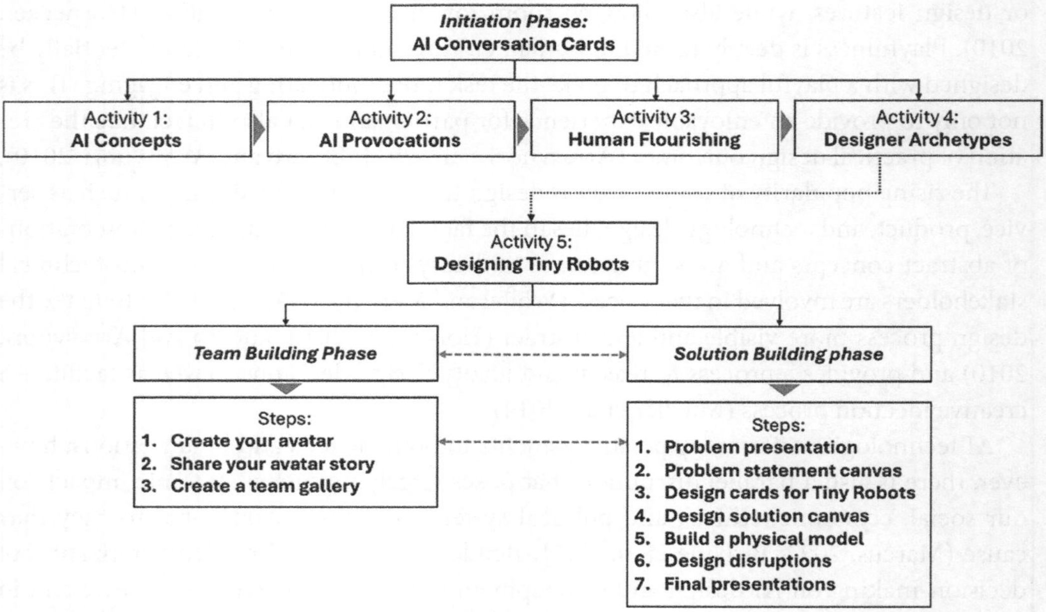

FIGURE 7.1 Collaboration design tools based on Torbert's three-phase framework.

- The "Third Person" is more impersonal and "aims to create a wider community of inquiry" which we built into our third *Solution Building* phase that incorporates the Designing Tiny Robots card game and Design Sprint.

The three phases aim to engage citizens with the content by firstly understanding themselves, then moving into how they interact with others, and then shifting toward a collective enquiry on the bigger picture of social, economic, and political questions. The following sections of this chapter detail the results of this work. As is the case with all collaborative design methodologies, such as design thinking and design sprints, these methods are now open source and open to your continuous improvements and adaptions.

AI DESIGN INITIATION PHASE – CONVERSATION CARDS

Four decks of ten conversation cards were developed to initiate stakeholder awareness and knowledge sharing on AI design concepts and the implications for our human, social, and planetary systems. These card decks are as follows:

- **AI concept cards** compromise prompts on different AI technology design concepts.
- **AI provocations cards** comprise the negative consequences of AI technologies.
- **Human flourishing cards** that depict questions on how our human and social systems may be affected.
- **Designer archetypes cards** that prompt reflection on personal feelings and attitudes toward working with AI.

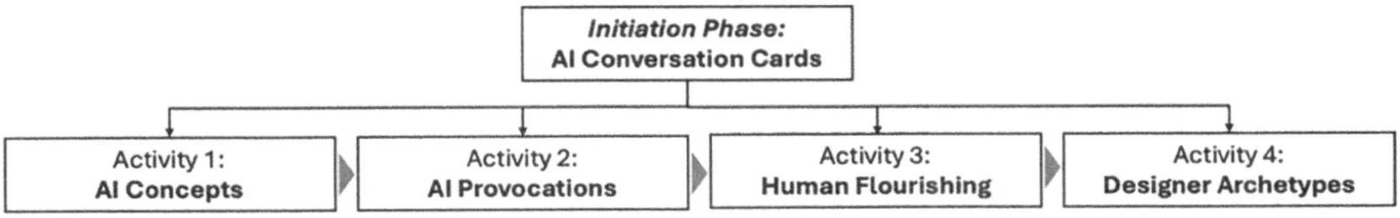

FIGURE 7.2 The four activities of the initiation phase.

The four key activities in the initiation phases, as depicted in the flowchart in Figure 7.2, are detailed in the sections below.

Activity 1: AI Concept Cards

Ten AI concept cards were developed based on the key elements of AI systems design that arose out of a detailed literature review on factors essential to human–machine collaboration (Raftopoulos and Hamari, 2023) and were subsequently modified after several years of testing in the field. Given the significant depth and breadth of topics that can be chosen for this deck, only ten were selected for the practical reasons of not having an unwieldy number of cards that need to be managed by workshop facilitators and participants. This is similar to other approaches that aim to engage your stakeholders with the content rather than overwhelm them with the technical detail (Ghajargar and Bardzell, 2022). This then becomes a post-activity session in having your team build onto this deck of cards so that it is tailored to your organization's specific needs.

The concept cards were intended as conversation starters or to open a field of inquiry among stakeholders at the early stages of exploring AI; they were not intended to be fully comprehensive on the topic. The ten key concepts included in this deck are human–machine collaboration, transparency, cybersecurity, data curation and model building, intelligence, co-creation, speculative worlds, human agency, leadership, and AI technology. A description of each concept was provided on the card, as well as a "how might we…" question to prompt a team discussion. A digital download is provided for you with this book, and an example of AI concept cards is shown in Figure 7.3.

How to Play with the AI Conversation Cards

There are several ways this activity can be used to engage your stakeholders with AI concepts. A suggestion of some of the more productive ways my team of researchers and I have found to be effective is as follows:

- **Set up your activity for success** by providing your team or organization with an initial briefing of the AI project in your organization and the intent of this workshop or activity. It's important that this is done to provide clarity on context and expectations in line with the objectives of enabling AI in your organization.
- **Prepare by creating an inviting and welcoming space for your gathering.** The ideal room setup is with chairs and tables out of the way – this is a stand-up exercise. Have chairs available around the edge of the space for those who need them.

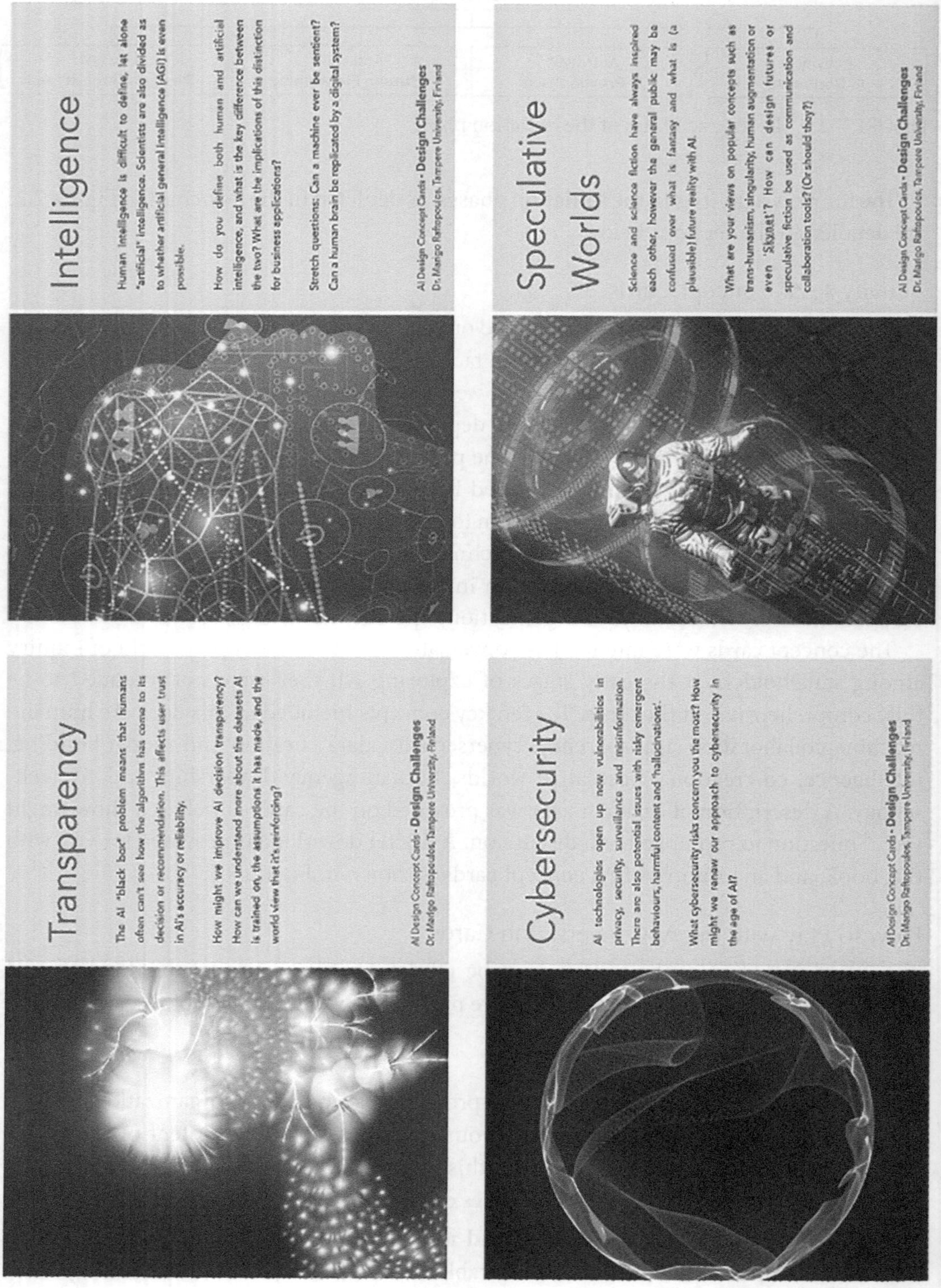

FIGURE 7.3 Four examples of AI concept cards.

Organize black marker pens and post-it notes in three different colors. On the walls have three sheets of butcher's paper headed with the following headings:

- What have you learned?
- What excites you vs what concerns you?
- How can we as a team improve our learning and prepare for an AI future?

- **Prepare by having all the cards laid out on a table** – either face up so they can see them and self-select or go for a more random and challenging approach and have the cards laid face down.
- Depending on the number of participants, ask your team to self-organize into smaller groups of three to five.
- **An energy booster group exercise** would be a bonus at this point, so people are energized and relaxed with a boost of serotonin and dopamine. They are not machines.
- When the group is ready, ask a member of each team to **select a card** from the table and return to the group for a discussion. Allow ten minutes for a free stand-up discussion among the team on the card they have selected. A stand-up is deliberately used to break from the entrained thinking that is associated with sitting at a desk or table, and making the teams feel less trapped by allowing for somatic movement and "thinking on their feet."
- After ten minutes, ask participants to share what they discussed in their small team session with the larger group. The teams will have discussed different cards, so encourage participants to ask probing questions of the other teams, and to contrast and compare with their own experiences and discussions.
- Next, ask each participant to take a moment and (a) write a post-it note on their personal response to the questions on the card, then (b) place the post-it notes on the butcher's paper on the walls. Allow five to ten minutes.
  - A reminder of the questions they focus on are: *What have you learned? What excites you vs what concerns you? How can we as a team improve our learning and prepare for an AI future?*
  - Have these all on a single color to represent the discussion on the "AI concept" cards – the other cards on provocations and flourishing will have a different color.
  - Facilitate a short discussion of five minutes exploring the common themes and points of differences between the post-it notes.
- Look for themes that are common across all the concept cards. You may see things emerging, such as:
  - Things we don't know.
  - The benefits and opportunities of using AI.
  - The fears or concerns of using AI.

- Run this session for three rounds so each small group processes three cards (several cards will be picked up by different teams over a session, and that is okay, as perceptions will shift over time). The running time for each card is 20 minutes, so over the period of an hour, you will have each group processing three cards. This will provide for a lot of team conversation and data capture on the perceptions of AI concepts.
- Alternatively, you can run one round using this deck, then two other rounds using the AI provocation cards and the human flourishing cards (discussed below), if you only want to keep the conversation card sessions for all three decks down to an hour.
- At the end of the session, ask your gathering to develop an action list of three things your organization needs to act on now to prepare for the age of AI, or for a specific project you are working on in your organization.
- It is preferable to have the conversation card sessions facilitated by someone who is perceived to be impartial and not pursuing an agenda, as this will enable a better free flow of contribution.

This is best as a face-to-face exercise, but if you're working with remote teams, this exercise can be replicated in online collaboration tools such as Miro. I have found that some teams want to refer to their favorite LLM on their phones for answers. Gently remind them that this session is about exercising their humanness (we already know that LLMs will have an answer). This is more of a tricky situation than you may think. There are widespread reports of citizens losing their ability to think and process information without the use of LLMs, which is leading to cognitive decline. Therefore, it's good to carve out time to allow the human brain to do its thing in these special activities.

Remember that there are no right or wrong answers, and everyone needs to express their views and opinions without judgment. There will be much contrast and ambiguity in team responses to the concepts, and even emotions and conflict about some of the content raised. Hold space for this. See if common ground can be reached on team or organizational action, or whether agreement can be reached on placing a "watch this space" for things that your organization does not yet have a definitive answer or position on.

This session provides insight into how you can be more effective in building and enabling human–machine systems in your organization. Silencing dissent and disagreement, particularly after we have explored all he complex issues in the previous chapters, will only get you more of the same dysfunction prevalent in our organizations today.

How Participants Feel after Working with the Conversation Cards

In the development and testing of the three decks of the conversation cards, a thematic analysis was conducted on the feedback given by participants. Participants were asked open-ended questions to reflect on their use of the cards (Raftopoulos, 2024). There were four key clusters of themes that emerged in the post-session surveys on what resonated with participants during the sessions:

1. **Kickstarting the process.** This cluster included themes of enjoying the fun and positive start to the workshop process and the use of effective warm-up for an organization-wide introduction to AI.
2. **Facilitating knowledge generation and sharing.** This cluster included views on how the cards provided useful, engaging introductions to AI concepts, informational reference points to anchor the workshop, and providing an effective introduction to specific AI topics and technologies.
3. **Facilitating interaction and experiences.** This cluster included themes on how the cards assisted in stimulating rich human conversations, facilitating learning and awareness of the AI topics and their issues, and challenging participants in their thinking about how AI is designed. A key theme in this cluster was the fundamental enjoyment of the tactile and tangible nature of handling and using the cards.
4. **Assistance needed**. This cluster some participants felt the need for additional support and encouragement on the topic of AI. This included needing a deeper understanding of why the cards were limited to these ten items, or that the definitions on the cards needed more clarity for beginners. This feedback was prevalent from participants with less experience or knowledge in the domain and required more guidance from their teams and the facilitator. This was a great opportunity to prompt them to ask clarifying questions and for the team to assist with knowledge sharing in a safe and encouraging environment.

Examples of participant feedback in their own words regarding the AI concept cards illustrate these themes:

- "These concepts were new for me, hence very helpful."
- "I really enjoyed the rich conversations with the people on my team who came from diverse backgrounds."
- "Gives you an idea for the technological base, which is really useful for understanding the user perceptions and readiness. I need to use this for my client-side meetings."
- "A fun way to explore complex topics."
- "I had to ask some dumb questions but I'm glad I did. Turns out they weren't so dumb after all."

Activity 2: AI Provocations Cards

The next round of the conversation card activity is on the topic of AI provocations, and the name is exactly what it does – provoke an emotional response in your participants. Ten AI provocation cards were developed based on the key barriers or negative consequences of AI technologies prevalent in extant literature (Marcus, 2022; Birhane et al., 2021; Bender et al., 2021) as well as reflecting the key concerns raised by industry commentators in popular media. These include items such as the powerful negative consequences of AI development using one-word provocations. These include theft, oppression, carbonized, anti-democratic, deterministic, disembodiment, injustice, anti-ethical, control, and colonialism. For these cards, only a statement was made as an act of provocation for stakeholders to explore the adverse effects of AI technologies on our human and planetary systems. An example of AI provocation cards is shown in Figure 7.4.

In terms of how to pay with the AI provocation cards, see the process outlined under the section *How to Play with the AI Conversation Cards*.

Examples of participant feedback for the AI provocation cards illustrate how the cards fulfilled their purpose of provoking deeper thought on the negative consequences of AI issues:

- "These were great conversation starters on the negative issues; a lot of discussion can and should be had around AI consequences."
- "As the name suggests, it 'provoked' us to look at the problems as well as the solutions."
- "Made me realize that it's important to address user concerns. I can now see that AI design needs to address these issues. I just didn't appreciate this before."
- "I was uncomfortable at first, I thought these cards were too negative. But then I saw others on my team feel so passionately about some of the issues on the cards. They opened my eyes to all the consequences."

Activity 3: Human Flourishing Cards

Ten human flourishing cards were developed based on our literature review and leveraged the increasing concerns of human flourishing in the digital era, popularized by the seminal work by VanderWeele (2017). The human flourishing concepts in this deck included items such as curiosity, mindfulness, purpose, knowledge, connection, the future of work, creativity, and empathy. Each card posed three questions for the teams to discuss. These were:

1. In the age of AI, how do I build my (card name)?
2. What needs to change for this to happen?
3. Who advances and who is left behind?

The tenth card in this set is "you," which is a good card to end the session on all three conversation card decks. The "you" card asks three personal questions:

1. In the age of AI, how do I…?
2. What is your burning question?
3. What do you need to know to answer this question?

An example of Human Flourishing cards is shown in Figure 7.5.

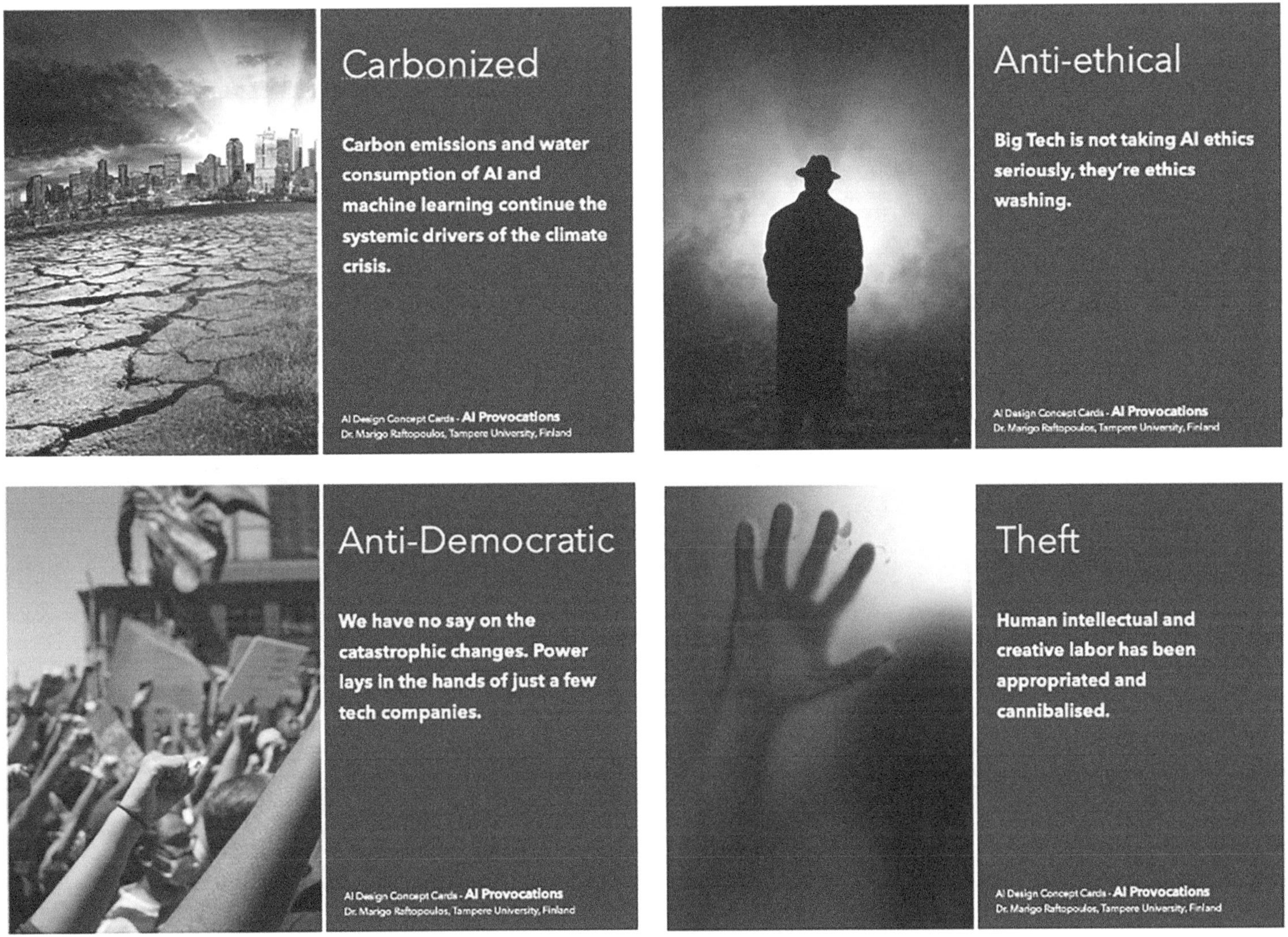

FIGURE 7.4 Four examples of AI provocation cards.

FIGURE 7.5 Four examples of human flourishing cards.

In terms of how to play with the AI human flourishing cards, see the process outlined under the section *How to Play with the AI Conversation Cards*. As this is the last deck to be explored in the conversation cards session, end with every participant using the "you" card.

Examples of participant feedback centered around stimulating thought and conversation on human topics uncommon in AI design practices:

- "It was challenging thinking about the consequences of AI on humans and flourishing. Made me realize AI will change us."
- "This was a hopeful lens; we talked about how AI can transform the way we think about knowledge and education, e.g., it's about asking the right questions."
- "I used to think it was just bad luck if AI takes your job. I now think we can, and should, influence that. It shouldn't be a foregone conclusion that AI eats us."
- "This was both sad and happy. Sad that it might be out of our control. Happy that it might actually be in our control."
- "Technology does not have the right to reduce us like this. No one signed up for this."

The most interesting outcomes of the session on human flourishing cards are that participants felt a greater sense of empowerment over the collective right to express their concerns but also to seek to influence outcomes.

Activity 4: Citizen Archetypes

In the final set of conversation cards, nine key archetypes or personas were developed from the data derived from our research on cognitive frames, detailed in Chapter 6. The use of archetypes is extensive in the HCI, games, and service design domains, influenced by the work of Cooper et al. (2007) on goal-directed design, as well as in business applications, largely influenced by the work of Mark and Pearson (2001) in strategic marketing. The nine archetypes we derived from the research presented in Chapter 6 are illustrated in Figure 7.6.

This is an engaging exercise that asks everyone in your gathering to identify which citizen archetype they identify with when it comes to using AI at work. Use of archetypes in this exercise provides psychological safety. It provides an engaging and safe medium to express their inner concerns and identify their own individual mindsets and orientations. Participant feedback from developing the Citizen Archetypes card sessions centered around the benefits of stimulating open conversations around differences in opinion and feelings toward AI:

- "These were very disarming, thank you. We were all present and accounted for."
- "I am all of these. Right now, with AI, I'm just Anxious."
- "It helped having the card to help me speak up. I didn't feel so alone."

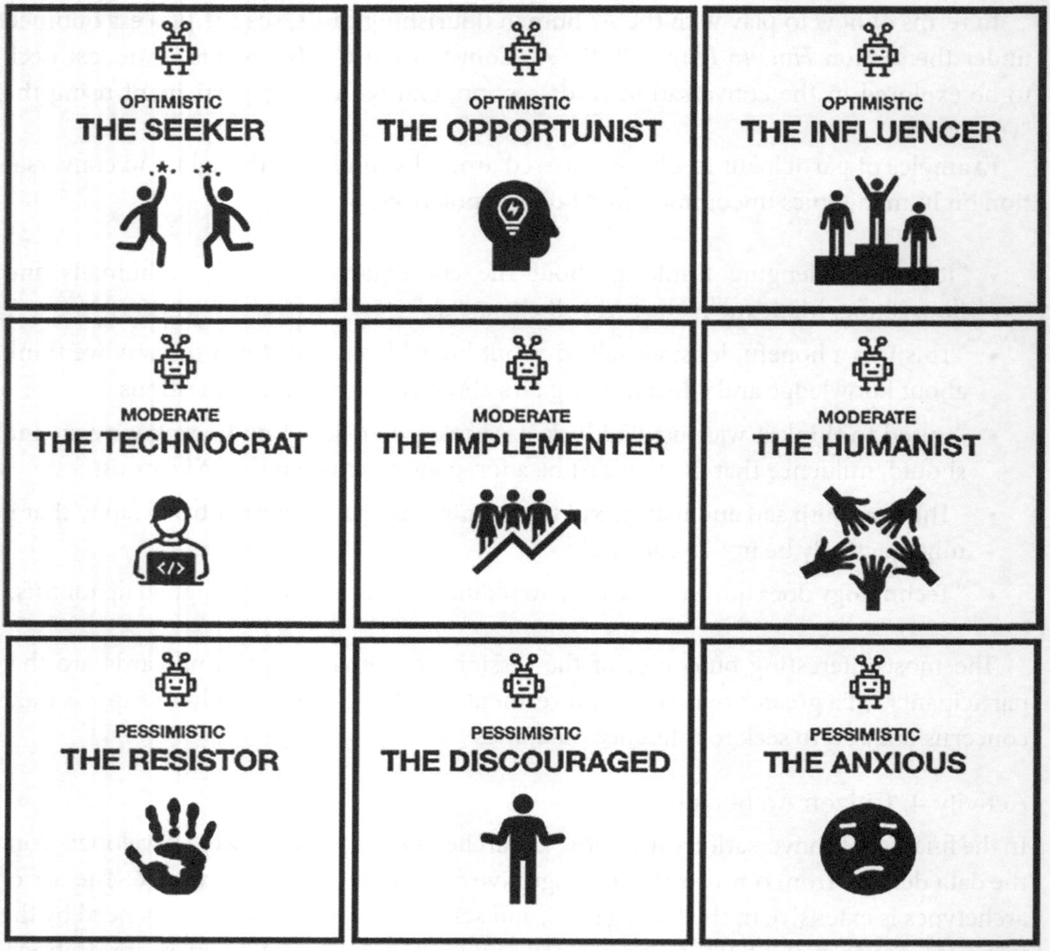

FIGURE 7.6 The nine AI citizen archetypes.

- "I got a big feeling of 'yikes' in this session, I thought we were all Seekers, apparently not. Good to know!"

To extend the exercise, participants can also be given blank cards to make up their own citizen archetype (with a name plus a drawing). The outcomes of this tend to be a combination of the nine cards and individualized to their own unique outlook. This is often a fun and engaging extension of the exercise when people are allowed to individualize their situation.

The four card-based activities can be used as an introductory session to AI at work, and they also serve as a warm-up for Activity 5 of Designing Tiny Robots. It is best held a week before Tiny Robots to allow time for reflection on the learnings raised during the conversation cards.

Activity 5: Designing Tiny Robots

Activity 5 is focused on the Designing Tiny Robots card game, which has been developed as a stand-alone design sprint. This activity moves participants from Torbert's (1998) "first person" stage that builds an "enquiring approach," into the next stage of "enhanced awareness" by increasing participants' level of challenge through application of new knowledge. As depicted in Figure 7.7, this is done in two phases.

The first is a teambuilding phase that personalizes the experience of co-creating human–machine systems by getting to know yourself and each other as teammates. This entails commencing with a self-reflection exercise on building one's own AI designer avatar with *Lego Serious Play* blocks, nominating a personal design "superpower" that they bring to the workshop, and then a group exercise to share their stories. This then moves into Phase B, which is the hands-on solution-building phase.

Phase A: Teambuilding

Divide your gathering into smaller teams of approximately five people (depending on overall numbers) to undertake an AI design challenge. To start, we use a *Lego Serious Play* exercise (Kristiansen and Rasmussen, 2014) for participants to build their own avatar or persona of an *AI Designer* in your organization. You'll need to provide individual *Lego Serious Play* blocks and/or other craft materials for this exercise. In building their avatar, participants are given three simple instructions:

- Build a portable avatar of who you are and your personal problem-solving superpower. Your superpower is any kind of personal skill, strength, or attitude that can be used in solving complex challenges.
- Write out a card with your name on it to introduce yourself and your superpower/s.
- Share your model with your team members, then build a gallery of team strengths!

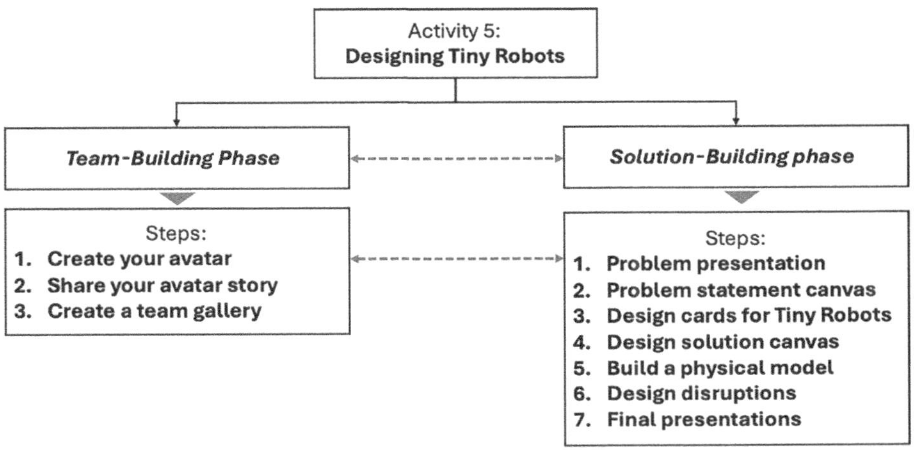

FIGURE 7.7 Activity 5: Designing tiny robots activity flow.

FIGURE 7.8 Example of a participant avatar (left) and my personal example (right).

Asking participants to offer a *personal superpower* is a playful means to bring their imagination and autonomy to the gathering in the early stages of an AI co-design challenge. Allow 15 minutes for everyone to build their avatars, then allow another 15 minutes for each team to share their avatars and superpower stories and create a team gallery of figurines for display. Examples are illustrated in Figure 7.8 of a participant avatar and notecard (left) and my own personal example (of me and my superpower contemplating my work in a Finnish forest) to create a connection with all participants in the gathering.

Participants are encouraged to keep the figurines on completion of the workshop, and we find that nearly everyone is keen to do so. On a psychosocial level, the figurines act as a talisman as a symbol to evoke the learnings of the workshop when they are back at their desk. I have received many photos from participants of their personal avatar sitting at their desk or beside their screen weeks after the workshop was run.

The reasons for this team-building phase are twofold. The first deals with potentially bringing innate designer bias out in the open. Second, it facilitates people's need to feel like they belong to a group working for a common purpose. This aims to establish openness, understanding, and empathy to create teamwork and workshop cohesion. This is also an argument for slow AI.

Participant feedback on building their AI designer avatar and sharing their personal story with their team centered around themes of personal enablement, which included enabling personal creativity, feelings of empowerment, enabling self-expression, and inviting personal involvement in the design project. An example of the emotion this generated can be seen in a few indicative quotes collected in our surveys, such as:

- "The avatar session ignited my creativity."
- "Such a good moment, it felt empowering."

- “It felt good to explain my avatar.”
- “Excellent way to encourage self-expression.”

Participant feedback on sharing team member stories and creating a gallery to symbolize their teamwork centered around building team dynamics. The themes included: getting to know each other, building empathy with team members, working effectively together as a team, and creating an interesting and fun experience. An example of the feelings this generated can be seen in a few indicative quotes, such as:

- “This allowed us to get to know our teammates.”
- “The method helped us relate to one another emotionally.”
- “This helped me build empathy toward them and this, in turn, helped us work more effectively.”

The team building phase is a short but essential exercise that runs for 30 minutes. On one level, this serves as a “warm-up,” but on a deeper level this opens enquiry into a deeper level of human connection and serves to broaden the field of vision and engagement for the creativity that is to come.

Phase B: Solution-Building

The solution-building phase is designed in a design sprint format that offers a fun and playful element to the AI system design process. This has been designed to better engage participants in learning about the key elements of AI systems design from a user's perspective. There are seven steps in the AI design sprint phase that has been tailored to introduce our specialty tools in the process. These include the *Designing Tiny Robot* card game, AI design canvases, and the building of physical low-fidelity prototypes of the solutions. The seven-step activity flow of the AI design sprint is as follows:

Step 1: Problem Presentation

At the beginning of the session, the gathering is divided into smaller teams of three to five people. A pre-prepared problem is presented for all teams to work on. Consistent with Design Thinking and Design Sprints, this initial experience is emphasized as a *demonstration exercise* and an AI learning experience. It's worth mentioning that in a live application of the methodology, the problem statement presentation will require more time for research and onboarding for all organizational stakeholders over a longer period.

Step 2: Problem Statement Canvas

Once the teams are presented with the problem statement, give them about ten minutes to discuss the depth and implications of the problem. Allow them to do additional research on the problem using a search engine or an LLM if they so choose but emphasize the need to keep this to a minimum, as the objective is to focus on human–human collaboration at this stage. An example of the problem statement canvas can be found in Appendix 1. After ten minutes, prime them for the next step.

Step 3: Design Cards for Tiny Robots

The Tiny Robot Design Cards were designed as a playful experience to engage your teams in learning and experimenting with different AI design ideas - and their potential consequences. Designing Tiny Robots was conceptualized as a design game. This game-like method provides scaffolding to structure stakeholders' design dialogues. The method also draws inspiration from design games, which are frequently used in the early phases of co-design projects in service design (Hannula and Harviainen, 2016; Hannula and Irrmann, 2016). The objective of the *Designing Tiny Robots* exercise is to design an AI-enabled solution to solve the given problem using the design constraints and challenges of the card game.

Each team should have its own deck of cards and be given time to handle and explore the deck. Humans are tactile and curious; let them explore for five minutes before we get to work. To begin the exercise, ask the teams to select one card from each deck of Task, Experience, and Touchpoint as illustrated in the examples in Figure 7.9.

An explanation of each card is as follows:

- A **Task** is the task or activity that the AI-enabled solution (or Tiny Robot) is to perform. There are eight cards in this set, which include recognize, personalize, predict, recommend, data mine, design or create, converse, and optimize. A brief description is provided to ensure participants receive a high-level awareness of the function of each of the AI-enabled tasks. The task card represents an AI technology that is the backroom engine of the functional solution.
- A **Touchpoint** is the interface technology the target citizen will be interacting with, and importantly, this is also the means by which the AI solution will collect or exchange data. The touchpoints included are social media, artificial assistant, beacon or sensor, virtual or augmented reality, wearables or implants, robots, surveillance cameras, and web/mobile/email. Most of the touchpoints in this deck are human to machine, but some can also be machine to machine.
- An **Experience** is the interaction or experience that is designed to nudge or trigger the target citizen to engage with the AI-enabled technology or its interfaces. Experiences include crowdsourcing ventures, digital games or simulations, community forums, digital quizzes or puzzles, marketing campaigns or competitions, status or recognition, escape room or treasure hunt, collection of points or badges, and loyalty rewards.
- Each team is also given one **get-out-of-jail card** per round, and this will allow them to swap one of the cards if they feel they're overly challenged trying to design an AI solution.
- The **Tiny Robots design card exercise** requires the team to place the cards face down on a table and randomly pick up one card from each set of **Task, Experience, and Touchpoint**. It should be noted that the design of the cards focused on human–machine interaction rather than machine–machine interaction. Due to the

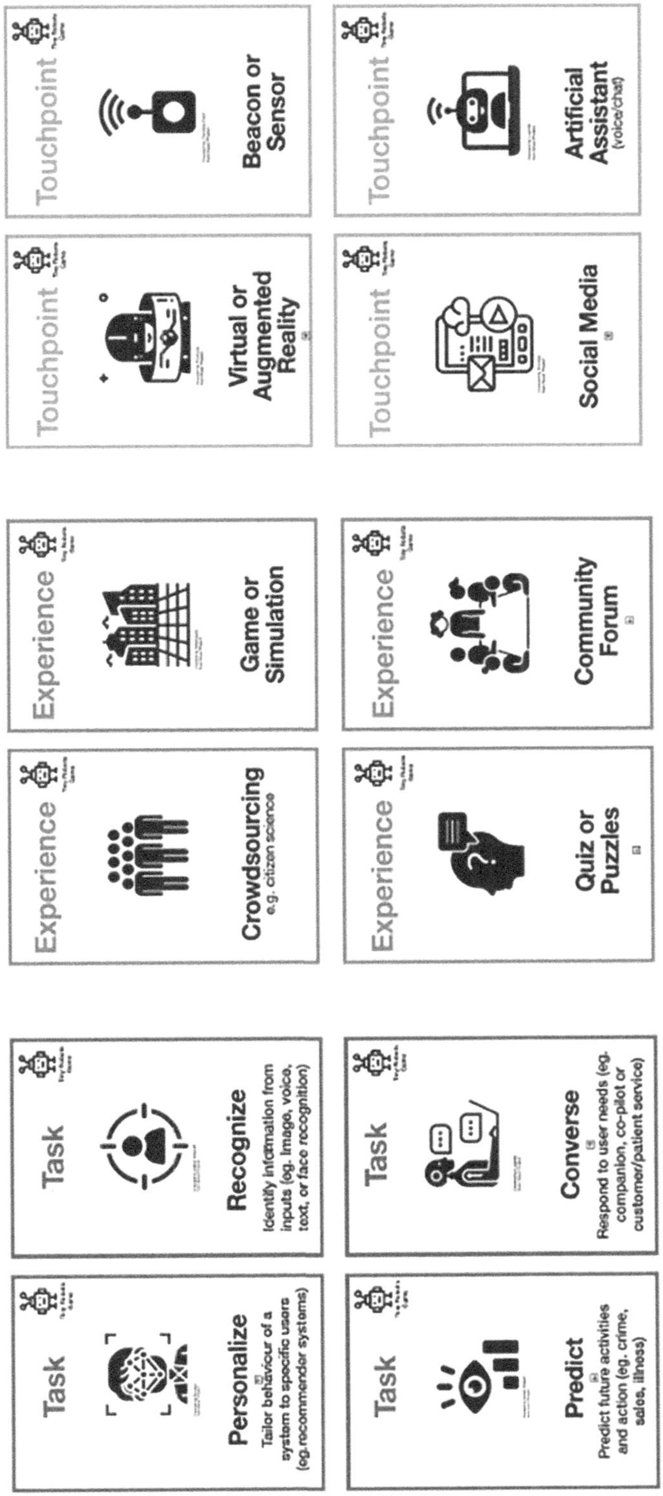

FIGURE 7.9 Examples of the tiny robot task, experience, and touchpoint cards.

challenging nature of the exercise, we also tried having the names of the cards face-up so participants had time to consider which cards they chose. This was important for groups who may have limited knowledge of different AI technology systems.

Two examples are given to participants of how these three elements work together – one positive and one negative. For example, the following simple negative scenario is presented:

- Problem statement: *How can a political party swing unsure voters?* Now pick up three Tiny Robot cards.
- Task: Personalize.
- Experience: Quiz.
- Touchpoint: Social Media.

An example potential solution could therefore be:

Build a fun and seemingly innocent quiz on "What personality type are you?" that is distributed on social media, specifically Facebook, to collect data and profile the user so we can send targeted, personalized advertisements to them about our party.

A second positive and wholesome example should also be given. The more examples given to the participants, the more likely they are to understand the flow of the game-like activity.

A standard design sprint exercise would run what they call "crazy eights," which is an exercise where teams are given limited time to be uninhibited and super creative to quickly create a pool of ideas, even if they are crazy or improbable. It's a great ideation exercise, and with the right team with the right coaching, simply amazing ideas are generated in this high-energy session.

If you feel you can do this with your team, then do so. However, I find, as many of my facilitator colleagues do, that many teams find the "crazy eight" exercise difficult to execute. Citizens are often frightened to make mistakes or look boring or uncreative in front of their colleagues. Often, many simply cannot easily ideate to the clock or in a room full of attention-seeking extroverts – and very often these can be the most creative individuals in the room. So, think carefully about what would work best with your gathering.

A possible solution to this is to ask each team to think two ideas for the set of cards. I call this **Good Robot Vs Bad Robot,** and as the name suggests, the challenge is to ideate at least one idea of a good or honorable use case, and at least one bad or evil example (let the team determine their own boundaries of good and evil). Either way, they'll figure out how the tech works, which is the objective of the introductory session. I find that this yields more ideas and hilarity than the "crazy eights" exercise.

Depending on the time you have available, run up to three sessions. That is, pick up one set of cards and ideate at least two ideas. Reshuffle, pick up another three, and ideate again. And then again for one last round. By the end of the three-round session, each team will have at least 6 ideas over 15–20 minutes. Ask them to pick their favorite idea to run with for the remainder of the AI design sprint.

This humble starter's deck, consisting of three sets of eight cards, will yield over 500 possible solutions for each design challenge. That's plenty to get you started. A great follow-up activity is to have your team design their own deck of Tiny Robot cards that are unique to the needs of your organization.

Step 4: Design Solution Canvas

The next task is to challenge the teams to flesh out their idea for an AI solution by drafting light-level notes in a design canvas over ten minutes. The canvas is provided in Appendix 2 and 3. This exercise can be done with or without the assistance of an LLM. In the first exercise in running this AI design sprint, I suggest you focus on building human–human connection and collaboration in this workshop. We know what LLMs can do; our aim is to reignite innate human creativity and create team bonds.

If you still wish to experiment with using LLMs in these sessions, then make a deliberate activity of it. First, let the team come up with their own ideas, then follow up by allowing them to ask their favorite LLM to ideate using the same cards. Compare and contrast the results in terms of the best or most interesting ideas, i.e., humans on their own, versus humans + machine together. You may need to allow more time for using LLMs in this design sprint, as crafting the best prompts may take some time.

Step 5: Build a Physical Model

In this session, teams are asked to bring their ideas to life by creating a low-fidelity model using the provided craft materials. Allow 30 minutes for this session. It's important to provide an ambient, liminal space in this environment, as people tend to become mesmerized by this session. Also noteworthy is that a lot of iteration of the original idea occurs at this time as subconscious elements come into play.

Examples of the models created by participants are provided in Figure 7.10. In our analysis of the AI physical models developed by the participants, we found what you can see as a concentration of anthropomorphic designs. Careful consideration needs to be made

FIGURE 7.10 Examples of tiny robot models.

of the materials provided for the build phase, as they can be suggestive or potentially lead participants toward anthropomorphic designs. For example, the provision of military type models can spark ideas of a combative situation in your organization, whether real or imagined.

Ramduny-Ellis et al. (2010) maintain that the nature of materials and tools provided to participants in a design space has a profound impact on the kinds of externalizations produced in creating the models. I therefore urge you to experiment by using different materials without the provision of anthropomorphic forms in the building materials to compare the outcomes in the solutions that are developed by your participants. Hearing the reasons or rationale for the different forms that are created is informative of the situation in your workplace, with your product, or with your brand.

We ran "think-aloud" sharing sessions (Yang, 2003) during the workshops, where we asked participants what they were working on while they were building their models. The results showed that participants were clear on the value and importance they placed on human–machine connectedness and collaboration that went beyond relating to AI as more than just a mechanical tool. This can be seen in the exhibits in the form of mechanical or non-biological materials attached or connected in some way to the human forms. There is symmetry in the designs and loosely connected subsystems, where integration always seemed challenged.

The subconscious mind makes connections that cannot always be verbalized, which raises the need for a deeper understanding of both conscious and subconscious factors in collaborative designs using engaging methods in this emergent and complex domain of AI technologies.

Such is the nature of entanglement.

Step 6: Design Disruptions!

After 30 minutes of model building, ask each team to provide an interim presentation of their solution and to get feedback from the other teams. Allow the gathering to visit each table while a presentation is made. The advantage of verbalizing a solution while presenting a physical model and then listening to feedback from the wider gathering is that it solidifies thought processes and provides further input into the design iteration process. After a five-minute presentation made by each team, we move to the disruption activity.

The last set of cards is elements that deliberately disrupt the "happy path" that is typical of the initial design of any digital solution. The disruption in this activity is designed to prompt participants to look deeper and question their design assumptions, their own biases, and learn the need to continuously tweak the design and function of AI systems to ensure their effectiveness and safety. An outline of the three decks of cards is illustrated in Figure 7.11 and described below:

- **Bugs** that are defined as problems associated with technological, design, or implementation limitations and challenges. Bugs included in this deck are bias, hostile

FIGURE 7.11 Examples of the disruption cards.

actors, uncanny valley, and breach. Only a small number of the most common bugs are used as we assumed only basic technical knowledge for this beginners deck. There is a bigger range of bugs that are dealt with by a specialist deck developed for AI software engineers. The intention with a general audience to give them a broad idea of the disruptions created by the more common bugs that may raise questions on the design or implementation decisions of AI-enabled systems.

- **AI ethics** are defined as the moral principles that govern human behavior or the conduct of a system's activity, which need to be honored or protected. In this deck of eight cards, we include transparency, human oversight, privacy and data governance, accountability, diversity, non-discrimination and fairness, societal and environmental well-being, technical robustness and safety, and human agency.
- **Cyber threats** are malicious acts intended to steal or damage data or disrupt the stability of a computer system. As is the case with the bug cards, we only included a small number of cyber threats in this deck to give a general audience a high-level awareness of these issues when designing or managing AI-enabled systems. These are social engineering, deep fake hacking, data poisoning, and data breach.

In the design disruptions activity, each team picks up a card from each deck of cyberthreats, ethics, and bugs, and then they are challenged to adjust their designs to deal with the problem. This can be played a few different ways. A disruption card can be selected one at a time or selected and dealt with all three issues at once (as is often the case in real life). Depending on the skill level of your teams and the objective of your session, you may only want them to deal with one or two of the disruption cards in a single session. An interesting play on this would be to select one card from each deck, then ask the teams to set priorities on which to work on first. An interesting reflection on this is to explore the team's assumptions made in deciding on that priority. Tip: As it turns

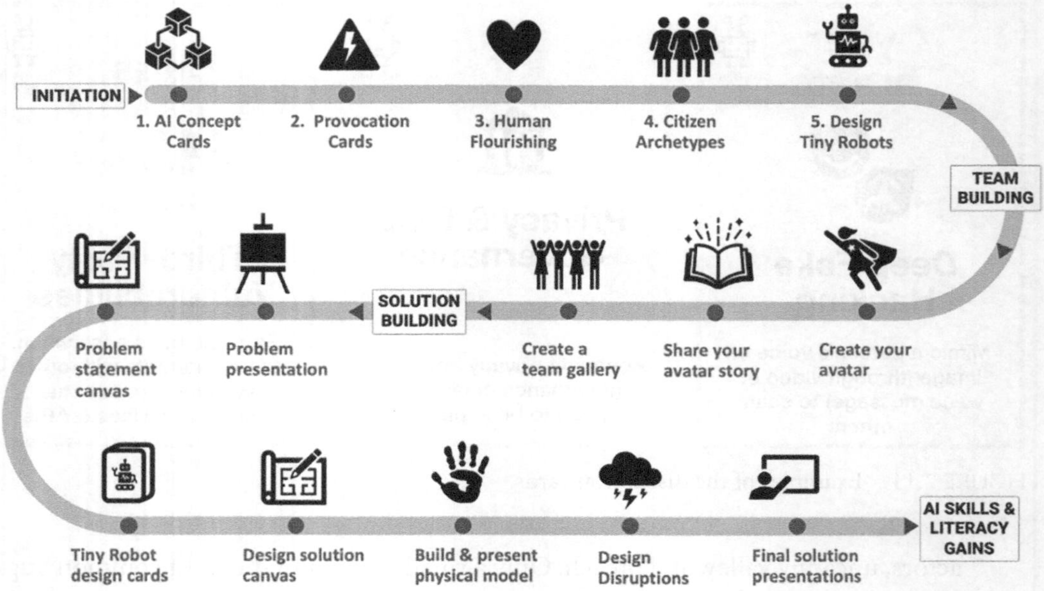

FIGURE 7.12 The activity flow of AI design tools.

out, ethics are seldom a priority, and if this arises in your workshop, use it as an opportunity for open discussion.

Step 7: Final Team Presentation of Solutions
This closing session is focused on participant reflection on the lessons learned about the different design elements reflected in the decks of cards. Each team is given five to ten minutes to present their AI solution to the wider gathering for feedback and closure.

This session also helps participants to take an informed approach to understanding how different combinations of technologies could work by making connections with the designs created by the other teams using a different set of cards.

The foundation behind the Tiny Robot design activity is to (a) encourage participants to work within design constraints in building AI solutions, (b) provide an engaging environment for participants to deeply question and understand the sample of cards that they drew, and (c) gain an appreciation of how a simple system is designed and integrated with one simple touchpoint, user experience, and technology.

A summary of the final activity flow of the 15 AI design tools and activities developed in this chapter is outlined in Figure 7.12.

AN OVERVIEW OF THE KEY ELEMENTS OF AI SYSTEMS DESIGN

The key objective of the *Designing Tiny Robots* activity is to engage stakeholders in the design of a simple human–machine system to expand the learning and awareness of the key elements of an AI system. The key to understanding AI systems design is to be clear on how the data exchanges and activity flows work in any given system, and this needs to be facilitated in the design sprint session. As depicted in Figure 7.13, the system's design strategy, data exchanges, and activity flows occur in three key parts:

- **Task to experience:** What is the nature of the overall system design? What are the strategic objectives of AI systems design and development? How is this system co-created or communicated to stakeholders? What are the ethical implications of this system?
- **Experience to touchpoint:** What is the nature of the user activation and data flows between the Touchpoint (interactive technology) and Experience (citizen engagement)? How is the target citizen nudged or activated to engage with the touchpoint? How is the data collected, processed, and stored? What are the ethical implications of this human–machine engagement?

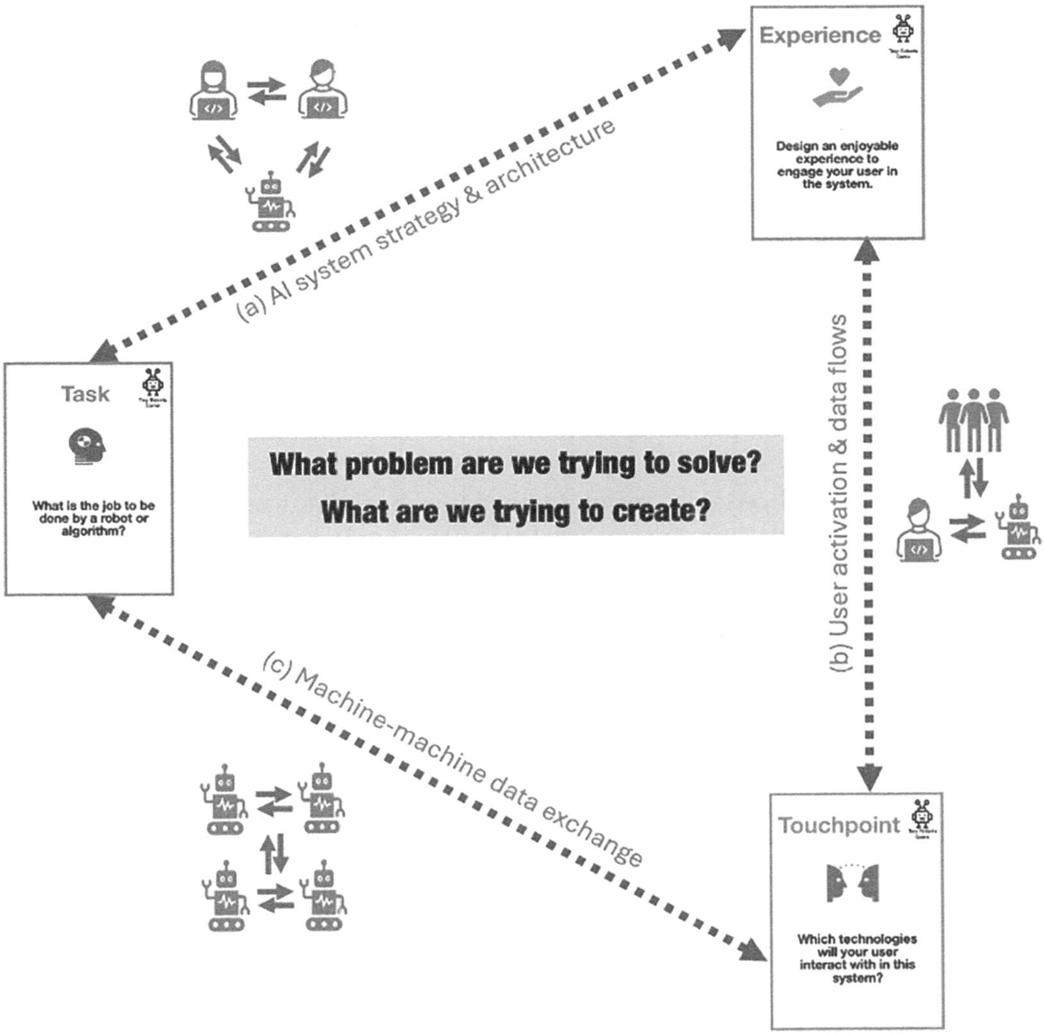

FIGURE 7.13 Tiny robot systems elements: system architecture, user activation, and data flows.

- **Touchpoint to task:** What is the nature of the machine-to-machine data exchange between the task and the touchpoint? How is the data collected, processed, and stored?

Central to this is the question of being clear on the problem that is being solved by this solution and the potential unintended consequences. To illustrate this, I will use the example of the creation of a building surveillance system (task) using a puzzle (experience) and sensors (touchpoint):

a) **Task to experience:** Using a surveillance card, the system strategy is to surveil citizens entering a building and only allowing entry to vetted employees or visitors. We want to create a welcoming and serene environment to avoid inducing fear or resistance. The problem to be solved is to secure the premises of the building.
b) **Experience to touchpoint:** Using a puzzle card, we will create a parterre garden maze from the street to the building. Light sensors will record movements of foot traffic, which will activate the surveillance cameras. The citizen experience is activated by following a set garden path to the building (which they can't jump over or cut through), so we can record all human movements. Once the citizen approaches the building, our facial recognition cameras will identify black-listed citizens by the time they arrive at the front desk. Security will automatically be notified. Employees will proceed straight to the scanner and scan their ID card. They will only be allowed through as long as they are on the green list.
c) **Touch point to task:** Data flows data and activity flows between all the connected and automated machine-to-machine items: movement sensors, facial recognition cameras, and card scanners. Human intervention will only be a call on security personnel if needed to expel a rogue citizen. One day, security personnel will be a team of robots.

This solution witll certainly 'secure the building' but what would the consequences be? Test every scenario with your stakeholders. The Tiny Robots Systems Elements diagram is provided in Appendix 2 and should be given to teams to think about their system interactions in this simple format.

In the following sections, we provide a series of detailed discussions on field notes and supporting research on design canvases, the hands-on build of models, and a review of participant feedback on the activities provided in this chapter. These field notes provide a useful guide on how to facilitate these sessions.

FIELD NOTES ON THE TINY ROBOT DESIGN CANVASES

The design canvases for the Tiny Robot design sprint were designed to provide scaffolding to aid participant thinking and creativity. They consisted of three canvases in this sprint, as provided in Appendices 1–4. A description of each is as follows:

- **The problem presentation**. Like all design sprint demonstration exercises, a short, prearranged case study is presented to the group. The more thorough approach involved contacting participants before the workshop to invite them to nominate a potential case for the gathering – the facilitator selected the most appropriate case.

- **The problem statement canvas.** On the day of the gathering, the problem statement canvas is completed by each team after the initial problem presentation and its discussion. It's important to have clarity of the problem whilst keeping it simple. As we learned in Chapter 6, many AI projects achieve suboptimal results due to a lack of clarity on the problem to be solved.
- **The design canvas.** This canvas gives structure to the process of ideating in building a model with three design cards. It's important that the potential solutions are initially recorded in writing or drawings on the canvas, then freely iterated during the following phases.
- **Disruptions canvas.** In this canvas, participants record their strategy on how they would respond to the challenges of the emergence of bugs, cyberthreats, or ethical issues, and make the necessary adjustments to their designs. These are important lessons on the adaptability that is needed to respond to changes in complex systems.
- **General perceptions of canvases.** Participants are generally comfortable with the format of the Tiny Robots design canvases due to their popularity based on the original work by Osterwalder and Pigneur (2010) and by design thinking, agile methodologies, and design sprint canvases. This serves as a good anchor for participants to gain confidence with something that they are familiar with. This offers a degree of psychological safety while using it as a springboard to delve into unfamiliar domains of AI technologies.

A cohort of participants tends to find working with canvases restricting, as it entails verbal and written conceptualizations of idea generation while sitting down at tables (while in full view of the creative materials waiting for them for the next activity). The canvases appeared to slow down some teams, particularly if one team member took "ownership" of writing up the ideas; other participants tended to retreat as they watched. This reticence is okay; people have different preferences in how they work.

Participants were often more enthusiastic in the hands-on building of their solutions and found that rapid iteration of ideas actually took place during the process of hands-on building or making – the teams then retrospectively made notes on their canvases after they were happy with their creations. *Thinking while doing* is backed by science and forms the foundational thinking behind many design approaches. Not everyone can rapidly iterate with pen and paper; some of the most creative participants think as they build a physical model with their hands.

FIELD NOTES ON BUILDING PHYSICAL MODELS OF TINY ROBOTS

External representations such as the building of physical prototypes and models are ubiquitous in design and all creative endeavors (Dix and Gongora, 2011) to provide a link between tacit and explicit knowledge, and between conscious and unconscious representation of thought and ideation. The ideation process has been claimed to be prenoetic (Gallagher, 2005), which refers to the human cognitive state or processes that occur before conscious thought or reasoning taked hold. It is about how the human body and its senses shape the mind. Creativity isn't just about deliberate thought and action; it's also about allowing subconscious or prenoetic processes to shape ideas before they become explicitly structured or logical. This is the human advantage over machines, so make the most of it.

Therefore, the building of physical prototypes in the Tiny Robots design sprint is also an embodiment of what the rational mind cannot yet articulate. This is a critical process in trying to untangle complexity to create more effective human–machine systems. It shines a light on our entanglements.

Using a sketch or a physical model with three design cards in a design process represents a single design possibility in a simple system. However, they also represent the beginning of the development of a whole set of other possibilities for the eventual product (Dix and Gongora, 2011). Sennett (2008) describes this process as a *conversation with materials* by taking a mental idea and giving it a physical form. This triggers different physical, social, and cognitive processes in those participating in the design process (Sennett, 2008).

These theoretical foundations have been the basis for popular design methodologies that include Design Thinking, Design Sprints, and *Lego Serious Play*. However, these excellent design products have become sanitized and rules-driven processes. The objective of this book is to revisit the philosophical and scientific foundations of how these methods enhance human creativity and bring them to the fore.

An example of how the materials were presented to participants as soon as they walked into the Tiny Robots workshop room can be seen in Figure 7.14. The intention here is to create a liminal space to heighten participant anticipation of an engaging, hands-on experience to heighten learning and creative processes.

There are several excellent drawing and sketching tools on the market that can replicate the Tiny Robots session to a degree. The group dynamics, connections, and psycho-social experiences between citizens however are not so easy to replicate using the software alone.

The building phase is a democratized process as everyone starts to build something during this session, then combines the ideas into a team solution. This is part of the reason participants are deliberately empowered by the session on building their own

FIGURE 7.14 Presentation of workshop materials to participants in a liminal space.

personal avatar at the very beginning of Activity 5, to ease them into the process of using their hands to build physical models, making the abstract more visible and tangible. The facilitator should ask probing questions of the teams to explain their designs so that they can "think-aloud" (Yang 2003) to add to the learning experience. However, don't weigh them down with too many questions while they are formng their ideas.

The facilitator should also explore the reasoning behind the anthropomorphic elements or the connections between mechanical and biological forms in the designs. Again, asking participants to "think-aloud" will give insight into the thought processes and hidden assumptions. This will range from design features, participant mood, emotion, and engagement experienced during the process. In design, biases and mental models are subliminal, and asking probing questions allows them to come to the surface for open examination.

Particularly interesting will be identifying what could not be articulated with anthropomorphic forms. For example, respondents would often say: "We didn't even think about it, it just happened that way." This is an excellent learning opportunity for hidden assumptions and preferences in systems design.

FIELD NOTES ON OVERALL PARTICIPANT FEEDBACK

Participant feedback was collected through interviews and surveys following the Tiny Robots design sessions.. Overwhelmingly, participants were positive and often enthusiastic about the engaging experience and process of learning about the AI system and creating a demonstration model. The common themes that emerged were (a) the enjoyment of being challenged by hands-on group design activities, (b) experimenting with a range of intuitive, informative, and tactile tools, and (c) working in a supportive, team-based environment.

In using the **Tiny Robot Design Cards**, a cohort of participants in the workshops (this ranges between 20% and 30% in any workshop) stated that they were challenged by working within these design constraints and needed more guidance or information. The reduction of human–AI system interactions down to the three elements of *Task, Touchpoint, and Experience* was not intuitive to this cohort and requires more explanation to think about human–machine interactions in this way. It is understandable that the average citizen may not be familiar with working with system design elements in this way. Equally, however, it was also observed that many of these participants had limited knowledge about the different AI technologies and how they are used in current business systems outside of generative AI. Once participants were coached through the challenge of the activity, they embraced the process and learning outcomes.

Participant feedback on the Tiny Robot design card exercises centered around the challenges and enjoyment of working within design constraints and how this can inspire ideation and different ways of thinking. Feedback from participants in their own words to illustrate these findings are as follows:

- "It was difficult to think about design constraints, but it made total sense by the end."
- "These were helpful prompts. I really liked that you could mix and match them to create multiple iterations for the same problem."

- "The cards inspired our thinking about the tiny robot design."
- "The cards were very intuitive and fun to use."

Overall, the majority of participants are enthusiastic about the **Building of Solutions phase** and the **Sharing of Solutions** phase of *Designing Tiny Robots*. There was a good level of information sharing between participants about their knowledge and perceptions of AI technologies. This was one of the objectives of this project: to have stakeholders share knowledge and ideas with each other. This is also consistent with Torbet's (1998) "third person" stage that seeks to create a wider community of inquiry among stakeholders.

In most sessions, we found that there is always a small number of participants who believe that they were personally "not creative" and feel some initial level of discomfort with making physical models. This is overcome with the encouragement from the facilitator and team members; as adults, we are unfortunately looking for "permission to play" when we should be "working." The process of engaging in teamwork during the *Tiny Robots* exercise helps these participants overcome their self-doubt and creative blockages.

The positive feedback from participants in the development of Tiny Robots confirms the importance of using a variety of interactive and creative exercises in modern digital systems design to externalize ideas on human–AI interaction; a notion supported by Dix and Gongora (2011). Creating an environment with a "permission to play" as an act that facilitates creativity and innovation is critical to this endeavor.

Feedback on the **building of physical models** focused on (a) productivity gained from visualizing the model, (b) being challenged to develop a physical model, (c) the process inspired greater levels of iteration and ideation when the idea was manifested into physical form, and (d) the enjoyment of the tactile elements of working with tactile materials.

- "I'm not good at this, but I enjoyed working with the team."
- "Loved it! This was easy to adopt and helps understand the technology design cycle."
- "Helped in better visualizing the problem and solution. We found that so much was subliminal. It wasn't written on the canvas, but it came out in the physical model we built. That blew me away."
- "A very useful and productive exercise that helped us to formulate 'out-of-the-box' ideas and crystallize solutions so rapidly!"
- "This was so much fun."

In the **sharing of solutions exercise**, participants reported on (a) how the process led to constructive design outcomes, (b) was a source for inspiration and teambuilding, and (c) gave them the feeling of being part of a group effort to collaborate on a solution.

- "It was interesting to listen to the different ways each team had in approaching the same problem. This was the best part."

- "This was a nice platform to share your ideas on AI. I enjoyed giving a playful 'pitch' of our solution which helped us all imagine the possible applications and commercial aspect of our ideas."
- "I was very impressed by the creativity and compassion of the proposed solutions. Forces you to think about team communication and the draft presentation early in the design phase."
- "I felt a sense of empathy with all the other teams in the conference room. We were all working on the same problem. We could have melded all our ideas together in the end for a fantastic overall solution."

CHAPTER INSIGHTS AND SUMMARY

The objective of this chapter was to explain how we might make AI systems design and development tangible, engaging, and understandable to a wide range of stakeholders in a process of co-creation. We developed and tested a variety of artifacts in the form of different AI design tools that can be used in the collaboration and co-creation of AI-enabled systems. These are provided in this chapter for you as a starting point to begin your exploration of the possibilities of AI.

There is still more work that needs to be done to investigate how we can improve AI systems to be more human-centered, transparent, and trustworthy. This is more than just an idealistic stance (not that there should be a problem with taking an idealistic stance). Human-centered, transparent, and trustworthy AI directly affects optimal citizen acceptance and implementation of AI-enabled technologies – and hence sets up the technology for success in your organization. Given the limitations and challenges that have been outlined in the preceding chapters, this is a business case to avoid the waste of failed AI projects by not only enabling the capabilities of the technology but also nurturing the human systems that enable it.

The approach and methodology of *Designing Tiny Robots* are in line with what Dix and Gongora (2011) describe as focusing on external representations of design so that we can make sense of tools for reflection and creativity, which will ultimately lead to improved design. Given the nature of human–machine entanglement, this is an important way to generate greater clarity and awareness of this complexity.

The different methods and tools presented in this chapter can be used in sequence or independently of each other. For example, the three sets of conversation cards work very well on executive teams that do not want to delve into the details of a system design. The key benefits these executives saw from the conversation cards were tools to facilitate deeper and often difficult conversations with internal teams and external stakeholders. For example, this exercise was used with a consulting firm in a discovery session with their clients to demystify AI technologies in an engaging, informative, and non-threatening environment.

It is important to take everyone on this AI journey. Consistent with the research on threat avoidance in Chapter 6, we found that a certain cohort of participants found it challenging to grasp AI concepts or to conceptualize human–machine interaction down to task/touchpoint/experience, and then to deal with bugs, cyberthreats, and ethics. Despite the AI domain being emergent and highly complex, endeavors still need to be made to democratize this knowledge to attain true collaboration and co-creation with a wide range of stakeholders. On a meta level, given technological disruptions to our social and planetary systems and citizens' social contract with our institutions, we owe this to society as a whole.

The positive feedback we've received on the *Designing Tiny Robots* exercise is an indication of the high value stakeholders place on collaboration and mutual learning in modern system design. However, the key challenge is that software development is a highly technical and complex production process. Given current practices, developers are unable to accommodate a more involved and time-consuming stakeholder co-creation practices, as it slows down the software production cycles and affects costs and time to market. Furthermore, stakeholder co-creation requires a different skill set that needs to be acquired by developers. In effect, this locks out the human, social, and public policy issues that emerge during co-creation practices.

On a technical level, current AI technology development is modular, fragmented, and difficult for developers to trace responsibility and accountability. For example, Widder and Nafus (2023) identified "dislocated accountabilities" that have been created by the modularity of roles and responsibilities and division of labor across different actors in the AI technology supply chain. Similarly, Schmidt et al. (2023) found considerable role ambiguity among developers of AI-based systems, which blurs the boundaries of system accountability. Within this environment, integrating stakeholder co-creation will be fraught with challenges.

This has led to calls by researchers to develop AI software development models that consider human-centered priorities early in the development cycle using novel computational tools (Hartikainen et al., 2023). It is well known that technical solutions to build business systems seldom consider the complexity of socio-technical interactions between stakeholders, and that these interactions have considerable impacts on organizations and society (Raisch and Krakowski, 2021). This is a vicious circle. Collaborative design slows down the development process, but a lack of collaborative design leads to lower technology effectiveness and acceptance.

While both researchers and practitioners believe that the current system of AI software development is unlikely to change any time soon (Widder and Nafus, 2023), human-centered design and collaborative elements like the artifacts developed in this chapter help to challenge the current system with opportunities to raise the bar for better practices. For example, the methods outlined in this chapter have the potential to supplement the development of AI Model Cards (Mitchell et al., 2019; Crisan et al., 2022) that are already implemented by many technology companies but could be refined to incorporate a collaborative approach with a wide range of industry stakeholders.

Reflecting on this work, it's useful to consider Ng et al. (2021) in their review of AI literacy as having three levels: knowing and understanding AI, using and applying AI, and evaluating and creating AI. This can be seen as a hierarchy in the level of understanding, where one level needs to be mastered before moving on to the next (Ng et al., 2021). This is not too dissimilar to Brennan and Resnick's (2012) three key dimensions of the *computational thinking framework* as people engage with content through design-based learning activities:

- **Computational concepts**. These are the preliminary computational concepts that designers become familiar with and engage early in the process.
- **Computational practices.** These are the practices designers begin to develop as they engage with the concepts to build solutions.
- **Computational perspectives.** These are the perspectives designers form about the world around them and about themselves through reflecting on the computational products they have designed.

The works presented in this chapter reflect this pattern of computational thinking that takes citizens through a structured process of concepts, practices, and perspectives in designing Tiny Robots. However, our business and technology sectors are only at the beginning of a renewed focus on what is required and necessary to incorporate these practices into AI development and deployment workflows. We offer our work as a contribution toward this collective endeavor.

CONCLUSION

Despite the potential of AI technologies to improve business performance, it has been widely reported as delivering limited returns on investment. This has been largely attributed to organizational enablement issues (Chapters 2, 5, and 6), as well as technology adoption issues among system users. One way to manage these limitations is to engage a wide range of stakeholders in the AI technology co-creation process that may account for a fuller range of the socio-technical interactions between stakeholders and thereby alleviate issues in relation to technology design, effectiveness, and adoption. In this chapter, we present a set of tools that can be used by researchers, organizational leaders, and project managers to better collaborate with stakeholders in developing more robust human-centered AI technology designs and enablement strategies. The greater challenge, however, remains that the current complexity of the AI software development value-chain and the high complexity in AI concepts are still challenging collaborative approaches to AI system design with a wide range of stakeholders.

ACKNOWLEDGMENTS

The author wishes to thank Audrey Thompson for her contribution to the creation of the workshop tools and processes. Thanks also to Tampere University, University of Oslo, and the Hawaii International Conference on Systems Sciences (HICSS) for hosting formal Tiny Robot workshops in the academic community. Deep thanks to Associate Professor

Dina Koutsikouri, Associate Professor Lena Hylving and Professor Juho Hamari for their support and encouragement on the research featured in this chapter.

This project has received funding from the European Union's Horizon 2020 research and innovation programme under the Marie Sklodowska-Curie Grant Agreement No. 101023024 for Augmented Humans.

REFERENCES

Arrasvuori, J., Boberg, M., Holopainen, J., Korhonen, H., Lucero, A., and Montola, M. (2011). Applying the PLEX Framework in Designing for Playfulness. In *Proceedings of 2011 International Conference on Designing Pleasurable Products and Interfaces (DPPI '11), ACM*, pp.179–186, New York, USA.

Bender, E. M., Gebru, T., McMillan-Major, A., and Shmitchell, S. (2021). On the dangers of stochastic parrots: Can language models be too big? In *Proceedings of the 2021 ACM Conference on Fairness, Accountability, and Transparency* (pp. 610–623).

Birhane, A., Kalluri, P., Card, D., Agnew, W., Dotan, R., and Bao, M. (2021). *The Values Encoded in Machine Learning Research*. http://arxiv.org/abs/2106.15590.

Brandt, E., and Messeter, J. (2004). Facilitating collaboration through design games. In *proceedings of the Eighth Conference on Participatory Design: Artful Integration: Interweaving Media, Materials and Practices*, pp.121–131.

Brennan, K., and Resnick, M. (2012). New frameworks for studying and assessing the development of computational thinking. In *Proceedings of the 2012 Annual Meeting of the American Educational Research Association, Vancouver, Canada* (Vol. 1, p. 25).

Cao, G., Duan, Y., Edwards, J. S., and Dwivedi, Y. K. (2021). Understanding managers' attitudes and behavioral intentions towards using artificial intelligence for organizational decision-making. *Technovation*, *106*, 102312.

Cooper, A., Reimann, R., and Cronin, D. (2007). *About Face 3: The Essentials of Interaction Design*. John Wiley and Sons.

Corbin, J., and Strauss, A. L. (2008). *Basics of Qualitative Research 3e*. Sage.

Crisan, A., Drouhard, M., Vig, J., and Rajani, N. 2022. Interactive model cards: A human-centered approach to model documentation. In *Proceedings of the 2022 ACM Conference on Fairness, Accountability, and Transparency* (pp. 427–439).

Dix, A., and Gongora, L. (2011). Externalization and design. In *Proceedings of the Second Conference on Creativity and Innovation in Design* (pp. 31–42).

Dwivedi, Y. K., Hughes, L., Ismagilova, E., Aarts, G., Coombs, C., Crick, T., Duan, Y., Dwivedi, R., Edwards, J., Eirug, A., Galanos, V., Ilavarasan, P. V., Janssen, M., Jones, P., Kar, A. K., Kizgin, H., Kronemann, B., … Williams, M. D. (2021). Artificial Intelligence (AI): Multidisciplinary perspectives on emerging challenges, opportunities, and agenda for research, practice and policy. *International Journal of Information Management*, *57*, 101994.

Farrow, E. (2021). Mindset matters: How mindset affects the ability of staff to anticipate and adapt to Artificial Intelligence (AI) future scenarios in organisational settings. *AI & Society*, *36*(3), 895–909.

Flanagan, M., and Nissenbaum, H. (2007). A game design methodology to incorporate social activist themes. *CHI*, San Jose, California, USA.

Friedman, B., and Hendry, D. G. (2012). The envisioning cards: A toolkit for catalyzing humanistic and technical imaginations. *CHI*, Austin, Texas, USA.

Gallagher, S. (2005). *How the Body Shapes the Mind*. Oxford University Press.
Ghajargar, M., and Bardzell, J. (2022). Making AI understandable by making it tangible: Exploring the design space with ten concept cards. In *Proceedings of the 34th Australian Conference on Human-Computer Interaction* (pp. 74–80).
Goodhue, D. L., and Thompson, R. L. (1995). Task-technology fit and individual performance. *MIS Quarterly, 19*(2), 213–236.
Hanelt, A., Bohnsack, R., Marz, D., and Antunes Marante, C. (2021). A systematic review of the literature on digital transformation: Insights and implications for strategy and organizational change. *Journal of Management Studies, 58*(5), 1159–1197.
Hannula, O., and Harviainen, J. (2016). Efficiently inefficient: Service design games as innovation tools. In Morelli, N., de Götzen, A., and Grani, F. (eds.), *ServDes 2016: Service Design Geographies*, 24–26 May, Copenhagen, Denmark. https://doi.org/10.21606/servdes2016.6
Hannula, O., and Irrmann, O. (2016). Played into collaborating: Design games as scaffolding for service co-design project planning. *Simulation & Gaming, 47*(5), 599–627.
Hartikainen, M., Väänänen, K., and Olsson, T. (2023). Towards a human-centred artificial intelligence maturity model. In *Extended Abstracts of the 2023 CHI Conference on Human Factors in Computing Systems* (pp. 1–7).
Hevner, A., March, S. T., Park, J., and Ram, S. (2004). Design science in information systems research, *MIS Quarterly, 28*(1), 75–105.
Hornecker, E. (2010). Creative Idea Exploration within the Structure of a Guiding Framework: The Card Brainstorming Game. In proceedings of TEI 2010.
IDEO. (2003). *IDEO Method Cards: 51 Ways to Inspire Design*. Palo Alto: IDEO.
Kerzel, U. (2021). Enterprise AI canvas integrating artificial intelligence into business. *Applied Artificial Intelligence, 35*(1), 1–12.
Kristiansen, P., and Rasmussen, R. (2014). *Building a Better Business Using the Lego Serious Play Method*. John Wiley and Sons.
Liang, H., and Xue, Y. (2009). Avoidance of information technology threats: A theoretical perspective. *MIS Quarterly, 33*(1), 71–90.
Lucero, A., and Arrasvuori. J. (2010). *PLEX Cards: A source of inspiration when designing for playfulness*. In proceedings of the 3rd International Conference on Fun and Games pp. 28–37, ACM, New York, USA.
Marcus, G. (2022). Artificial general intelligence is not as imminent as you might think, *Scientific American, June 6,* 2022. www.scientificamerican.com/article/artificial-general-intelligence-is-not-as-imminent-as-you-might-think1/ Accessed 6 November 2025.
Mark, M., and Pearson, C. S. (2001). *The Hero and the Outlaw: Building Extraordinary Brands through the Power of Archetypes*. McGraw Hill Professional.
Mikalef, P., and Gupta, M. (2021). Artificial intelligence capability: Conceptualization, measurement calibration, and empirical study on its impact on organizational creativity and firm performance. *Information & Management, 58*(3), 103434
Mitchell, M., Wu, S., Zaldivar, A., Barnes, P., Vasserman, L., Hutchinson, B., ... and Gebru, T. (2019). Model cards for model reporting. In *Proceedings of the Conference on Fairness, Accountability, and Transparency* (pp. 220–229).
Mueller, F., Gibbs, M.R., Vetere, F., and Edge, D. (2014). *Supporting the Creative Game Design Process with Exertion Cards. CHI 2014,* Toronto, Canada.
Muller, M. (2014). Curiosity, creativity, and surprise as analytic tools: grounded theory method. In Olson, J., and Kellogg, W. (eds), *Ways of Knowing in HCI*. Springer.

Ng, D. T. K., Leung, J. K. L., Chu, S. K. W., and Qiao, M. S. (2021). Conceptualizing AI literacy: An exploratory review. *Computers and Education: Artificial Intelligence*, *2*, 100041.

Osterwalder, A., and Pigneur, Y. (2010). *Business Model Generation: A Handbook for Visionaries, Game Changers, and Challengers* (Vol. 1). John Wiley and Sons.

Pumplun, L., Tauchert, C., and Heidt, M. (2019). A new organizational chassis for artificial intelligence – exploring organizational readiness factors. *European Conference on Information Systems*. Stockholm and Uppsala, Sweden.

Raftopoulos, M. (2024). Designing Tiny Robots: Engaging Stakeholders in Collaborative AI System Design. In *Proceedings of the 27th International Academic Mindtrek Conference* (pp. 121–132).

Raftopoulos, M., and Hamari, J. (2023). Human-AI collaboration in organizations: a literature review on enabling value creation. *The European Conference on Information Systems (ECIS) 2023 Research Papers. Kristiansand, Norway.*

Raisch, S., and Krakowski, S. (2021). Artificial intelligence and management: The automation–augmentation paradox. *Academy of Management Review*, *46*(1), 192–210.

Ramduny-Ellis, D., Hare, J., Dix, A., Evans, M., and Gill, S. 2010. Physicality in design: An exploration. *The Design Journal*, *13*(1), 48–76.

Schell, J. (2008). *The Art of Game Design: A Deck of Lenses*. Schell Games.

Schmidt, J. H., Bartsch, S. C., Adam, M., and Benlian, A. (2023). Accountability incongruence and its effects on AI developers' job satisfaction. *ECIS 2023 Research Papers*, 284. https://aisel.aisnet.org/ecis2023_rp/284

Sennett, R. (2008). *The Craftsman*. Allen Lane.

Shollo, A., Hopf, K., Thiess, T., and Müller, O. 2022. Shifting ML value creation mechanisms: A process model of ML value creation. *The Journal of Strategic Information Systems*, *31*(3), 101734.

Spies, R., Grobbelaar, S., and Botha, A. 2020. A scoping review of the application of the task-technology fit theory. In *Responsible Design, Implementation and Use of Information and Communication Technology: 19th IFIP WG 6.11 Conference on e-Business, e-Services, and e-Society, I3E 2020, Skukuza, South Africa,* April 6–8, 2020, Proceedings, Part I 19 (pp. 397–408).

Torbert, W. R. (1998). Developing wisdom and courage in organizing and sciencing. In Srivastva, S., and Cooperrider, D. (eds), *Organizational Wisdom and Executive Courage*. New Lexington Press, pp. 222–253.

Vakkuri, V., Kemell, K. K., Jantunen, M., Halme, E., and Abrahamsson, P. (2021). ECCOLA—A method for implementing ethically aligned AI systems. *Journal of Systems and Software*, *182*, 111067.

VanderWeele, T. J. (2017). On the promotion of human flourishing. Proceedings of the National Academy of Sciences, U.S.A., 31,8148-8156. https://doi.org/10.1073/pnas.1702996114.

Venkatesh, V., Morris, M. G., Davis, G. B., and Davis, F. D. 2003. User acceptance of information technology: Toward a unified view. *MIS Quarterly*, *27*(3), 425–478.

Waardenburg, L., Huysman, M., and Sergeeva, A. V. 2022. In the land of the blind, the one-eyed man is king: Knowledge brokerage in the age of learning algorithms. *Organization Science*, *33*(1), 59–82.

Wagner, D. N. 2020. The nature of the Artificially Intelligent Firm – An economic investigation into changes that AI brings to the firm. *Telecommunications Policy*, *44*(6), 101954.

Widder, D. G., and Nafus, D. (2023). Dislocated accountabilities in the "AI supply chain": Modularity and developers' notions of responsibility. *Big Data & Society*, *10*(1), 20539517231177620.

Wölfel, C., and Merritt, T. (2013). Method card design dimensions: A survey of card-based design tools. In P. Kotz et al. (Eds.), *INTERACT* 2013, part I, LNCS 8117, pp. 479–486. IFIP International Federation for Information Processing.

Yang, S. C. (2003). Reconceptualizing think-aloud methodology: Refining the encoding and categorizing techniques via contextualized perspectives. *Computers in Human Behavior*, *19*(1), 95–115.

CHAPTER 8

Provocations

There is as yet insufficient data for a meaningful answer.
The troubles of modern life come from being divorced from nature.

—ISAAC ASIMOV

INTRODUCTION

Providing a comprehensive book that covers every truth or theory about human–machine relationships is simply not possible. The previous seven chapters have offered insights into our technology entanglements from anthropological, sociological and eco-political perspectives. Along with thoughtful considerations of scientific progress in understanding the human-machine condition this book offers insight not only in terms of where we've come from, but also where we may be heading.

The References section at the end of each chapter will further help you understand the landscape as we currenlty know it, but the rest is up to you. And this is a challenge that you must take because of one little thing: no one really knows what is to come (and those who say they know are either bluffing or delusional). The trajectories we take are a choice, not the foregone conclusion that it's made out to be. Exercise your choice as a citizen to take decisive action to create the world you want and the world we need. To quote Joe Strummer, punk rock musician and activist: The future is unwritten; we are all authors of the future that is to come.

Yes, you can be a great organizational leader, run a profitable and effective organization that meets your stakeholders' expectations on financial targets, customer service, and environmental sustainability goals. You can achieve this through what we discussed as strategic sassiness, human fearlessness, organizational rewilding, and technology

DOI: 10.1201/9781003616566-12

reimagining. But you need to level up a notch to flourish in the age of AI. Toward this endeavor, I have five provocations for you.

AN INVITATION TO BE UNDISCIPLINED

The many years I spent in traditional "digital transformation" roles for corporate clients taught me many things, but the most critical was how quickly we lose meaning and resonance of an agreed strategic direction when we conform to normative language in our communications with stakeholders. This includes the guidelines we develop in how we conduct our work, and the metrics we use to measure if we have performed, as well as we had promised in "the plan". This normative language is the language of the MBAs, the politicians, the consultants, the academics, of human resources, and of public relations that quietly frame how we should all think, how to express thought, and how to perform toward desirable predetermined metrics. To be frank, this position will lead you on the road to nowhere in the age of AI. Now is the time for a shift.

As we learned in Chapters 3 and 4, humans have advanced through time by creating *boundary objects* for new tools, as well as developing *symbolic systems* and *systems of abstractions* to interpret and utilize emerging technologies – even in communities and societies that may be apprehensive about change. However, we are approaching a critical juncture where these established or legacy frameworks are becoming less effective at helping us understand our environment in the age of AI, instead serving to maintain and reinforce existing paradigms. Therefore, the key question leaders need to ask of themselves is how we challenge our thinking and our behaviors, especially when we're bound within the disciplines of our professions, trades and industries? My provocation here is to undiscipline yourself.

Anti-disciplinarity, as originally developed by Fred Moten and Stefano Harney (2013), represents a radical critique of academic disciplines and institutional knowledge production. Their concept challenges the very foundations of how knowledge is organized, legitimized, and controlled within universities and other institutional settings. At its core, anti-disciplinarity rejects the compartmentalization of knowledge into discrete academic fields. Moten and Harney argue that *disciplinary boundaries serve to fragment understanding and maintain hierarchical power structures*. They contend that disciplines don't merely organize knowledge neutrally; they actively police what counts as legitimate knowledge and who can be recognized as a legitimate knower. Given what we explored in Chapters 3 and 4, it is worth keeping in mind that if we want to nurture innovation in our organizations and promote human flourishing in the age of AI, we need to rise above all that which holds us back.

To intensify this provocation, anti-disciplinarity also carries a strong political dimension. Moten and Harney link disciplinary knowledge to colonial and racial violence, arguing that academic disciplines have historically served to exclude and marginalize certain forms of knowledge, particularly those emerging from Black and Indigenous communities. They see anti-disciplinary practice as a form of resistance to these exclusions.

The fugitive quality of anti-disciplinary work is crucial as it operates through what they call "fugitive planning," which involves creating alternative spaces and practices that exist both within and against established institutional structures. This practice of provocation can be used equally in corporate settings that, not coincidentally, share the same siloed mentality as academia.

This isn't simply about being *interdisciplinary* or *multidisciplinary* which is spoken of often in business and academia but rarely sees reliable commitment and follow-though. It is about fundamentally questioning the legitimacy of disciplinary organization itself. Their approach emphasizes improvisation, collaboration, and what they term "hapticality," which is a form of knowledge that emerges through touch, contact, and embodied interaction rather than through detached observation. This had been one of the inspirations for developing the Conversation Cards and the Designing Tiny Robots game presented in Chapter 7 as an invitation for stakeholder co-creation of AI systems. The physicality of the exercises and the tactile nature of the materials were reported by respondents as inspirational and a motivation to learn the material and to work collaboratively to reimagine problems and their possible solutions. I know we can push the envelope further if we put our collective heads together with these radical acts.

Anti-disciplinarity thus represents both a critique of existing knowledge structures and a proposal for alternative ways of thinking, learning, and being together that prioritize collective study over individual expertise and institutional validation. However, when Moten and Harney critique disciplines, they're not just talking about academic fields but about discipline as a form of social control or the ways institutions shape, constrain, and "discipline" both knowledge and bodies. Being "undisciplined" in this context becomes a form of resistance to these regulatory mechanisms.

Disputes about the nature, borders, and rationales of academic disciplines have a history as long as the disciplines themselves (Osborne, 2015), but at least academia has opened this for debate (despite little change to show for it). However, the division of academic disciplines is reflected in the disciplines we see in MBA programs, organizations, and government, are all borne of empire; it's up to us to take up the challenge of undisciplining ourselves into our practice.

Continuing on this theme, scholars such as Armiero et al. (2019) maintain that being undisciplined in academia could be part of a wider *societal purpose of radicalizing and transforming ways of thinking politically about the socio-ecological conditions of human and non-human existence.* They believe that there can be many forms of un-disciplining scholarship and ways of practicing it that challenge what they call "the oppressive disciplinarity of neoliberal academia" (Armiero et al., 2019). In other words, the current way we do things is part of the problem and is nowhere near the solution we need for systemic change. In an environment where the popular narrative of how AI will change and dominate the world and alter our way of life is a key scenario we are all facing – isn't it in our best interest to take this on as an exercise of risk mitigation and creative destruction?

To help you out here, I'll share an exercise I often run with executives. I have adapted the 10 items in the *undisciplining manifesto* and have refined and reworked them to suit both researchers and practitioners looking to undiscipline themselves to think outside of the confines of their respective fields. These are *radical thought experiments*. I have found that for us to change even just a tiny bit, we need to first truly imagine the full expanse of the impossible. The 10 thought experiments in undisciplining are as follows:

1. **Question your identity.** How might we expose the superimposed mental models that have shaped us?
2. **Everything is gendered, racial, and cultural.** How might we remove these blinkers that limit our thoughts and vision?
3. **Be naked.** How might we lift the masks that speak on our behalf, or the masks that you hide behind?
4. **Get expelled.** Better still, camouflage yourself and sabotage from the inside. How might we be anarchists and break things?
5. **Be a rebel.** How might we build a revolutionary agenda to produce new socio-technical realities?
6. **Undisciplined is a choice – but is grounded in empathy.** How might we build and support communities that want to reduce oppressive thoughts and practices?
7. **Undiscipline cannot become a new discipline.** How might we prevent the creation of yet another paternalistic system of control?
8. **Undisciplined is a move toward disobedience.** How might we start to transgress in order to be undisciplined?
9. **Being undisciplined implies having fun.** How might we build and maintain fun and joy in the process of unbecoming (and avoid becoming paramilitary)?
10. **Being undisciplined is a process of liberation; one will never be completely undisciplined.** How might we keep ourselves honest and in tune with what it means to be human and connected?

I have run this exercise with many different teams, and the results have been wild, to say the least. Much can't practically be implemented (and is not the point in any case), but the intellectual and emotional freedom generated through the joy of being unencumbered has been priceless – but to many people, these ideas and thought experiments may also feel threatening, so you need to be gentle. However, *the general idea is to make people feel uncomfortable* – this is the essence of the creative destruction of the things we cannot see that are holding us back as individuals, organizations, and communities.

Use your imagination to develop props for each of the thought experiments and allow your people to immerse themselves in character. Please have it professionally facilitated, as the emotions that are generated can sometimes be difficult for a novice to manage when a passionate group of people is involved in psychologically challenging exercises. Very often, we ask the groups to sit with their thoughts and discomfort, as solutions are nearly always not easy to come by in the short term. Very often, ideas and insight emerge days or weeks later from our subconscious.

Don't underestimate the power of these thought experiments to plant a seed. I'll repeat what I said above; for us to change even just a tiny bit, we need to first truly imagine the full expanse of the impossible.

AN INVITATION FOR ARTISTIC INTERVENTIONS

While the use and impact of AI in the arts is a book in itself, in this section, I'm focusing on how to use the creative arts to provoke attention and conversation, and if well handled, constructive action. First, a comment about how many artists around the world are actively taking measures to defend their creative works from being exploited by generative AI systems. Their actions range from public campaigns and legal advocacy to bring public attention to the issues. Visual artists began protesting generative AI in 2022, and then the protests extended to other creative domains such as writers, filmmakers, actors, and musicians, claiming that AI posed an existential threat to their livelihoods. High-profile artist lend their support to the movement, which includes Pearl Jam, Nicki Minaj, Billie Eilish, Stevie Wonder, Elvis Costello, and several others, calling upon AI developers, tech companies, and platforms to stop using AI to infringe on their creative art (Edwards, 2024).

Creative artists were the canary in the coalmine for the first of the professional "white collar" workers to experience considerable job losses, loss in the meaning of work, and experience the direct theft of their work as generative AI models scraped their "data" without permission.

The creative arts are a dynamic space for examining and expressing the impact of AI on society, creativity, and technology in terms of the positive as well as the negative impacts. Both traditional artists and new media creators are now using visual arts to communicate complex ideas about AI, provoke dialogue, and invite viewers to reflect on how AI is reshaping our world. For example, the themes often explored in AI-related visual art are:

- **Identity and Agency:** How does AI affect our sense of self and creative voice? Who "owns" the product of a collaboration between human and machine?
- **Surveillance and Data:** Artworks visualize the pervasive presence of data collection and algorithmic decision-making.
- **Imagination and Future:** Sci-fi landscapes are blended with commentary on possible futures shaped by AI.
- **Emotional Resonance:** Some artists probe whether machine-generated art can evoke the same emotional impact as human-made work.

This was the reasoning behind the use of visual and tactile mediums in the design of my *AI Design Cards* and the *Designing Tiny Robots Cards* presented in Chapter 7.

Artistic expression has been one of the most poignant ways to express the human-technology condition, particularly for its potent visceral effects on citizens as all our senses are engaged when interacting with art. For example, the ***Broken Machines and Wild Imaginings*** exhibition resulting from an *AI Anarchies* workshop in Berlin in 2023

(AI Anarchies, 2023) that engaged a wide range of performance, visual and musical artists to explore the full spectrum of the impact of AI on our lives, from AI as a tool of subjugation to AI as companions and tools for pleasure. All the installations were provocations for deep thinking on the relationships between humans and technology, and on the questioning of their ethical implications. Artists have long explored the relationship between humans and technology to express ideas about progress, societal changes, and the very nature of creativity (Messer, 2024) and this medium provides a provocative and accessible means to explore complex issues with your stakeholders.

In another example, Korean eyewear giant Gentle Monster launched a campaign, ***Unopened: The Probe***, which was a year-long project developed in-house by the Gentle Monsters' Robotics Lab (Figure 8.1). The campaign's objective was to provoke viewers into questioning the future of the human–robot relationship. Gentle Monster worked with over 100 in-house artists, including specialists in robotics and kinetic art, to develop this probe. They described their installations as *cultural experimentations*, and this helps them connect with the concerns, fears, and fascinations of their customer base.

Many independent artists have turned to social media to either protest the theft of art to train generative AI models or to share prompting ideas, their gen AI art with other like-minded artists using these works. Other artists are using generative AI to portray the destructive side of AI, such as creating fantasy artwork depicting cyborgs and transhumanism in ghoul and horror-like styles such as Zack London's work with the creative studio, *Gossip Goblin*, on Instagram (London, 2025). However, this is more than a "criticism" of AI, it's using AI as a *force multiplier* to tell stories and prompt introspection about the human psyche, the worlds we have created, and their consequences.

The message here is to encourage you to think like an artist in expressing your business strategy or in inviting participation in co-creating your strategy with stakeholders to create emotional resonance. As an example, after we completed a recent *Designing Tiny*

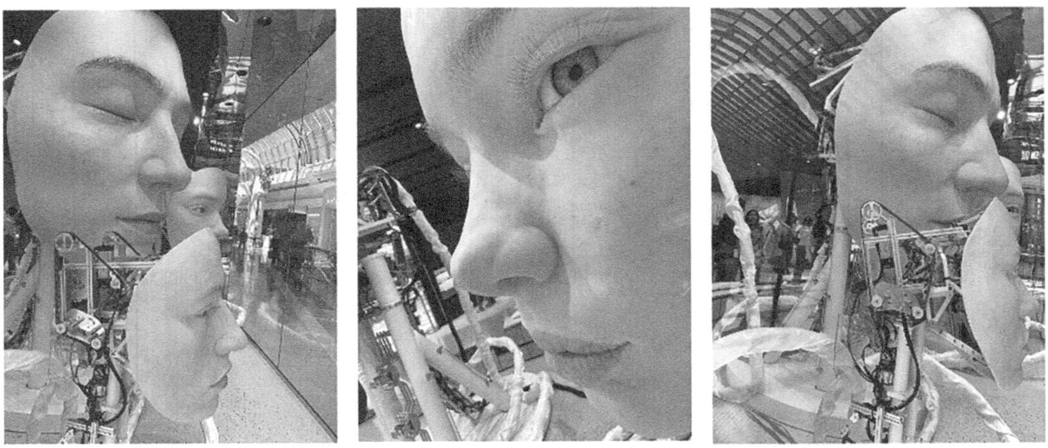

FIGURE 8.1 Gentle Monster's retail display.

Source: Photos taken by the author.

Robots workshop, I encouraged participants to upload their written outcomes into an AI music generator for it to create a song and generate lyrics and music for the strategy we were working on (for example, we used Suno, but there are many others). Participants were either horrified or overjoyed after being confronted by what their strategy actually *sounded like* to an outsider, to a machine. Exploring those emotions on how they felt threatened or emboldened was valuable and made it more deeply personal than a strategy workshop would have on its own.

In a personal example, I engaged a young graphic artist for his interpretation of the topics on the Tiny Robots cards. While I used standard icons for the original card designs (as depicted in Chapter 7), I asked the artist for his emotional interpretations. A sample of the two cards is provided in Figure 8.2. During stakeholder testing of the new cards, the response to the designer's cards were much more visceral compared the utilitarian designs of the original deck. Art has many deeper, unspoken layers and symbols that touch our subconscious.

The message for this provocation is to be creative and artistic, as this will help us ease out of entrenched thinking and inspire greater feeling and emotion, which is a source of truth for citizens, and the human comparative advantage relative to machines. When we explore the world through art, our subconscious comes into play. This helps us break free from rigid patterns of thought, allowing us to access deeper feelings and emotions that can reveal profound truths about ourselves and our experiences. When we allow ourselves to feel deeply through creative expression, we often uncover insights about ourselves and the world that logical thinking alone cannot provide. For example, engaging in activities like painting or listening to music can bring forth unexpected memories or emotions, unveiling hidden aspects of our inner lives. By exploring the world through art, we invite our subconscious to participate, making our discoveries richer and more meaningful.

FIGURE 8.2 Artist's interpretation of surveillance (left) and cybersecurity (right).

Source: Illustrations by Lucas Davies (used with permission).

AN INVITATION TO TAKE AI ETHICS SERIOUSLY

In Chapter 7, we introduced a set of ethics cards as a tool to raise awareness of key issues inherent in AI systems that need active monitoring and proactive action. These are provided again in Figure 8.3. The invitation here is to extend this work of using ethics cards and adopt ***value-sensitive design (VSD)***, which is a co-design method used throughout the design phases of intelligent AI systems (Liao and Muller, 2019; Umbrello and de Bellis, 2018; Umbrello and van de Poel, 2021) and has been an important method used in digital technology development for over a decade.

VSD is defined as a theoretically grounded approach to the design of technology that accounts for human values in a principled and comprehensive manner throughout the design process (Friedman et al., 2013). The importance and relevance of VSD is underpinned by the argument that information systems are intentionally or unintentionally informed by the moral values of their makers (van den Hoven, 2007).

We identified many case studies during our research where organizations had adopted a design philosophy that embedded values into the design of artificial agents at the early stages of AI development, largely driven by the high-risk stakes of unmitigated AI design (Umbrello and de Bellis, 2018; Longo et al., 2020; Riebe et al., 2024). Incorporating universal human values in AI design assists in managing the current challenging areas in the domain of transparency, explicability, accountability, and bias. To this point, there are many design approaches with VSD at their core that can be utilized (Leikas et al., 2019; Robertson et al., 2019; Zicari et al., 2021).

FIGURE 8.3 Key AI ethics principles.

As an example of how a focus on AI principles need not be an academic exercise – but can be used to build, protect and promote business value – consider Figure 8.4, which illustrates how a global food and agribusiness company has rolled out AI ethics in its organization.

The company has over 18,000 employees in over 100 countries and treats AI as an important potential tool that can help them become more productive, cost-effective, and innovative. Their AI governance framework incorporates AI ethics in six key areas:

- AI policy that manages legal and policy issues.
- An internal AI lab that tests AI experiments in a sandboxed environment before releasing them into their organization.
- Each employee has been issued with an AI passport and must undertake mandatory training (for example, using generative AI as a beginner's course) before they can use any AI tools in their work.
- The organization has a self-managed AI community on their intranet where interested employees share ideas on the latest tools and how they are using them in their work.
- The IT department has an AI Security Framework.
- The Audit Group runs an AI Ethics committee that advises the board and leadership teams on high-level issues on their AI deployments, AI risk management, and in preparation for what is on the horizon.

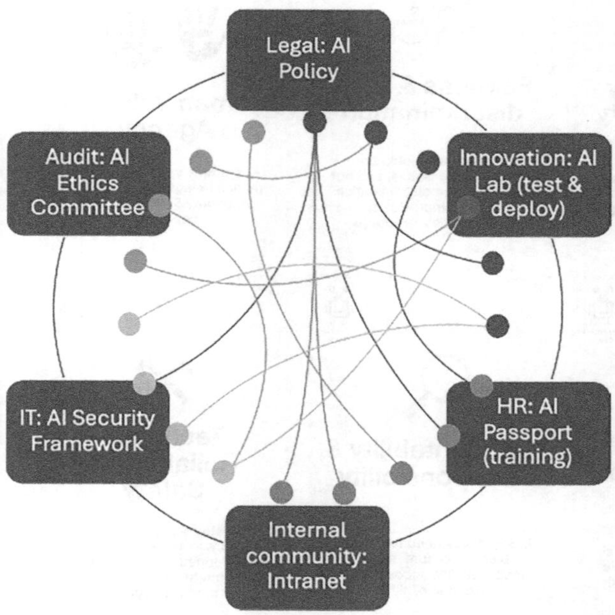

FIGURE 8.4 Managing AI ethics in practice (global food and agribusiness company).

This organization is large and well-resourced and can afford to put the effort into all the key areas that will enable them to optimize their use of AI in an ethical and managed manner. However, organizations of every size can learn something important from this model and implement what they can to enhance their value creation objectives.

There are many arguments that can be made for promoting ethics for their own innate value, but AI ethics often become a "tick the box" exercise. Stronger ethics policies and governance frameworks can help companies mitigate (but not completely circumvent) AI incidents and vulnerabilities, as policies must be supported by robust implementation, including clear governance, risk management, and technical safeguards. A comprehensive ethical framework helps address issues like bias and privacy, but it must be embedded into the entire AI lifecycle to prevent unpredictable behaviours and potential harm, especially when interacting with security risks. In short, ethics creates and protects business value.

AN INVITATION TO PROMOTE HUMAN FLOURISHING

Our collective understanding of **human flourishing** is well established, as the research has been extensive and consistent. In Harvard's Global Flourishing Study, human flourishing is defined as living in a state in which all aspects of a person's life are good (VanderWheele, 2017). The study's objectives were to measure various aspects of human flourishing in workplace, medical, educational, and government settings to shape policies to actively promote it. The study identified six key domains of well-being that are nearly universally desired across cultures (the survey reached 200,00 people in 22 countries). These six **domains of well-being** are as follows:

- Happiness and life satisfaction
- Mental and physical health
- Meaning and purpose
- Character and virtue
- Close social relationships
- Financial and material stability

Five of these six domains focus on humans as social, curious, and spiritual creatures engaged with self-improvement and interaction with community. The sixth domain focuses on the material means to (sometimes) enable the other five. The question we therefore need to ask is: can the era of artificial intelligence contribute the human flourishing? The answer is yes, of course, it can, but it can also take it away.

We can see from the six key domains of well-being that while AI and digital technologies in general can be used to contribute to human flourishing, the dominant paradigm of technology ownership and use is to drive efficiencies and to extract wealth from individuals and society as a whole (Zuboff, 2019). Ngwenyama et al. (2025; 2024) describe this as being entrapped by a digital rationality that espouses that all things digital are best and that digitalization is inevitable. Critics would go as far as to say that we are entrapped in a neo-liberal ideology and producing technological artefacts based on "science fiction" narratives without societal debate and consensus (Rowe et al., 2023; Koutsikouri et al., 2024).

As we discussed in Chapter 2, public opinion on the future of AI on the planet falls on a wide spectrum that ranges from **utopian scenarios** (humans will have all their needs taken care of and may only need to work two days a week, if at all) to **dystopian scenarios** where the public fears the end of humanity and society as we know it. This public discourse is entrenched and is a very difficult place to build a united community vision of how human flourishing can be nurtured. Furthermore, the utopian vision becomes harder to defend when considering the massive transfer of wealth that has taken place over the last 100 years and the increasing concentration of ownership of global income-producing assets. For example, data from *inequality.org* and several economic studies show that in the USA, the wealthiest 5% own 66% of the wealth, and this is a result of decades of steep increase in wealth since the 1970s (Zucman, 2019), and over this period of time, the inequality of wealth distribution has increased dramatically (Saez and Zucman, 2020).

These problems appear to have been exacerbated by technology. Moll et al. (2022) found that new technologies accrued wealth to high-skilled labor and to owners of capital. Expansions in technology and automation are also linked to increasing inequities in the distribution of income and wealth and lead to stagnant wages, particularly for those at the bottom of the distribution. These aren't ideal conditions for human flourishing.

Against this backdrop, and without a clear unilateral policy direction to alter this trend, citizens' concerns over AI taking over their jobs with no guarantee of a social security safety net appear to be a real possibility. In this scenario, are leaders expecting a ROI from AI to improve from the current low levels highlighted in Chapter 2? How will this scenario exacerbate the enablement issues highlighted in Chapter 5? and the cognitive frames of threat avoidance in Chapter 6?

These are important, provocative questions for your leadership teams. In such contexts, it's up to researchers and business leaders to take the initiative. In their research in this domain, Koutsikouri et al. (2024) offered the following questions as calls to action for the information systems research community:

- Can and should we take on a critical responsibility to shape digital technology and use it for the promotion of human flourishing and the public good?
- How can we place technology's impact on human flourishing into focus to inform responsible technology design and sustainable socio-technical systems?
- How might we take a critical stance against the unquestioned adoption of digital solutions in our domain, paying attention to sociotechnical processes (where human flourishing plays a greater role)?

- Should researchers take a greater personal responsibility for setting the future direction and better disseminate research regarding the possibilities and challenges in building better futures where humans can flourish and live well?

The original and ongoing work on the Harvard studies on human flourishing, VanderWheele (2017; 2024) concludes that we need to practice a deeper consideration and understanding of human purpose and virtue, as these may contribute not only to a broader and more profound individual flourishing but also to a better functioning society as well.

INVITATION TO PLAY WITH CRITICAL POST-HUMANISM

In Chapter 4, we identified that critical posthumanism offers a powerful lens for interrogating the assumptions embedded in contemporary AI technologies in the way they are designed and the sociotechnical systems in which they are embedded. Critical posthumanist questioning helps us to expose limiting thoughts and assumptions and explores the implications of emerging AI technologies, the interdependence of all actors in an ecosystem, and the agency of nonhumans (which includes technology). The summary of the key critical post-humanist principles from Chapter 4 is as follows:

1. Intelligence is distributed throughout the ecosystem.
2. Arrest archaic assumptions and mindsets.
3. Technology is not a tool but a relational, entangled network.
4. Non-human actors have agency (not sentience).
5. Beware of structural inequality and normative thinking.
6. We are all responsible for sustained planetary outcomes.
7. Beware of techno-optimism and techno-solutionism.
8. There are many ways of knowing.

Some of these may sound difficult to accept or put in practice, but I urge you to ***play with the material*** as you would with the provocation of being undisciplined. This can be an exercise to challenge our mechanistic thinking about the world and help us embrace a future of increasing complexity and ambiguity. In exploring these principles, I recommend you undertake what my colleagues Ryan and McWaters (2023) call ***Radical Acts***. They suggest that *most radical acts are deceptively small and intimate. It's more about motivating and paying attention in a time-starved world.* Ryan and McWaters ask: How can we shake things up in a kind and fun-loving way? This is what you need to ask of yourself and your teams. For this provocation, my recommendation is to play with the material. Use it for body storming, enactments, or improv exercises. Use them to challenge your designs from our *Designing Tiny Robots* exercise. Above all, keep these principles at the back of your mind when looking to design or implement a human–machine system in your organization or when an AI solutions provider is presenting you with their proposal.

CONCLUDING REMARKS

It's tempting to view these provocations as negative. They are in fact critical, and *critical thinking* is what we all need right now to see through the AI hype so that we can better understand and enable this amazing technology responsibly and set it up for success – without compromising human flourishing.

Early **humans were compassionate and cooperative beings** living in supportive communities. Contrary to popular belief, they didn't engage in constant war and battles with each other (Bregman, 2020). Older anthropological studies had us believe in the killer ape theories, which depicted early humans as warring, competitive; however, as Bregman (2020) points out, not a single archaeological site suggests that early human foragers fought against each other. Homosapiens' survival and success as a species is largely attributed to their capacity for cooperation and social learning, and these abilities allowed them to overcome challenges, innovate, and adapt to diverse environments (Harari, 2014; Boyd and Richerson, 2009).

It's in our DNA to be benevolent, co-operative, and peaceful beings, and this has been in our DNA long before we learned to become hostile when it comes to fighting for what we perceive to be *our right* to planetary and geographic resources or think that these resources *belong to us* when they might actually belong to someone else (Patou-Mathis, 2020). These are learned behaviors and attitudes derived from Empire; they're social constructs that serve the vested interest of a few. They are perceptions that have been shaped by our environment and are part of a belief systems that tell us stories about how to interpret our world. The good news is that we have the capacity to rise above this; therefore, it has now become a choice about what we do next.

I'd like to come back to where we started, with the theme for Chapter 1, which is a quote from Samuel Beckett's *Waiting for Godot*: ***What are we here for, that is the question***. This is the final provocation that I'll leave you with.

REFERENCES

AI Anarchies (2023). Broken Machines & Wild Imaginings. https://aianarchies.net/ Accessed 7 November 2025).

Armiero, M., Barca, S., and Velicu, I., (2019) Undisciplining Political Ecology: A Minifesto https://undisciplinedenvironments.org/2019/10/01/undisciplining-political-ecology-a-minifesto/ last accessed 12 July, 2025.

Boyd, R., and Richerson, P. J. (2009). Culture and the evolution of human cooperation. *Philosophical Transactions of the Royal Society B: Biological Sciences*, *364*(1533), 3281–3288.

Bregman, R. (2020). *Humankind: A Hopeful History*. Bloomsbury Publishing.

Edwards, B. (2024). Billie Eilish, Pearl Jam, 200 artists say AI poses existential threat to their livelihoods: Artists say AI will "set in motion a race to the bottom that will degrade the value of our work." Ars Technica. https://arstechnica.com/information-technology/2024/04/billie-eilish-pearl-jam-200-artists-say-ai-poses-existential-threat-to-their-livelihoods/ Accessed 7 November 2025.

Friedman, B., Kahn, P. H., Borning, A., and Huldtgren, A. (2013). *Value Sensitive Design and Information Systems* (pp. 55–95). https://doi.org/10.1007/978-94-007-7844-3_4

Harari, Y. N. (2014). *Sapiens: A Brief History of Humankind*. Random House.

Koutsikouri, D., Hylving, L., Raftopoulos, M., Ngwenyama, O., Rowe, F., and Tona, O. (2024). Human flourishing in the digital age: What responsibilities does/should researcher (s) have? Perspectives from the AIS Community. *Communications of the Association for Information Systems*, *55*(1), 178–192.

Leikas, J., Koivisto, R., and Gotcheva, N. (2019). Ethical framework for designing autonomous intelligent systems. *Journal of Open Innovation: Technology, Market, and Complexity*, *5*(1). https://doi.org/10.3390/joitmc5010018

Liao, Q. V., and Muller, M. (2019). *Enabling Value Sensitive AI Systems through Participatory Design Fictions. arXiv preprint arXiv:1912.07381.*

London, J. (2005). Home page. www.gossipgoblin.studio/ Accessed 7 November 2025.

Longo, F., Padovano, A., and Umbrello, S. (2020). Value-oriented and ethical technology engineering in industry 5.0: A human-centric perspective for the design of the factory of the future. *Applied Sciences*, 10(12), 4182.

Messer, U. (2024). Co-creating art with generative artificial intelligence: Implications for artworks and artists. *Computers in human behavior: artificial humans*, 2(1), 100056.

Moll, B., Rachel, L., and Restrepo, P. (2022). Uneven growth: automation's impact on income and wealth inequality. *Econometrica*, *90*(6), 2645–2683.

Ngwenyama, O., Kanita, N., and Rowe, F. (2025). Can Generative AI Contribute to both productivity gains and human Flourishing, and in fine satisfaction at work? Research on GitHub Copilot use in Software Development.

Ngwenyama, O., Rowe, F., Klein, S., and Henriksen, H. Z. (2024). The open prison of the big data revolution: False consciousness, faustian bargains, and digital entrapment. *Information Systems Research*, *35*(4), 2030–2058.

Osborne, P. (2015). Problematizing disciplinarity, transdisciplinary problematics. *Theory, Culture & Society*, *32*(5–6), 3–35. https://doi.org/10.1177/0263276415592245

Patou-Mathis, M. (2020). Ideas: The origins of violence. *The UNESCO Courier*, *2020*(1), 38–41.

Riebe, T., Bäumler, J., Kaufhold, M. A., and Reuter, C. (2024). Values and value conflicts in the context of OSINT technologies for cybersecurity incident response: a value sensitive design perspective. *Computer Supported Cooperative Work (CSCW)*, 33(2), 205–251.

Robertson, L. J., Abbas, R., Alici, G., Munoz, A., and Michael, K. (2019). Engineering-based design methodology for embedding ethics in autonomous robots. *Proceedings of the IEEE*, *107*(3), 582–599. https://doi.org/10.1109/JPROC.2018.2889678.

Rowe, F., Jeanneret Medina, M., Journé, B., Coëtard, E., and Myers, M. (2023). Understanding responsibility under uncertainty: A critical and scoping review of autonomous driving systems. *Journal of Information Technology*, DOI: 02683962231207108.

Ryan, L., and McWaters, V. (2023). *Radical Acts: Unconventional Wisdom for Shaking Things Up*. Beyond the Edge Publishing.

Saez, E., and Zucman, G. (2020). The rise of income and wealth inequality in America: Evidence from distributional macroeconomic accounts. *Journal of Economic Perspectives*, *34*(4), 3–26.

Umbrello, S., and de Bellis, A. F. (2018). A Value-Sensitive Design Approach to Intelligent Agents. https://ssrn.com/abstract=3105597

Umbrello, S., and van de Poel, I. (2021). Mapping value sensitive design onto AI for social good principles. *AI and Ethics*, *1*(3), 283–296. https://doi.org/10.1007/s43681-021-00038-3.

Van den Hoven, J. (2007, November). ICT and value sensitive design. In *The Information Society: Innovation, Legitimacy, Ethics and Democracy: Proceedings of the Conference*

"Information Society: Governance, Ethics and Social Consequences," University of Namur, Belgium 22–23 May 2006 (pp. 67–72). Springer US.

VanderWeele, T. J. (2017). On the promotion of human flourishing. *Proceedings of the National Academy of Sciences, U.S.A., 31*, 8148–8156.

VanderWeele, T. J. (2024). Flourishing and the scope of medicine and public health. *Journal of Epidemiology and Community Health, 78*(7), 466–470.

Zicari, R. v., Ahmed, S., Amann, J., Braun, S. A., Brodersen, J., Bruneault, F., Brusseau, J., Campano, E., Coffee, M., Dengel, A., Düdder, B., Gallucci, A., Gilbert, T. K., Gottfrois, P., Goffi, E., Haase, C. B., Hagendorff, T., Hickman, E., Hildt, E., … Wurth, R. (2021). Co-design of a trustworthy AI system in healthcare: Deep learning based skin lesion classifier. *Frontiers in Human Dynamics*, 3. https://doi.org/10.3389/fhumd.2021.688152

Zuboff, S. (2019). Surveillance capitalism and the challenge of collective action. In *New Labor Forum* (Vol. 28, No. 1, pp. 10–29). Sage Publications.

Zucman, G. (2019). Global wealth inequality. *Annual Review of Economics, 11*(1), 109–138.

Appendices

Appendix 1: Tiny Robots Problem Statement

Creating Tiny Robots: Problem Statement

What problem are we trying to solve? (Make a concise statement!)

PRESENT

What is the current situation or problem?

Who are the target users or audience in need of a solution?

PAST

How has this situation been managed in the past?

What worked well? What didn't work well?

FUTURE

What are the opportunities to do things differently?

What do we want to achieve (desired outcomes)?

What are the key challenges we may face in building new solutions?

Appendix 2: Tiny Robot Exercise 1

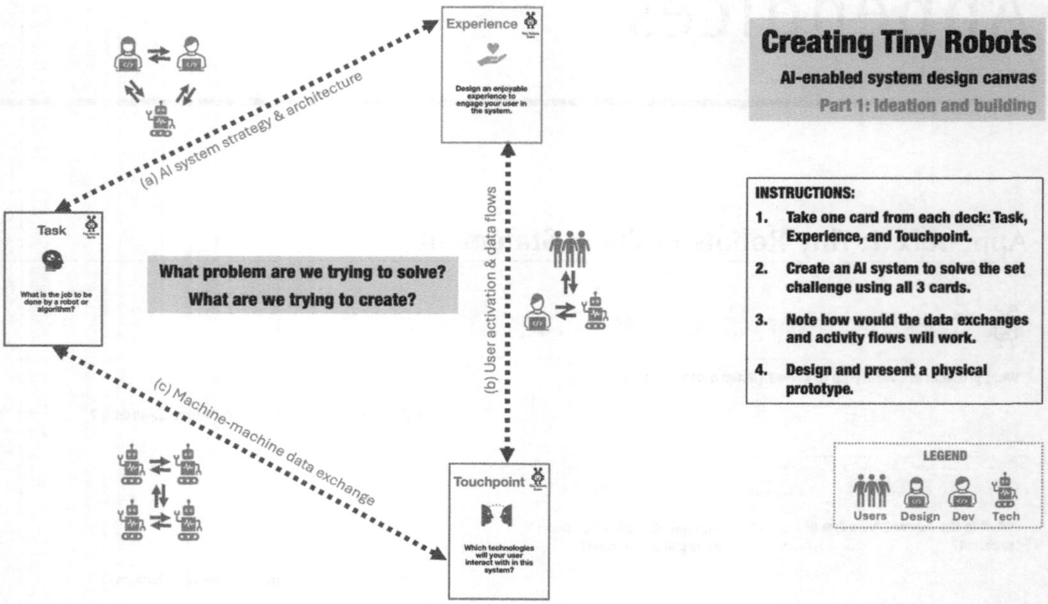

Appendix 3: Tiny Robots Design Canvas

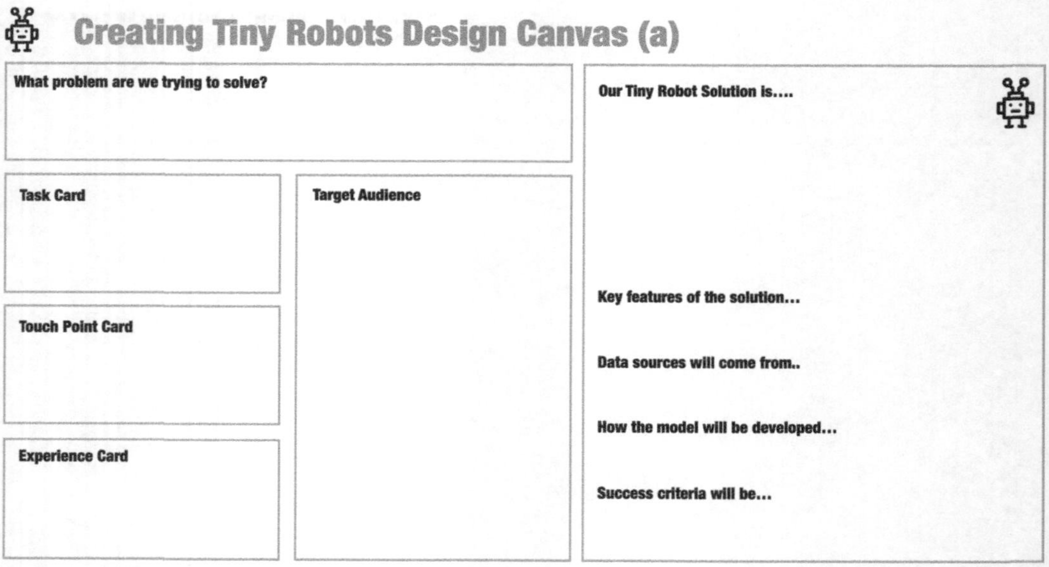

Appendix 4: Tiny Robot Exercise 2 (Bugs Canvas)

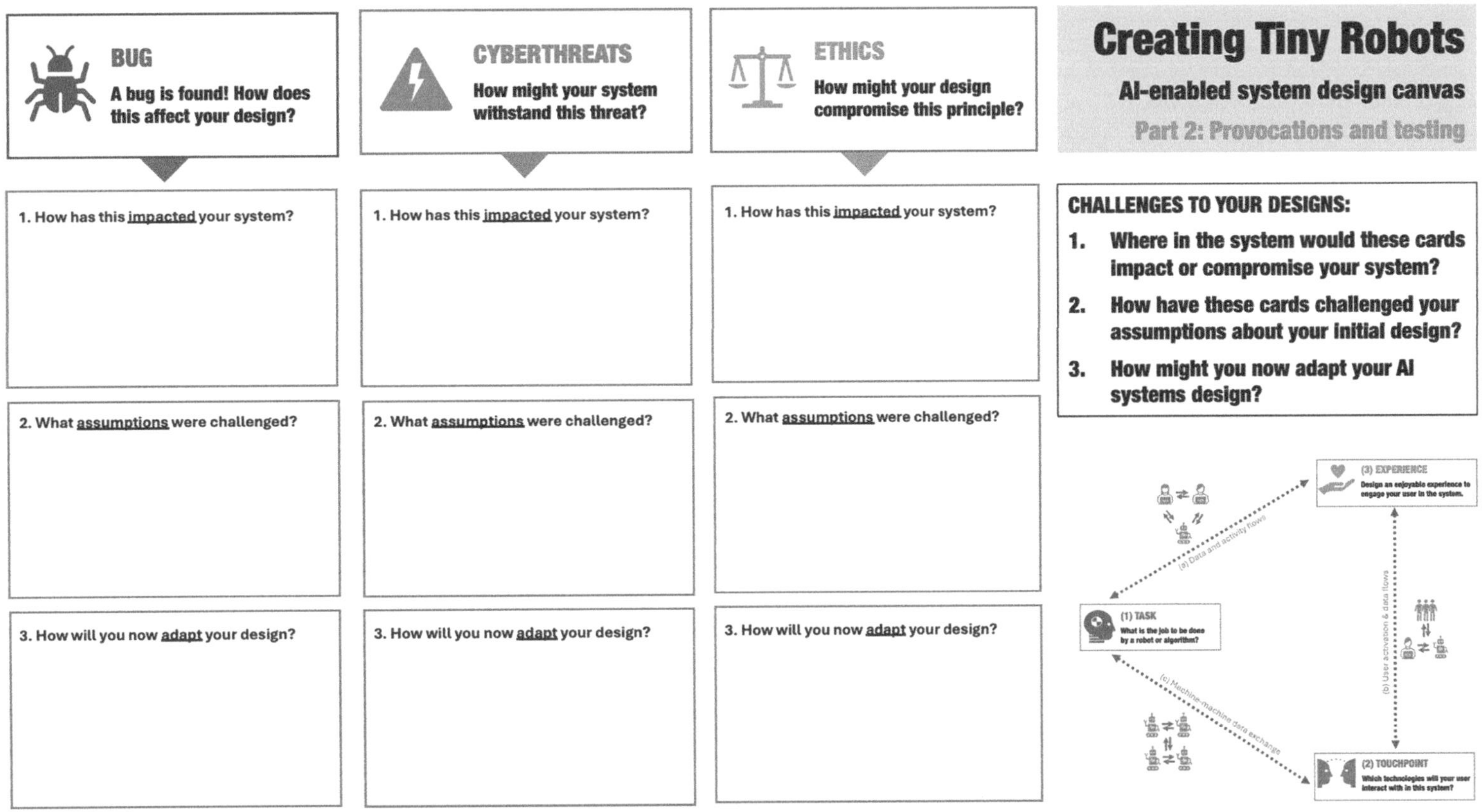

Index